BREAKING FREE

A CROSS-CULTURAL ANTHOLOGY

JOHN BOROVILOS

Prentice Hall Canada Inc.

Prentice-Hall, Inc., Englewood Cliffs, New Jersey
Prentice-Hall International, Inc., London
Prentice-Hall of Australia, Pty., Ltd., Sydney
Prentice-Hall of India Pvt., Ltd., New Delhi
Prentice-Hall of Japan, Inc., Tokyo
Prentice-Hall of Southeast Asia (PTE) Ltd., Singapore
Editora Prentice-Hall do Brasil Ltda., Rio de Janeiro
Prentice-Hall Hispanoamericana, S.A., Mexico

ISBN 0-13-307430-7

Publisher: Donna MacCallum
Managing Editor: Linda McGuire
Production Editor: Elizabeth Siegel-Masih
Production Co-ordinator: Sharon Houston
Permissions: Angelika Baur and Karen Taylor
Text and Cover Design: Carole Giguère
Cover and Internal Illustration: Tracy Walker
Composition and Typesetting: Hermia Chung

Canadian Cataloguing in Publication Data

Main entry under title:

Breaking free: a cross-cultural anthology

ISBN 0-13-307430-7

1. Short stories, Canadian (English).*
2. Canadian fiction (English) – 20th century.*
3. Canadian poetry (English) – 20th century.*
4. Short stories. 5. Fiction – 20th century.
6. Poetry, Modern – 20th century. I. Borovilos,
John, 1946–

PS8233.B7 1994   C811'.5408   C94–932028–5
PR9194.4.B7 1994

Printed and bound in Canada by D. W. Friesen
    3 4 5 6 DWF 00 99 98

Policy Statement
Prentice Hall Canada Inc., School Division, and the author of *Breaking Free: A Cross-Cultural Anthology* are committed to the publication of instructional materials that are as bias-free as possible. This anthology was evaluated for bias prior to publication.
    The editor and publisher also recognize the importance of appropriate reading levels and have therefore made every effort to ensure the highest degree of readability in the anthology. The content has been selected, organized, and written at a level suitable to the intended audience.

To my students, who teach me well,
To my friends and family, who support me,
and
To Anita and our children, always…

CONTENTS

CONTENTS BY ROOTS/RESIDENCE/SETTING

120	British Columbia / Okanagan	British Columbia	North America
122	Minjerribah / Australia	Australia	Australia
124	Manitoba	Quebec	Igavik, Bay of Ungava
134	Germany	Germany	Germany
140	Poland / Ohio / Ontario	Prince Edward Island	Ontario
151	Iraq	Austria	Iraq
157	Romania / Saskatchewan	Saskatchewan	Saskatchewan
160	China (Shanxi)	China	China
170	Scotland / California / Canada	Saskatchewan	Canada
175	Ukraine / Nova Scotia / Ontario	Nova Scotia	Poland / Canada
178	China / California	California	California
189	Portugal	Portugal	Canada
194	Greece / Manitoba	Ontario	Manitoba
205	India	India	India
210	Ontario	Ontario	Ontario
214	Egypt	Egypt	Egypt
218	Iceland / Manitoba	British Columbia	Canada
228	South Korea	South Korea	South Korea
234	Ontario	Ontario	Canada
238	Saskatchewan	British Columbia	Canada
243	Indiana	United States	United States
254	Columbia	Mexico	Columbia
262	Nova Scotia / New Brunswick	New Brunswick	New Brunswick

TO THE STUDENT

"There is no such thing as truly universal literature, partly because there are no truly universal readers."

—Margaret Atwood: *Second Words*

"...the mental talents of this side of the world, in an ecstasy of contemplation of their own cultures, have found themselves without a proper means to interpret us. One realizes this when they insist on measuring us with the same yardstick with which they measure themselves."

—Gabriel García Márquez: *Nobel Prize Address*

An exciting new world—a post-modern world—is emerging from the great winds of profound change and conflict swirling endlessly around us. The world we have known is being transformed into a global village where understanding a culture and a people thousands of kilometres away will be equally as important as understanding one's next-door neighbour. We have a critical choice to make. Either we can retreat from the challenges that this new world will create, or we can actively confront them, becoming clear-eyed citizens of both our own country and our world.

To evolve into more responsible global citizens, we must be prepared to be critical of long-held assumptions, "break free" of well-worn clichés and stereotypes, and acquire a better understanding of people from outside our own immediate community and culture. In effect, we should begin to use a different "yardstick" by which to "measure" ourselves, our world, and also the printed page that attempts to mirror all of us.

The stories and poems in this cross-cultural anthology have been included to help you to compare and contrast different cultures and attitudes, and reflect upon contemporary issues. Many of the selections will reveal "difference" as a way of gaining greater understanding of and empathy with others, while underscoring the need for seeing commonalities—the ties that bind us as a human race. You will have an opportunity to read and think about ideas and themes which many cultures share: family relationships and adolescence; changing gender roles; education, school, and work; love and healing; reactions to violence and death; "marginalized" peoples; humour and irony; politics and protest; power and manipulation; and the need for courage and self-respect.

The "Entry Points" following each selection challenge you to develop a critical, inclusive, cross-cultural perspective. They will encourage you to question biases and assumptions you may have about Canada and the world, and provoke you to see both difference and uniformity in order to gain a more balanced perspective on many "truths."

Amidst this whirlwind of change, *you* will be in control of events instead of events being in control of you. Using literature with new insights and new perspectives, you will make new meanings, and remake, like a magician, the world into a better place. That is the challenge of the post-modern world. That is the challenge of the voices in this book. That is *your* challenge.

— *John Borovilos*

ACKNOWLEDGEMENTS

Having a vision is one thing; making it real is quite another. A book makes things real: concepts come to life, emotions are captured, relationships are formed, the spirit soars.

Making things real, making a book, takes time and takes belief, but it also takes the encouragement and belief and expertise of others. Those precious others include students and colleagues at Riverdale, Malvern, and Danforth who enthusiastically encouraged my work; the reviewers from across Canada for their sensible and insightful comments; the staff at Prentice Hall, from publishers to designers, for their confidence and creativity; and, always, Anita. But, most of all, I must express my deepest gratitude to Linda McGuire, my editor, who believed in the project from the very start and always kept pushing for the finest book possible. Her excitement for literature and new ideas was a dream come true. A vision come true.

Prentice Hall Canada Inc. wishes to express its sincere appreciation to the following Canadian educators for contributing their time and expertise during the development of this anthology.

Avril Chalmers, Teacher, Port Moody Senior Secondary School, British Columbia

Judith F. Clark, Teacher, North Surrey Secondary School, British Columbia

Dr. James Greenlaw, Teacher, Georgian Bay Secondary School, Ontario

Lynn Ibsen, Department Head — English, Exeter High School, Ontario

Noreen Jeffrey, Teacher, Marion M. Graham Collegiate, Saskatchewan

Carol Mayne, Teacher, St. Francis Xavier High School, Alberta

Michael McMorrow, English Department Head, Monsignor Johnson Catholic Secondary School, Ontario

Harry Neufeld, Teacher, West View Secondary School, Alberta

Stephan Sierakowski, Head of English, Lester B. Pearson Collegiate Institute, Ontario

John Syvitski, English Department Head, Miles Macdonell Collegiate, Manitoba

Sherril A. Webb, Teacher, Halifax West Senior High School, Nova Scotia

Inclusion of a person in this list does not necessarily indicate endorsement of the text.

LIES

YEVGENY YEVTUSHENKO

Telling lies to the young is wrong.
Proving to them that lies are true is wrong.
Telling them that God's in his heaven
and all's well with the world is wrong.
The young know what you mean. The young are people.
Tell them the difficulties can't be counted,
and let them see not only what will be
but see with clarity these present times.
Say obstacles exist they must encounter
sorrow happens, hardship happens.
The hell with it. Who never knew
the price of happiness will not be happy.
Forgive no error you recognize,
it will repeat itself, increase,
and afterwards our pupils
will not forgive in us what we forgave.

Translated by Robin Milnar-Gulland and Peter Levi

1 In your own words, explain what you think the poet means by the word *lies*? Write out words or phrases that may be considered synonymous with the word *lies*. Check a thesaurus and try to distinguish the connotations of the different words.

2 Why do adults sometimes "lie" to young people? What are their motivations? Why do young people sometimes lie? Is it *always* right to tell the truth?

3 Why does the poet make the point that "the young are people"? Who might not think of them as people? Why?

4 Analyze and discuss the last four lines of the poem with particular emphasis on the concept of "forgiveness." Why do you think the poet says that "pupils will not forgive in us what we forgave"? Do you agree?

5 Define "satire." How might the concept of satire apply to this poem?

6 Many Canadian ministries of education consider "critical thinking" to be one of the most important skills for students to acquire. In a group, with reference to the poem, discuss this concept and its importance to our present "information society."

7 It is often said that "ignorance is bliss." Do you agree? Relate your answer to the poem.

8 Write an article for your school newspaper on the topic: "Telling lies to the young is wrong."

9 Read the poem, "Stereotype" (page 55). How are "stereotypes" forms of lies?

THERE WAS ONCE

MARGARET ATWOOD

— There was once a poor girl, as beautiful as she was good, who lived with her wicked stepmother in a house in the forest.

— Forest? *Forest* is passé, I mean, I've had it with all this wilderness stuff. It's not a right image of our society, today. Let's have some *urban* for a change.

— There was once a poor girl, as beautiful as she was good, who lived with her wicked stepmother in a house in the suburbs.

— That's better. But I have to seriously query this word *poor*.

— But she *was* poor!

— Poor is relative. She lived in a house, didn't she?

— Yes.

— Then socio-economically speaking, she was not poor.

— But none of the money was *hers*! The whole point of the story is that the wicked stepmother makes her wear old clothes and sleep in the fireplace—

— Aha! They had a *fireplace!* With *poor*, let me tell you, there's no fireplace. Come down to the park, come to the subway stations after dark, come down to where they sleep in cardboard boxes, and I'll show you *poor!*

— There was once a middle-class girl, as beautiful as she was good—

— Stop right there. I think we can cut the *beautiful*, don't you? Women these days have to deal with too many intimidating physical role models as it is, what with those bimbos in the ads. Can't you make her, well, more average?

— There was once a girl who was a little overweight and whose front teeth stuck out, who—

— I don't think it's nice to make fun of people's appearances. Plus, you're encouraging anorexia.

— I wasn't making fun! I was just describing—

— Skip the description. Description oppresses. But you can say what colour she was.

— What colour?

— You know. Black, white, red, brown, yellow. Those are the choices. And I'm telling you right now, I've had enough of white. Dominant culture this, dominant culture that—

— I don't know what colour.

— Well, it would probably be *your* colour, wouldn't it?

— But this isn't *about* me! It's about this girl—

— Everything is about you.

— Sounds to me like you don't want to hear this story at all.

— Oh well, go on. You could make her ethnic. That might help.

— There was once a girl of indeterminate descent, as average-looking as she was good, who lived with her wicked—

— Another thing. *Good* and *wicked*. Don't you think you should transcend those puritanical judgemental moralistic epithets? I mean, so much of that is conditioning, isn't it?

— There was once a girl, as average-looking as she was well-adjusted, who lived with her stepmother, who was not a very open and loving person because she herself had been abused in childhood.

— Better. But I am so *tired* of negative female images! And stepmothers—they always get it in the neck! Change it to step*father*, why don't you? That would make more sense anyway, considering the bad behaviour you're about to describe. And throw in some whips and chains. We all know what those twisted, repressed, middle-aged men are like—

— *Hey, just a minute!* I'm *a middle-aged—*

— Stuff it, Mister Nosy Parker. Nobody asked you to stick in your oar, or whatever you want to call that thing. This is between the two of us. Go on.

— There was once a girl—

— How old was she?

— I don't know. She was young.

— This ends with a marriage, right?

— Well, not to blow the plot, but—yes.

— Then you can scratch the condescending paternalistic terminology. It's *woman*, pal. *Woman.*

— There was once—

— What's this *was, once?* Enough of the dead past. Tell me about *now.*

— There—

— So?

— So, what?

— So, why not *here?*

ENTRY POINTS

1 In this piece of experimental fiction, a storyteller is continually interrupted while attempting to relate a traditional fairytale. Why? How would you characterize the "listener"?

2 To what *exactly* is the listener objecting? Give examples of the objections and analyze them. Do you agree or disagree with the listener's objections? Elaborate on your response.

3 Define the term "political correctness" with your group. You may need to do library research. Explain how Atwood is satirizing political correctness in this story. Do you agree with her attitude? Discuss with your group.

4 With your group, comment on and assess the following two of the listener's generalizations as they relate to other literature you have read:
(a) "Description oppresses."
(b) "Everything is about you."

5 Read Yevgeny Yevtushenko's poem "Lies" (page 1). Do you think the storyteller in "There Was Once" is lying? Do you think the listener is lying? Who is telling the truth in this dialogue?

6 If you were the storyteller, how would you have reacted to the listener's objections? Write a diary entry in which you, as the storyteller, express your feelings about the listener.

7 Choose a partner from your class and role-play the storyteller and the listener, incorporating your own reactions into the exchange. As your dramatic dialogue evolves, search for opportunities for compromise.

8 Write a modern fairytale which uses "politically correct" language throughout—or rewrite a traditional fairy tale like "Goldilocks" or "Hansel and Gretel" using "politically correct" language. Recite to the class in a dramatic manner as though your classmates were little children.

9 Margaret Atwood's story is typically post-modern in that it is both experimental in its form and is "self-reflexive," that is, it comments on its own storyline. Write a story using this form, perhaps to comment on a social issue such as violence, political corruption, or drug abuse. (For more information about post-modernism, see page 267.)

10 Relate and compare the theme of language and image in this story to the theme of politics and image in "The Image Maker" (page 7).

THE IMAGE MAKER

TONY BELL

"Obie, the P.M. was just asking about you."

O'Brien stands at the window, in a dressing gown and slippers, pretending not to hear. He takes a sip from his glass of Dewar's and stares at the Edmonton sunset. From the twenty-fourth floor, the view is striking: precise, fiery layers of red, orange and amber play out endlessly on the horizon. He had forgotten about the sunsets, the sharp light that defines the West, that makes each shape stand out from its surroundings. In Toronto, the winters are sunless, each day a separate journey from partly cloudy to overcast to widely scattered drizzle. Haze melts into fog; shapes dissolve into shifting blurs. O'Brien loves Toronto, revels in its diffuse, murky light. He dislikes coming West, dreads the vast, oppressive prairie sky, the cold, gray, direct landscape. No nuances, no evasions; he feels exposed.

Young Jeffrey, one of the tour organizers, stands impatiently in the doorway, waiting to organize him. "The P.M. wants to know if you've watched his speech yet."

"No, I haven't," yawns O'Brien. He holds up the bottle of Dewar's. "I was just girding myself."

"Well, hurry up, eh, he has to give it again after dinner."

O'Brien nods amiably. "Dinner. Good idea, Jeffrey. Call Room Service."

"Come on, Obie, there isn't time."

O'Brien scoffs at his concern. "Of course there's time. The election isn't till next year. And after that, who knows, you may have all the time in the world."

Jeffrey shifts his feet uncomfortably. "What're you talking about? The last polls were very encouraging. Even you can't deny that."

O'Brien smiles, says nothing. He knows better than to argue with Jeffrey about polls. Jeffrey believes utterly in polls; he believes in nothing but polls. If the polls were to tell him he was Jesus Christ, he would start speaking in parables.

O'Brien finishes his drink and pours another. It has been six days since he joined the Prime Minister's tour—six days going on sixty. O'Brien always drinks more when he's out West. Because of the climate, he tells anyone unwise enough to ask. This time it is the truth. He has the beginnings of a cold and tonight the temperature will plummet to minus thirty. At minus thirty, it is a poor joke to ask, "Celsius or Fahrenheit?" The blood congeals in such weather; shoulders hunch under the weight of ice crystals; faces contract into masks of pain. Only the light remains unaffected, bouncing sharply off the crystals, forming jagged, blinding rainbows in front of O'Brien's eyes. In Toronto, the weather tomorrow will be overcast and thirty-five degrees. O'Brien knows this without asking: in Toronto, December is always overcast and thirty-five degrees, with small craft warnings and a chance of drizzle-turning-to-sleet. After six days in Edmonton, O'Brien longs to hear about the small craft warnings.

Jeffrey still waits with fidgety impatience for him to view the tape. "Why don't we watch it while we eat?" O'Brien suggests.

"There isn't time, Obie, it's urgent. I said I'd get back to him in half-an-hour." O'Brien sighs. Everything is urgent with Jeffrey; he is doomed to spend his life trying to catch up to where he thinks the present should be. For he has plans, Jeffrey does, he is a man to be watched. He dresses impeccably in suits he can't afford; he neither drinks nor smokes. One day he will run for a seat in the Commons and win, Jeffrey has no doubt of it, but first he must spend the requisite number of years grovelling at the feet of the Party, collecting I.O.U.'s.

Unable to procrastinate any longer, O'Brien inserts the tape of the Prime Minister's speech into the V.C.R. Jeffrey picks up the phone to call Room Service. "What shall I ask for?"

O'Brien shrugs. "I'm not fussy. Anything you like—just no salt. I'm tired of being treated like an icy road."

Jeffrey murmurs something that sounds like "Why me?" and dials. O'Brien turns on the T.V. and slumps into one of the hotel's expensively uncomfortable chairs to watch the Prime Minister's address to the Chamber of Commerce.

"Shall I turn up the volume?" Jeffrey asks. "It's not very loud."

"It's all right. I've heard it before." Actually, he hasn't heard this particular speech before, but it doesn't matter. O'Brien seldom listens to the actual words when his clients are speaking. There's no point. He knows the average listener remembers only a small percentage of what he hears, and even then he gets it back-to-front. No, O'Brien would rather focus on the timbre of the voice, the rise and fall of inflection, the use of emphasis, the timing and appropriateness of a gesture. Perceptions are everything, and O'Brien scrawls his perceptions on a memo pad as he watches: *Don't wear gray—it makes you look drab. And get a new razor—remember Nixon? Keep cameras on the right if you can—your right profile's much more sincere. Voice is too low, tires your audience. Get it up more—you sound like an undertaker. Ventriloquist mouth—move the upper lip, drop the jaw. Don't point—you look threatening. Gesture with open hand, reach out, draw them in. Don't smile so much—they know you don't mean it.*

"How about salad?" Jeffrey asks.

"Fine—but no dressing. And another bottle of Dewar's."

"Doesn't Scotch have salt?"

O'Brien ignores him and continues writing: *Don't talk about the deficit. It's gloomy and it bores the hell out of people. Après-nous le deluge. Stick to tax reform. Keep telling them how much you'll save them. And stop rubbing your hands—it makes you look guilty....*

O'Brien puts the Prime Minister on pause so he can reread his comments. Over the last six days, he has noted a certain petulance, hostility even, creeping into his assessments of the Prime Minister. Because of the weather, he tells himself.

Jeffrey's shadow looms over his notes and he quickly covers them. Jeffrey feigns offence: "What's the big secret? We're all in this together."

"Some of us are in deeper than others, Jeffrey."

"What, you think I'd run around telling people what I know?"

"Of course not. I just don't want *anyone* to know." What isn't known can't be used, is O'Brien's maxim. He ignores Jeffrey's look of scorn and returns to his notes. He knows that Jeffrey dislikes him and says so emphatically to the other organizers. But he also knows that Jeffrey *asked* to work as his aide during the tour, believing that he could pick up some of O'Brien's secrets for his own use—his own future campaigns. However, three days of spying has yielded him nothing. O'Brien has no intention of sharing his secrets, mainly because he has no secrets to share, only the illusion of a secret, which is infinitely more powerful than the real thing.

O'Brien stares at the frozen image of the Prime Minister's face on the T.V. screen—caught in the middle of the word "hope." "The hope of something-or-other"—O'Brien can't remember the context. The expression reinforces the rhetoric: lips pushing forward in the forceful *oh* sound; brows rising with authority; hands reaching out to reinforce the words. In motion, the persona of assured confidence. Only the still image catches the grimace behind the eyes—the politic worm caught on his own hook.

He notices that Jeffrey, too, is studying the Prime Minister's face, perhaps wondering what O'Brien finds in it. O'Brien can guess what Jeffrey will say later to the other aides: *"You should see that crazy bastard. Every day, same thing. He doesn't even listen to the speeches. He just hits the pause button and stares at the screen."*

"Jeffrey, is that a silk tie you're wearing?"

"What, this? Yeah. Armani. You want one?"

"No, I want yours. I want to give it to the Prime Minister before his speech tonight. His wife keeps buying him paisley, but it bleeds on T.V."

"And what am *I* supposed to wear?"

O'Brien unfreezes the Prime Minister and resumes scribbling. "If anybody decides to film you, Jeffrey, I'll give you mine."

"Sure, the way *you* dress? I'll bet you don't even own a tie."

"That's because I'm not running for anything, am I? Now stop interrupting."

Jeffrey looks accusingly at the face on the screen for a moment, then gives in and slowly removes his tie. "I hate this tour," he fumes. "We've got so many aides along there aren't enough people to give orders to. And what's the point of it? I mean, it's not as if we've got anything to announce. We're just here because we're here, y'know, because it looks good. You'd think he's in the middle of a campaign or something."

That's because he *is* in the middle of a campaign, thinks O'Brien. Ever since the last election. Campaigning is what the elected do best, enjoy most. Looking to the future. The visionary rhetoric. The smiles and the laying on of hands. Seeking affirmation—getting it, too, some of them. Only to spend the next four years trying, with increasing desperation, to find the moment again—the brief euphoria of acceptance and possibility.

The comments come faster as the camera closes in on the Prime Minister's face, causing the pen to skip erratically across the page: *Don't look down, keep the gaze level. You're getting flashback—more pancake on the forehead. And you're pausing too much—don't pause—don't let them think you can't find the words. Just keep going, even if you have nothing to say, keep the gaze level, don't let them see the doubt. Use the eyes, smile, even if you don't mean it, don't let the face go blank, don't let the voice fade—they'll think the well is dry, they'll think you used it up getting to where you are. Don't look down, they'll see the dizziness—*

O'Brien stops. Even he can't read the scrawl anymore; he closes and uncloses his hand several times, but a slight jangling feeling remains. He stands, tears off the sheet of paper, crumples it, and puts it in his pocket, out of Jeffrey's view. Then he picks up his drink and returns to his station at the window. It's barely five o'clock and already the sun is gone; only a thin bloody vein is left to hold off the night. He watches as a plane glides in for a landing at the Municipal Airport, and again he counts the minutes until his flight leaves....He hasn't been sleeping, that's his problem; he never sleeps well when he's away from home. He feels his precious equilibrium slipping away.

He picks up the earlier page of comments, adds *Don't look down, keep the gaze level* at the bottom, and concludes with *Break a leg*. He puts the sheet in an envelope, looks at Jeffrey, and decides to seal it. Jeffrey shakes his head and attempts to appear world-weary: "If you trust me that much, why don't you just hand it to the Prime Minister yourself?"

"There isn't time, Jeffrey. I have to start packing."

"Packing? Where're you going?"

"Back to Toronto."

"Tonight?"

"I'm taking the Red-Eye." In his mind he's already there, the next morning, easing his car through the morning rush on the 401, looking for the Don Valley turnoff, thinking of the breakfast Peggy will have waiting for him when he arrives; the children just out of bed, wandering sleepily into the kitchen, and their excitement at seeing him back....

Jeffrey's expression is a mix of outrage and envy.

"How come you get to go home early?"

"I'm a free agent, Jeffrey. The Party doesn't own me. I still have other clients."

"Lucky you," Jeffrey pouts. "You'll be asleep in Toronto while the rest of us are stuck out in the boonies. Have you seen the new itinerary for tomorrow?"

"Yes," says O'Brien and inwardly counts his blessings. Tomorrow, when O'Brien is catching up on his sleep in Don Mills, the Prime Minister will be travelling. The Alberta Outback within ten steps of the Yellowhead Highway. Breakfast in Vegreville. Lunch in Vermilion. Dinner at Lloyd. It is good to be seen travelling. Travelling implies movement, gives the illusion of action. It looks good on the six-o'clock news. The objective is clear: "To find out what the people are thinking." But the people aren't thinking anything. The people are waiting for the polls to tell them what to think, or failing that, the Prime Minister. But the Prime Minister is waiting for the polls to tell him what people are waiting to hear. But the polls don't collect thoughts; they take pulses, weigh feelings, discern moods. Ask not what the people are thinking tonight. They think nothing: they feel endlessly; they yearn hopelessly. They love, they hate, with precious little in-between. What does the West want? The Party has come west to ask. *They want to kill us, Prime Minister, they want blood. They say we've let them down. Our mistake was in ever letting them up. They want justice, Prime Minister, they want revenge...with sunsets and clear light and endless horizons...with Room Service, beer and pizza, burgers and soggy french fries...a revenge of hypertension. We've lost the West, Prime Minister; it was never ours to begin with.*

"You really think so?"

Jeffrey's voice startles O'Brien; he must have been thinking aloud. He attempts to brush aside the comment: "I dunno. Maybe we have. But then so have all the other parties. The fact is, Jeffrey, I don't think the West wants to be found."

"How can you say that?" says Jeffrey. "Last week's poll was much better. Much more encouraging. We're holding our own."

"Against what?"

"What do you mean?"

O'Brien shrugs, retreats to his drink.

"Holding our own," insists Jeffrey. "More than holding our own. Until tomorrow, that is…." He laughs bitterly, remembering the new itinerary. "We're going to spend twelve hours on a bus so we can listen to a bunch of farmers tell us we're not giving 'em enough handouts."

O'Brien tries to sound sympathetic: "But Jeffrey, think of all the photo-ops for the P.M. in those great outdoors. Framed against the prairie sky. The strong man making his lonely, difficult decisions." Already Jeffrey appears to be brightening at the prospect. "Just see to it they don't make him wear a baseball cap."

Room Service arrives. Bits of lettuce doused in oil, with black olives, feta cheese, anchovies, and a side order of garlic bread. O'Brien feels his blood pressure rising at the sight.

"You have it, Jeffrey. I'm going to pack." But he is already packed. There is nothing left to do but stare at the night and wait for his plane. The blackness stretches endlessly, seeps inward as well. There aren't even any highrises to block his view, to provide a comforting perspective. He pours himself another drink and watches as pins of light appear against the darkening background, only a few at first, then seemingly all at once, filling the sky with a thousand knifepoints. Not at all like Toronto. In Toronto, in winter, a star is an event, a soft smudge filtered through gauze. He calls his children to the window to wish on them. But here…it must be the weather or his cold that twists his thoughts so. Even the Northern Lights seem sinister: massive shrouds skulking about for victims. He mustn't think this way—it's counter-productive. In Toronto, he wouldn't think this way. In Toronto, he doesn't even have windows in his office.

He turns to find Jeffrey watching him. Jeffrey is always watching him, probing for weaknesses that can be used against him one day. O'Brien points to the envelope. "You'd better deliver that," he says.

"Yes, I'd better." But Jeffrey makes no effort to leave. Instead, he holds the envelope up to the light in an attempt to see the contents.

"So much for urgency," says O'Brien.

Jeffrey shrugs and puts the envelope in his pocket. "You know, the Prime Minister must think a lot of you, bringing you along just so you can tell him what kind of tie to wear."

"Yes, I suppose he does," allows O'Brien.

"And not just the P.M. I hear you have lots of clients."

O'Brien can guess where the inquiry is leading, but he has no intention of making it easier for Jeffrey.

"Some clients, yes."

"Are they all politicians?"

"Some are. Most are in business."

This is more than O'Brien has ever confided to Jeffrey; Jeffrey quickly sits down, eager to pursue the opening.

"What exactly do you sell them, anyway?"

O'Brien holds out his palms as if the answer is obvious. "I don't sell them anything. You could say I teach them how to buy."

"Buy? What do you mean? Buy what?"

"You'll have to pay me to find out."

But Jeffrey will not be dismissed so lightly. "I might take you up on that one day," he says earnestly.

O'Brien shrugs, drinks, says nothing.

"How about it, Obie? You think you could get me elected?"

"To what?"

"C'mon, be honest, do you think I've got the makings of a politician?"

O'Brien looks askance at Jeffrey, then gravely offers him the bottle of Dewar's. Jeffrey shakes his head and waits for a better answer. O'Brien sighs and wishes he could wake up and find himself on the plane.

"How old are you Jeffrey?"

"Twenty-six."

"Do you have a girlfriend?"

"Are you kidding? With this job? There isn't time."

"You should make time, Jeffrey. Find a girlfriend. A wife, preferably. A couple of kids, a house in the suburbs, a nice long commute. I can recommend it."

Jeffrey takes a deep breath to keep his anger from flaring; he makes a final attempt to get through to O'Brien. "Okay, I admit, maybe I am being premature. But don't underestimate me, Obie. A few years from now, I'll be ready to make my move, and that's when I'm gonna call you. I've seen what it takes to get elected. That's why I respect your ability, Obie. You're the best. Just don't underestimate me, that's all."

"Don't worry, Jeffrey. I don't underestimate you." O'Brien underestimates many things, many people—it is the nature and the despair of his business—but he has never underestimated Jeffrey. He has no doubt that Jeffrey will end up exactly where Jeffrey wants to be. But not with *his* help—O'Brien draws the line at Jeffrey. When he looks at Jeffrey, O'Brien knows it is time for him to quit his business, before he sacrifices even more of himself than he has already.

Jeffrey is smiling now: he feels a breakthrough of sorts has been made. O'Brien has recognized his potential. With O'Brien in his corner, anything is possible.

He remembers the envelope in his pocket, but it is no longer a chore to him. "I guess I'd better get this downstairs." He starts to leave, but half way out the door he suddenly remembers something, something he'd been holding all week in reserve. He had intended to use it as a kind of flattery if the need arose; but now that O'Brien understands him, Jeffrey can display his sincerity instead. "You know, a number of the fellas were sitting around at lunch yesterday discussing the last campaign. We were trying to pick out the main thing you did to put us over the top."

"The *main* thing? Maybe you should start with the Prime Minister," suggests O'Brien.

But Jeffrey knows better. He smiles and ignores the comment. "One theory was that you got him to slow down and lower his voice—you know, so he sounded more statesmanlike. But then somebody else said it was the fact you fixed up his French accent so he was more marketable in Quebec—"

"What about you, Jeffrey? What did you say?"

"Me?" shrugs Jeffrey modestly. "I said it was a combination of things. The contact lenses. The new hairstyle. The suits. You were finally able to get the female voters to sit up and take notice."

O'Brien manages an approving nod. "Yes, you're right, Jeffrey. All of you are right. It *was* the contact lenses. And the accent. And the speech training. It was all of those things." O'Brien holds up his glass in salute, as Jeffrey, content now, his week with O'Brien no longer a waste, leaves with the envelope.

And, of course, it was none of those things, muses O'Brien. They were all just part of the ritual, the elaborate placebo designed to make the candidate believe. *Believe in O'Brien, never doubt, O'Brien is the expert, O'Brien knows all, trust O'Brien's judgment and victory is assured. O'Brien is the magician, don't ask what he has up his sleeve, just appreciate that you are part of the magic.* It is only after victory that the doubting begins. *It was me all along*, concludes the candidate. *O'Brien was just the spur, the rabbit's foot, part of the ride.* Once elected, he avoids O'Brien, prefers reports in sealed envelopes to face-to-face meetings. O'Brien becomes dispensable; the elected can act alone. But his faith in himself never matches the faith he once had in O'Brien.

O'Brien knows all this before it happens; he keeps his counsel and waits for a new slate to seek him out. And they will, he has no doubt of it. Tonight he'll go home, tomorrow he'll sleep, and the next day he'll be asked to spend his magic on someone else. It is only here, confronted by the view from the twenty-fourth floor, that he realizes how small and self-deluding his magic really is....

Once, during O'Brien's first trip west, when the idea of travel still excited him, the Prime Minister's campaign bus broke down just outside of Plamondon, a small town north of Edmonton. O'Brien spent the night there—volunteered, in fact, as it gave him the chance to meet with some of the local people. They were farmers, most of them, ethnic Russians who referred to themselves as Old Believers because they did not accept the reforms of the Orthodox Church. In the course of an evening, O'Brien learned a great deal about their world, which was flat and motionless and much nearer to heaven than his own. But not quite near enough, for between heaven and earth there were still the stars to contend with. The Old Believers called them "devil's teeth," and said they preyed upon unwary souls, living or dead. It was more than a quaint story told to visitors, it was a part of their faith: Live simply, keep your head down, and at night bolt the door to keep out the devil and his teeth. O'Brien admired the Old Believers for their conviction; they could pray in front of strangers as if it were a natural human function. In winter, they prayed mostly for the return of the sun each morning.

Now, whenever he is forced to come out West, O'Brien feels himself being wrenched back into the Old Believers' world. He pours another drink and stares at the darkness, and understands why it is they pray so fervently. To have to spend each night in the maw of those stars…? Eighteen hours of night in winter, to have to look up at one's face in the window, the grimace in the window, and dream of those teeth, poised behind the eyes?

Tomorrow, the Prime Minister will travel. It is good to be seen travelling, everyone agrees. He will set out under stars and return under stars; but in between—if the Old Believers' prayers are answered—he will pose in the sunshine and make speeches and put his faith in the polls. And if the polls are encouraging, he may even start speaking in parables again.

O'Brien finishes his drink and slowly draws the curtains. He sits in the uncomfortable chair, puts his feet on the coffee table, and starts whistling an old tune from the sixties as he waits for the hours to pass. It doesn't matter that he no longer has faith in the polls or in anything else: tomorrow he will be home again; tomorrow he won't need it. In Toronto, there are no stars in winter; the fog and the haze and the drizzle provide a civilizing veil. Instead of the devil, there is only airport parking and the 401 and the Don Valley to endure before reaching the turnoff, bolting the front door, pulling down the blinds and…sleep.

In his dreams he never leaves his bed.

ENTRY POINTS

1. "Jeffrey believes utterly in polls; he believes in nothing but polls." In specific terms, how would you characterize Jeffrey? To what extent do you think the general population is influenced by polls? To what extent are *you* influenced by polls? Discuss thoroughly with your group.

2 Explain the following passage: "O'Brien has no intention of sharing his secrets, mainly because he has no secrets to share, only the illusion of a secret, which is infinitely more powerful than the real thing." Why does Jeffrey want O'Brien's "big secret"? *Is* illusion more powerful than reality?

3 Read and reflect on Yevgeny Yevtushenko's poem, "Lies" (page 1). Now, analyze and discuss with your group how O'Brien, a public relations consultant, sees and tells "truths."

4 O'Brien repeatedly compares Edmonton, Alberta, with Toronto, Ontario—places where the author himself has lived. Do you think the differences he notes are valid and fair? Do Canadians, generally, tend to overstate their regional differences and understate their commonalities? Discuss thoroughly with your group and share your thoughts with your class.

5 Why does the author include the anecdote about the "Old Believers" farmers and the "devil's teeth" near the end of the story? What impact did this incident have on the "image maker"?

6 Write a letter to the editor of a magazine or newspaper in which you comment on (a) the influence of polls and "image makers" on Canadians; (b) the need for truth and honesty in our elected officials; or (c) the need for greater and more open communications between East and West Canadians.

7 What is *your* image? How do you think others view you? How would you change your image? How important is substance over image to you?

8 (a) O'Brien declares, "I don't sell them anything. ...I teach them how to buy." Comment on this statement and relate it to your studies in media literacy.

    (b) You are O'Brien. Design a series of video or magazine advertisements in which you create an "image" of a certain type. With reference to the target audience's needs and wants, analyze why the "image" of the advertising campaign is or is not successful.

9 For further ideas on political manipulation and image makers, view the following American films: *The Candidate*; *Bob Roberts*; and *Dave*. See also the British television series, *House of Cards*, based on the Michael Dobbs novel of the same name, and its sequel series, *To Play the King*, also based on the same novel.

THE EX-MAGICIAN FROM THE MINHOTA TAVERN

MURILO RUBIÃO

> Bow down thine ear, O Lord, and hear me:
> for I am poor and needy.
>
> Psalms, LXXXVI:1

Nowadays I'm a civil servant, which is not my greatest misfortune.

To be honest, I was not prepared for suffering. Each man, on reaching a certain age, is perfectly equipped to face the avalanche of tedium and bitterness, since from his early childhood he has become accustomed to the vicissitudes of daily life through a gradual process of continual vexation.

This did not happen to me. I was cast into existence without parents, without infancy or adolescence.

I found myself one day, with light gray hair, in the mirror of the Minhota Tavern, a discovery which in no way frightened me, any more than it astonished me to take the owner of the restaurant out of my pocket. He, rather perplexed, asked me how could I have done such a thing.

What could I answer, given my situation, a person who lacked the least explanation for his presence in the world? I said to him that I was tired, that I was born tired and weary.

Without weighing my answer or questioning me any further, he made me an offer of a job, and so I began, from that time on, to entertain the clientele of the establishment with my magical activity.

The man himself, however, failed to appreciate my habit of offering onlookers a variety of free lunches, which I would mysteriously draw forth from the inside of my own jacket. Judging it to be not the best of transactions merely to increase the number of customers—without a corresponding growth in profits—he introduced me to the impresario of the Andalusian Circus Garden, who, when told of my aptitudes, offered to hire me. First, however, he was advised to take certain precautions over my tricks, since I might just decide to distribute free admissions to the performances.

Contrary to the pessimistic expectations of my first employer, my behavior was exemplary. My public engagements not only thrilled multitudes, but brought in fabulous profits for the company owners as well.

Audiences, in general, received me rather coolly, perhaps because I failed to present myself in tails and a top hat. But as soon as I began involuntarily to extract rabbits, snakes, lizards from a hat, spectators tingled with excitement, above all in the last number, when I would cause an alligator to appear from the tips of my fingers. Then, by compressing the animal from both ends, I changed him into an accordion and brought the act to its close by playing the Cochin China National Anthem. Applause would burst forth from all sides, under my remote gaze.

The manager of the circus, observing me from a distance, was exasperated by my indifference to the public's acclaim, especially when it came from the younger children who would show up to clap for me at Sunday matinees. Why be moved, though, if those innocent faces, destined to endure the suffering inflicted upon any man's coming of age, aroused no pity in me, much less any anger, over their having everything I longed for but did not myself possess: birth, and a past.

As I grew more popular, my life became intolerable.

At times, sitting in some café, stubbornly observing the populace filing past on the sidewalks, I would end up pulling doves, gulls, skunks out of my pocket. The people around me, judging my behavior to be intentional, invariably broke into shrill peals of laughter. I would stare at the floor dejectedly, and mutter against the world and birds.

Whenever, absentmindedly, I happened to open my hands, curious objects slid out of them. On a certain occasion I surprised myself by pulling one shape after another out of my sleeve. In the end I was completely surrounded by strange shapes, without any idea of what purpose to attribute to them.

What could I do? I looked all around me, my eyes pleading for some kind of help, in vain, an excruciating state of affairs.

Almost always, if I took out my handkerchief to blow my nose, I astonished those nearby by pulling a whole bedsheet out of my pocket.

If I fidgeted with the collar of my coat, a large buzzard would immediately appear. On other occasions, while trying to tie my shoelaces, snakes would slither out of my trousers. Women and children started screaming. Guards came over, bystanders crowding around, a scandal. I would have to report to police headquarters and listen patiently while I was prohibited by the authorities from any further setting loose of serpents on public thoroughfares.

I raised no objection. Timid, I humbly mentioned my condition of magician, reaffirmed my intention not to bother anyone.

I became accustomed, at night, to waking up quite suddenly in the middle of a sound sleep, with a loud bird flapping its wings as it took flight from my ear.

On one of these occasions, completely furious, and resolved never again to practice magic, I cut off my hands. To no purpose. As soon as I moved, they reappeared, fresh and perfect, on the ends of the stump of each arm!

I had to resolve my despair somehow. After weighing the matter carefully, I concluded that only death would put a proper end to my misfortune.

Steadfast in my decision, I took a dozen lions out of my pockets and, crossing my arms, waited for the moment when I would be devoured. They did me no harm. Surrounding me, they sniffed at my clothes and, eyeing the landscape, slunk away.

Next morning they were back again and sat themselves provocatively before me.

"What do you expect from me, stupid animals?" I roared indignantly.

They shook their manes sadly and pleaded with me to make them disappear.

"This world is tremendously tedious," they declared.

I failed to restrain my outright rage. I killed them all, and began to devour them myself. I had hopes of dying the victim of a fatal indigestion.

Misfortune of misfortunes! I suffered an enormous stomachache, and continued to live.

This failure only multiplied my sense of frustration. I left the city limits and went off in search of the mountains. Reaching the highest peak, which dominated the dark abyss, I relinquished my body to space.

I felt no more than a slight sensation of the closeness of death— almost at once I found myself suspended from a parachute. With difficulty, battering myself against rocks, maimed and grimy, I finally returned to the city, where my first step was to acquire a pistol.

At home again and lying on my bed, I raised the weapon to my ear. I pulled the trigger, expecting a loud report and the pain of the bullet tearing through my head.

There was no shot, and no death: the handgun turned into a pencil.

I rolled to the floor, sobbing. I who could create other beings had no means to liberate myself from existence.

An expression I overheard by accident, out on the street one day, brought me renewed hope of a definitive break with life. From a sad man I heard that to be a civil servant was to commit suicide little by little.

I was in no condition to determine which form of suicide was best suited to me: slow or quick. As a result, I took a job in the Department of State.

1930, a bitter year, longer than those that followed the first manifestation I had of my existence, back in the mirror at the Minhota Tavern.

I did not die, as I had hoped to. The greater my afflictions were, the greater my misfortune.

While I was a magician, I had had very little to do with people—the stage always kept me at a comfortable distance. Now that I was obliged to have constant contact with my fellow creatures, it was necessary to understand them, and to disguise the repugnance they aroused in me.

The worst of it was that, my duties being rather trivial, I found myself in the position of having to hang around uselessly for hours at a stretch. Idleness led to my resenting the lack of a past. Why was it only me, among all those existing before my very eyes, who had nothing to recall? My days floated in confusion, mixed with a few paltry recollections, the small plus of three years in existence.

Love, which came to me by way of another civil servant, her desk close to mine, distracted me for a time from my worries.

Momentary distraction. My restlessness quickly returned, I struggled with uncertainties. How was I to propose to this colleague of mine if I had never made declarations of love, nor had a single amorous experience?

1931 began cheerlessly, with threats of mass dismissals in our department and a refusal by the typist to consider my proposal. Faced with the possibility of being discharged, I tried somehow to look after my own interests. (The job mattered little to me. I was simply afraid of leaving behind a woman by whom I had been rejected, but whose presence slowly became indispensable to me.)

I went to the supervisor of our section and announced that I could not be fired because, after ten years in the department, I now possessed job security.

He stared at me for some time in total silence. Then, frowning at me, he said he was astonished by my cynicism. He would never have expected anyone with only one year of service to have the audacity to claim ten.

To prove to him that my attitude was not frivolous, I rummaged through my pockets for some documents corroborating the authenticity of my claim. Stunned, I managed to pull out only a crumpled piece of paper, the fragment of a poem inspired by the breasts of the typist.

Anxiously, I turned all my pockets inside out, but found nothing more....

I was forced to admit defeat. I had trusted too much in my powers to make magic, which had been nullified by bureaucracy.

Nowadays, without the aforementioned and miraculous gift of wizardry, I am unable to relinquish the very worst of human occupations. I lack the love of my typist companion and the presence of friends, which obliges me to frequent solitary places. I am often caught attempting to remove, from the inside of my clothes with my fingers, little things which no one glimpses anyway, no matter how attentively they gaze.

They think that I'm crazy, chiefly when I toss into the air those tiny objects.

I have the impression that a swallow is about to disengage itself from my fingertips. I sigh aloud, deeply.

Of course, the illusion gives me no comfort. It only serves to intensify my regret not to have created a total magical world.

At certain moments, I imagine how marvelous it would be to extract red, blue, white, and green handkerchiefs from my body, fill the night with fireworks, turn my face to the sky and let a rainbow pour forth from my lips, a rainbow that could cover the earth from one extremity to the other. Then the applause from the old men with their white hair, and from gentle children.

Translated by Thomas Colchie

ENTRY POINTS

1. The story is written in a style common to many Latin American writers: magic realism. This style of writing, which blends fantastic elements (bizarre situations, dreams, superstition, and absurd or strange humour) with realistic elements (recognizable characters, dialogue, and setting), was often used by these writers to create parables in order to fool state censors and comment critically on problems in their own countries: devastating hunger and poverty, political and artistic oppression, social injustice, and military dictatorships. Cuban writer Alejo Carpentier, put it this way: "For what is the story of Latin America if not a chronicle of the marvellous in the real."

(a) What is "marvellous" (fantastic, magical, absurd) in this story? Be specific.

(b) What is "real"?

(c) What point(s) do you think Rubião is making about (i) his society, (ii) his government and its bureaucracy, and (iii) the state of human nature caught in an inhuman state? Discuss the implications of these points for our own society.

2 Why, according to the ex-magician, is being a civil servant the "greatest misfortune"? Do you think his ideas are fair or cynical? Why does he then claim that he wants to keep this job? Do you believe his claims? Ideally, what do you think civil servants should be like?

3 How does the epigraph from Psalms give us a solid clue about the thematic intentions of Rubião? In what way is the "ex-magician" and others like him "poor and needy"?

4 In the previous story (page 7), the "image maker," O'Brien, suggests that others perceive him as a "magician": "O'Brien is the magician, don't ask what he has up his sleeve, just appreciate that you are part of the magic." Why does the narrator of this story, a Brazilian civil servant, call himself an "ex-magician"? How is he similar to and different from the Canadian, O'Brien?

5 Why does the ex-magician's "magic" disappear? Who is more "magical"—the "ex-magician" or the "image maker"? Share your thoughts with your group.

6 "It only serves to intensify my regret not to have created a total magical world." What could the "ex-magician" have done with his powers? Imagine yourself to have magical powers. Write a short paper or script in which you outline what would be in your "total magical world."

7 Write a short story in which you use the elements of "magic realism" to criticize a social or political problem in your own country.

8 For a satiric view on civil servants, view the British television series, *Yes, Minister*, and its sequel, *Yes, Prime Minister*.

9 Compare the view of government's effect on the individual in this story with the view in Franz Kafka's short story "The Hunger Artist," and his classic novel, *The Trial*.

CALGARY AS A CHRISTMAS TREE IN FEBRUARY

ELIZABETH BREWSTER

The critic quotes Sam Johnson
against numbering the streaks of the tulip;
yet I remember a certain candy-striped tulip
like a red-and-white peppermint stick
and remember buying it with three other tulips
on a spring day

special special
after a cold winter in Ottawa.

I wish I could remember exactly,
wish I had counted the stripes
and put them down in a notebook.

There are tulip-trees also
native to Canada

and other trees
flowering dogwood, grey birch,
lodgepole pines, tamarack, hemlock,
balsam fir, grand fir.
I can never tell one spruce from another
but all different.

I was surprised when someone told me
there aren't any daisies on the prairie.
The commonest flower, I thought,
but not here.
A foreign flower, has to be explained.
In Canada daffodils are garden flowers,
don't grow like Wordsworth's
running wild and dancing
hardy as dandelions.
I hadn't seen one when I read his poem
back in Grade Seven in Minto, New Brunswick,
but knew well enough what he was talking about.

A regional writer, Wordsworth,
a Cumberland man
out-of-place in London and Cambridge,
wrote from his special place
his special time
prosaically, uneconomically,
a cumbrous style, like the heavy
landscape he came from,
only sometimes lightened by
a dancing like Layton's
butterfly on a rock.

Does the writer become universal
by striving to be so?

"Shine, Poet, in thy place
and be content,"
said Wordsworth

Or write of Paterson, New Jersey,
the corner of Bloor and Yonge Street
in Toronto,
the beautiful, polluted Saint John River
or Saskatchewan (there's nowhere like it,
so at least one song-writer says)

this place, this moment,
seen by one person, not Mankind
or even Woman.

In the Calgary Airport
the windows face West toward the foothills
(a range of blue pyramids
or solidified waves)

Not quite the same airport as in Winnipeg.
Almost, but not quite, the same souvenirs
in the airport shops.
The piped-in music is recognizably
"The Sidewalks of New York."

All flights are the same flight—
nearly?
But I look down at Calgary at 6:35 PM
on February 18, 1978
and see a city I have never seen
a tree of light
a dark pine with yellow Christmas candles.

Is a country a region?
Is a city a region?
Is a city a flower?
Is Calgary a pine
or a mountain ash
with shining berries?

In Saskatoon
on the way home from the airport
the hitch-hiker in the back seat of the car
says he was one of four survivors
from the plane crash last week,
took this flight from Vancouver
to prove to himself he could fly another time.
He was nervous during the flight
but able to enjoy his dinner.

We agree
No two flights are the same

1 (a) Why does Brewster disagree with Sam Johnson's notion "against numbering the streaks of the tulip"? Why does she remember so vividly "a certain candy-striped tulip"?

   (b) Do you remember a "special special" day in *your* life when you wish you had experienced an event or situation more fully? Write as *fully* as you can of this experience, using specific details.

2 Why does she call William Wordsworth (1770–1850), who was one of England's greatest poets, a "regional writer"? Is this meant to be an insult or a compliment in her view? Explain. Look up and read Wordsworth's classic, "The Daffodils."

3 In a group, discuss and interpret stanzas 8, 10, and 11 in reference to Brewster's ideas about "special experiences," similarities, and differences. Pay particular attention to the following lines:

   (a) *wrote from his special place*
       his special time
   (b) *"Shine, Poet, in thy place*
       and be content,"
   (c) *this place, this moment,*
       seen by one person, not Mankind
       or even Woman.

4 "Does the writer become universal by striving to be so?" Answer this rhetorical question in your own words and with reference to this and other poems in this anthology. What is the point Brewster is making throughout the poem about "difference"?

5 Margaret Atwood, one of Canada's most admired writers, said in her book of critical essays, *Second Words* (1982), that "There is no such thing as a truly universal literature, partly because there are no truly universal readers." How does this poem illustrate Atwood's principle about universality and difference?

6 This poem speaks of the importance of really seeing the specific and different realities behind people and things, even if they seem to be very similar: "No two flights are the same." Write a poem or a short prose piece in which you describe your city or town in two different ways just as Brewster has "seen" Calgary. Just as Brewster has done ("Is Calgary a pine or a mountain ash...?"), use metaphors as part of your description.

SKIPPER

ALDEN NOWLAN

Skipper was the youngest of the five sons of Ethel and Rupert Syverson. As a small boy, Skipper, like each of his brothers before him, feared and hated his father and entered into a wordless pact of mutual defence with his mother.

Rupert, as he himself said, was a hard man. For sixty hours in every week, he carried deal at the sawmill, balancing the long, green boards on a leather-padded shoulder and bearing them from the trimmer saw to the lumber piles. Weeknights he lounged about the kitchen, sluggish and sullen, until nine o'clock, then went to bed. In his father's presence, Skipper adopted his formal manners, as though before a stranger; he walked softly and seldom spoke. In conversation with his mother, Skipper spoke of "Rupert," never of "Father." For his part, Rupert demanded obedience but otherwise left his son pretty much alone. On Saturday night, like almost all of the mill hands, Rupert went to town and came home, violently drunk, at two or three o'clock the following morning.

When with his drinking companions, Rupert was sportive and exuberant. But when he came home drunk, he cursed his wife, called the boys brats and wished they were kittens so that he could sew them in a sack weighted down with rocks and drown them. On several occasions, he beat Ethel with his fists, and once he kicked her and sent her sprawling while Skipper stood by, screaming. Many times, he yanked

Skipper out of bed in the dead of night and, on one pretext or another, flogged him with a cowhide strap. Often, if the weather was warm, Ethel led Skipper out into the night and they hid, wrapped in each other's arms, on the hillside overlooking the house until Ethel felt certain that Rupert's rage had been extinguished by sleep.

In a curiously dispassionate way, Skipper hated his father. He loathed the mill where Rupert worked himself into dumb exhaustion. He detested the men who came for his father with rum bottles hidden under their overall bibs. On numerous occasions between his sixth and fourteenth year, he vowed to his mother that never, as long as he lived, would he taste strong drink.

Ethel fostered those aspects of Skipper's character which Rupert most despised. While a little lad in cotton shorts and a polo shirt, Skipper often brought her bouquets: handfuls of violets or bunches of mayflowers or daisies. She never took such gifts for granted; they touched her deeply, like presents from a lover.

She encouraged Skipper to daydream. She had done this with his brothers before him. When he grew up, she said, he would be a clean, sober man who would wear a white shirt and necktie to work. He would go far away from the village and, of course, his mother would accompany him. Perhaps he would never become rich—but he would be a gentleman.

Skipper listened attentively to all that she told him. She was his guide and his refuge. A snivelling brat, Rupert called him when he saw him clinging to Ethel's skirts. His daydreams were foolishness, Rupert snorted. When Skipper grew up, he would go into the mill, as his father and grandfather had done before him. He would become hard, because a man had to be hard to survive. And if there was any man in him, when Saturday came he would get drunk, because the ability to drink was one of the measures of a man.

Skipper told his mother that he would die rather than allow this to happen to him. Often, at night, Ethel slipped into his room and lay on the bed beside him, and listened to him whisper his thoughts, feelings and ambitions.

He liked to play with crayons. She bought him a watercolour set. To Rupert's vocal disgust, he spent many evenings making pictures at the kitchen table. On Ethel's infrequent visits to town, she bought him books. First, Hans Christian Andersen. Later, *Robinson Crusoe, Kidnapped* and *Treasure Island*. She rejoiced to see him run his fingers affectionately along the edges of the pages.

In Skipper, Ethel saw her last hope. His elder brothers had followed the old, brutal pattern to its conclusion. Harold, for example, had left school at fifteen to go into the mill. There he had learned to drink. At eighteen he got a girl in trouble and had to marry her. By the time he was twenty-two, they had four children. Ethel's daughter-in-law told her that now every Saturday night he came home roaring drunk like his father. The others, for whom she had once had such high and splendid hopes, were much like Harold. They were not different from any of the men who worked in the mill and lived in the village. Ethel's love for them had been soured by disappointment and hurt. Sometimes, thinking of what they had done with their lives, she almost hated them.

In the summer of his twelfth year, Skipper killed a sparrow with a sling-shot. Ethel looked upon this as an omen. To his astonishment, she wept and berated him. For several days, following this incident, she refused to speak to him.

For his fourteenth birthday, Rupert gave him a .22 calibre rifle. This gift, Ethel knew, had been inspired not by affection but by the knowledge that she would hate it. Sick at heart, she saw Skipper go hunting birds with his father. He came back dragging a partridge, a poor, bloody thing with dead, fear-crazed eyes. She could not bring herself to refuse to cook it, but she would not taste the meat. And she detested her son when she observed the gusto with which he attacked a greasy drumstick. "That Skipper's a dead shot for sure," Rupert boasted, eyeing his wife slyly. Skipper grinned, relishing his father's praise. For the first time, the man and the boy had established a bond of fellowship.

Still, she refused to believe that he would be like the others. It was not until the fall of his sixteenth year that she was for certain what the future was destined to bring.

It was Saturday night. Skipper had gone to town with the boys, something he did frequently now. Most of these boys had left school and gone into the mill. Ethel harboured a dark suspicion that they were already learning to drink. She knew that they fought with their fists and picked up strange girls. She had warned Skipper about them. "Be careful, honey," she had said. He had patted her hand, reassuringly, and she had hated the amusement she detected in his eyes.

She was waiting up for him when he got home. Rupert had not come back from town. Ethel sat in the kitchen and listened to her son's movements in the porch. He was trying to be very quiet, she knew. The knowledge that she was going to surprise him gave her a strange sensation of triumph.

"Hi, Mama," he said as he opened the kitchen door. He wore his cap at a rakish angle, like the boys who worked at the mill. There were mud-stains on the sleeves of his jacket.

"Skipper..." she began.

"Yeah?" He continued to grin, swaying back and forth on his heels.

She got up from her chair and went over to him. She inhaled deeply, smelling his breath. Skipper laughed. "Yeah, Mama, I guess maybe I been drinking," he said.

She put her hand on his shoulders. "Skipper! You promised."

He shrugged. She had a momentary vision of him coming to her in his shorts and polo shirt, his hands filled with flowers.

"I'm a big boy now, Mama."

She returned to her chair and sat there, staring sightlessly at the floor. He shuffled his feet on the linoleum. "Look Mama," he said. "I was talking to Bill Spence tonight."

Bill Spence was the foreman at the mill. *Don't say it*, she prayed silently. *Please don't say it.*

"He says he might be able to find a job for me."

"Yes." She would not argue. She would not try to reason with him. Already she had given up. For the fifth time, she had been defeated.

"We need the money, Mama."

"Yes."

"I didn't tell him yes and I didn't tell him no."

"No."

"Are you listening to me, Mama?"

"Yes."

He burst into laughter. "I just thought of something funny," he explained.

"What?"

"Oh, it doesn't matter." He laughed again. "The old man really tied one on tonight. I ran into him in town. Drunk as a skunk."

In his voice, there was a strange alloy of contempt and empathy. Never before had she heard him use this tone of voice in speaking of his father.

Wearily, she rose and headed towards the stairs. "I'm going to bed now, Skipper."

"Okay, Mama. I guess I'll wait up for the old man." He threw himself into a chair at the table and lit a cigarette. For an instant, she hated him and wished that it were within her power to hurt him as he had hurt her. Then there was only the emptiness of defeat.

"You used to sit in that same chair and paint watercolours," she said.

He had not been listening. "Huh?" he said.

"Be careful of fire."

"Sure, Mama."

"Good night, Mama."

Ethel got into bed and switched off the light. In a little while she heard Rupert arrive. Then for a long time she lay in the darkness, listening to the man and his son laughing together at the other end of the house.

ENTRY POINTS

1 "As a small boy, Skipper…feared and hated his father…."
(a) Were Skipper's fear and loathing justified?
(b) Why do you think his father behaved as abusively as he did?

(c) Early on, how did Skipper react to and defend himself in such abusive circumstances? Could he have done anything more or anything differently in defending himself?

2 Describe Skipper's relationship to his mother in his early years. Why does this relationship begin to change after Skipper turns twelve?

3 Rupert, Skipper's father, believed that Skipper "would become hard, because a man had to be hard to survive." Discuss the following questions with your group and report your group's responses to the class:
(a) To what degree is this a correct assumption in today's world? To what degree is this a limiting stereotype?
(b) Why won't or can't Rupert accept difference in his sons?
(c) How would you define what a "man" is?

4 Investigate child and spousal abuse in your library's vertical files. Write a persuasive editorial in which you argue or debate this statement: "Although both highly negative, psychological abuse may be more damaging to its victims than physical abuse because of its long-term consequences on a person's choices and life."

5 "A child's life is determined by his/her parents." Debate this statement with your group keeping in mind the concepts of free will and pre-destination. You might want to develop your arguments with reference to other works such as William Shakespeare's *Romeo and Juliet*, Marilyn Halvorson's *Cowboys Don't Cry*, and John Wyndham's *The Chrysalids*, Michael Anthony's *Green Days by the River*, and J. D. Salinger's *The Catcher in the Rye*.

6 In role as Skipper, write a letter to a "Youth Clinic" column in which you outline your problems with your abusive father. As the columnist, write a response in which you suggest possible solutions.

7 "Ethel got into bed and switched off the light." Write an interior monologue in which you articulate Ethel's "emptiness of defeat." Present your monologue to the class.

8 Write a short story in which a teenager makes a decision which fulfills his/her early dreams and ideals, rising above all challenges and obstacles.

CANE IS BITTER

SAMUEL SELVON

In February they began to reap the cane in the undulating fields at Cross Crossing estate in the southern part of Trinidad. "Crop time coming boy, plenty work for everybody," men in the village told one another. They set about sharpening their cutlasses on grinding stones, ceasing only when they tested the blades with their thumb-nails and a faint ping! quivered in the air. Or they swung the cutlass at a drooping leaf and cleaved it. But the best test was when it could shave the hairs of your leg.

Everyone was happy in Cross Crossing as work loomed up in the way of their idleness, for after the planting of the cane there was hardly any work until the crop season. They laughed and talked more and the children were given more liberty than usual, so they ran about the barracks and played hide and seek in those canefields which had not yet been fired to make the reaping easier. In the evening, when the dry trash was burnt away from the stalks of sweet juice, they ran about clutching the black straw which rose on the wind: people miles away knew when crop season was on for the burnt trash was blown a great distance away. The children smeared one another on the face and laughed at the black streaks. It wouldn't matter now if their exertions made them hungry, there would be money to buy flour and rice when the men worked in the fields, cutting and carting the cane to the weighing-bridge.

In a muddy pond about two hundred yards east of the settlement, under the shade of spreading laginette trees, women washed clothes and men bathed mules and donkeys and hogcattle. The women beat the clothes with stones to get them clean, squatting by the banks, their skirts drawn tight against the back of their thighs, their saris retaining grace of arrangement on their shoulders even in that awkward position. Naked children splashed about in the pond, hitting the water with their hands and shouting when the water shot up in the air at different angles, and trying to make brief rainbows in the sunlight with the spray. Rays of the morning sun came slantways from halfway up in the sky, casting the shadow of trees on the pond, and playing on the brown bodies of the children.

Ramlal came to the pond and sat on the western bank, so that he squinted into the sunlight. He dipped his cutlass in the water and began to sharpen it on the end of a rock on which his wife Rookmin was beating clothes. He was a big man, and in earlier days was reckoned handsome. But work in the fields had not only tanned his skin to a deep brown but actually changed his features. His nose had a slight hump just above the nostrils, and the squint in his eyes was there even in the night, as if he were peering all the time, though his eyesight was remarkable. His teeth were stained brown with tobacco, so brown that when he laughed it blended with the colour of his face, and you only saw the lips stretched wide and heard the rumble in his throat.

Rookmin was frail but strong as most East Indian women. She was not beautiful, but it was difficult to take any one feature of her face and say it was ugly. Though she was only thirty-six, hard work and the bearing of five children had taken toll. Her eyes were black and deceptive, and perhaps she might have been unfaithful to Ramlal if the idea had ever occurred to her. But like most of the Indians in the country districts, half her desires and emotions were never given a chance to live, her life dedicated to wresting an existence for herself and her family. But as if she knew the light she threw from her eyes, she had a habit of shutting them whenever she was emotional. Her breasts sagged from years of suckling. Her hands were wrinkled and callous. The toes of her feet were spread wide from walking without any footwear whatsoever: she never had need for a pair of shoes because she never left the village.

She watched Ramlal out of the corner of her eye as he sharpened the cutlass, sliding the blade to and fro on the rock. She knew he had something on his mind, that was how he had come silently and sat near to her pretending that he could add to the keenness of his razor-sharp cutlass. She waited for him to speak, in an oriental respectfulness. But from the attitude of both of them, it wasn't possible to tell that they were about to converse, or even that they were man and wife. Rookmin went on washing clothes, turning the garments over and over as she pounded them on a flat stone, and Ramlal squinted his eyes and looked at the sun.

At last, after five minutes or so, Ramlal spoke.

"Well, that boy Romesh coming home tomorrow. Is six months since he last come home. This time, I make up my mind, he not going back."

Rookmin went on scrubbing, she did not even look up.

"You see how city life change the boy. When he was here the last time, you see how he was talking about funny things?"

Rookmin held up a tattered white shirt and looked at the sun through it.

"But you think he will agree to what we are going to do?" she asked. "He must be learning all sorts of new things, and this time might be worse than last time. Suppose he want to take creole wife?"

"But you mad or what? That could never happen. Ain't we make all arrangements with Sampath for Doolsie to married him? Anyway," he went on, "is all your damn fault in the first place, wanting to send him for education in the city. You see what it cause? The boy come like a stranger as soon as he start to learn all those funny things they teach you in school, talking about poetry and books and them funny things. I did never want to send him for education, but it is you who make me do it."

"Education is a good thing," Rookmin said, without intonation. "One day he might come lawyer or doctor, and all of we would live in a big house in the town, and have servants to look after we."

"That is only foolish talk," Ramlal said. "You think he would remember we when he comes a big man? And besides, by that time you and me both dead. And besides, the wedding done plan and everything already."

"Well, if he married Doolsie everything might work out."

"How you mean if? I had enough of all this business. He have to do what I say, else I put him out and he never come here again. Doolsie father offering big dowry, and afterwards the both of them could settle on the estate and he could forget all that business."

Rookmin was silent. Ramlal kept testing the blade with his nail, as if he were fascinated by the pinging sound, as if he were trying to pick out a tune.

But in fact he was thinking, thinking about the last time his son Romesh had come home...

It was only his brothers and sisters, all younger than himself, who looked at Romesh with wonder, wanting to ask him questions about the world outside canefields and the village. Their eyes expressed their thoughts, but out of some curious embarrassment they said nothing. In a way, this brother was a stranger, someone who lived far away in the city, only coming home once or twice a year to visit them. They were noticing a change, a distant look in his eyes. Silently, they drew aside from him, united in their lack of understanding. Though Romesh never spoke of the great things he was learning, or tried to show off his knowledge, the very way he bore himself now, the way he watched the cane moving in the wind was alien to their feelings. When they opened the books he had brought, eager to see the pictures, there were only pages and pages of words, and they couldn't read. They watched him in the night, crouching in the corner, the book on the floor near to the candle, reading. That alone made him different, set him apart. They thought he was going to be a pundit, or a priest, or something extraordinary. Once his sister had asked: "What do you read so much about, *bhai*?" and Romesh looked at her with a strange look and said, "To tell you, you wouldn't understand. But have patience, a time will come soon, I hope, when all of you will learn to read and write." Then Hari, his brother, said, "Why do you feel we will not understand? What is wrong with our brains? Do you think because you go to school in the city that you are better than us? Because you get the best clothes to wear, and shoes to put on your feet, because you get favour from *bap* and *mai*?" Romesh said quickly, "*Bhai*, it is not that. It is only that I have left our village, and have learned about many things which you do not know about. The whole world goes ahead in all fields, in politics, in science, in art. Even now the governments in the West Indies are talking about federating the islands, and then what will happen to the Indians in this island? But we must not quarrel, soon all of us will have a chance." But Hari was not impressed. He turned to his father and mother and said: "See how he has changed. He don't want to play no games anymore, he don't want to work in the fields, he is too much of a bigshot to use a cutlass. His brothers and sisters are fools, he don't want to talk to them because they don't understand. He don't even want to eat we food again, this morning I see he ain't touch the *baghi*. No. We have to get chicken for him, and the cream from all the cows in the village. Yes, that is what. And who it is does sweat for him to get him pretty shirt to wear in Port of Spain?" He held up one of the girls' arms and spanned it with his fingers. "Look how thin she is. All that is for you to be a big man, and now you scorning your own family?" Romesh got up from the floor and faced them. His eyes burned fiercely, and he looked like the pictures of Indian Gods the children had seen in the village hall. "You are all wrong!" He cried in a ringing voice. "Surely you, *bap*, and you, *mai*, the years must have taught you that you must make a different life for your children, that you must free them from ignorance and the wasting away of their lives? Do you want them to suffer as you have?" Rookmin looked like she was going to say something, but instead she shut her eyes tight. Ramlal said: "Who tell you we suffer? We bring children in the world and we happy." But Romesh went on, "And what will the children do? Grow up in the village here, without learning to read and write? There are schools in San Fernando, surely you can send them there to learn about different things besides driving a mule and using a cutlass? Oh *bap*, we are such a backward people, all the others move forward to better lives, and we lag behind believing that what is to be, will be. All over Trinidad, in the country districts, our people toil on the land and reap the cane. For years it has been so, years in the same place, learning nothing new, accepting our fate like animals. Political men come from India and give speeches in the city. They speak of better things, they tell us to unite and strive for a greater goal. And what does it mean to you? Nothing. You are content to go hungry, to see your children run about naked, emaciated, grow up dull and stupid, slaves to your own indifference. You do not even pretend an interest in the Legislative Council. I remember why you voted for Pragsingh last year, it was because he gave you ten dollars—did I not see it for myself? It were better that we returned to India than stay in the West Indies and live such a low form of existence." The family watched Romesh wide-eyed. Ramlal sucked his clay pipe noisily. Rookmin held her youngest daughter in her lap, picking her head for lice, and now and then shutting her eyes so the others wouldn't see what she was think-ing. "There is only one solution," Romesh went on, "We must educate the children, open up new worlds in their minds, stretch the horizon of their thoughts…" Suddenly he stopped. He realised that for some time now they weren't listening, his words didn't make any sense to them. Perhaps he was going about this in the wrong way, he would have to find some other way of explaining how he felt. And was he sufficiently equipped in himself to propose vast changes in the lives of the people? It seemed to him then how small he was, how there were so many things he didn't know. All the books he'd read, the knowledge he'd lapped up so hungrily in the city, listening to the politicians making speeches in the square—all these he mustered to his assistance. But it was as if his brain were too small, it was like putting your mouth in the sea and trying to drink all the water. Wearily, like an old man who had tried to prove his point merely by repeating, "I am old, I should know," Romesh sat down on the floor, and there was a silence in the hut, a great silence, as if the words he'd spoken had fled the place and gone outside with the wind and the cane.

And so after he had gone back to the city his parents discussed the boy, and concluded that the only thing to save his senses was to marry him off. "You know he like Sampath daughter from long time, and she is a hard-working girl, she go make good wife for him," Rookmin had said. Ramlal had seen Sampath and everything was fixed. Everybody in the village knew of the impending wedding…

Romesh came home the next day. He had some magazines and books under his arm, and a suitcase in his hand. There was no reception for him; everyone who could work was out in the fields.

He was as tall as the canes on either side of the path on which he walked. He sniffed the smell of burning cane, but he wasn't overjoyful at coming home. He had prepared for this, prepared for the land on which he had toiled as a child, the thatched huts, the children running naked in the sun. He knew that these things were not easily forgotten which he had to forget. But he saw how waves of wind rippled over the seas of cane and he wondered vaguely about big things like happiness and love and poetry, and how they could fit into the poor, toiling lives the villagers led.

Romesh met his sisters at home. They greeted him shyly but he held them in his arms and cried, "*Beti*, do you not know your own brother?" And they laughed and hung their heads on his shoulder.

"Everybody gone to work," one girl said, "and we cooking food to carry. Pa and Ma was looking out since early this morning, they say to tell you if you can come in the fields."

Romesh looked around the hut in which he had grown up. It seemed to him that if he had come home after ten years, there would still be the old table in the centre of the room, its feet sunken in the earthen floor, the black pots and pans hanging on nails near the window. Nothing would change. They would plant the cane, and when it grew and filled with sweet juice, cut it down for the factory. The children would waste away their lives working with their parents. No schooling, no education, no widening of experience. It was the same thing the man had lectured about in the public library three nights before in the Port of Spain. The most they would learn would be to wield a cutlass expertly, or drive the mule cart to the railway line swiftly so that before the sun went down they would have worked sufficiently to earn more than their neighbours.

With a sigh like an aged man Romesh opened his suitcase and took out a pair of shorts and a polo shirt. He put these on and put the suitcase away in a corner. He wondered where would be a safe place to put his books. He opened the suitcase again and put them in.

It was as if, seeing the room in which he had argued and quarrelled with the family on his last visit, he lost any happiness he might have had on coming back this time. A feeling of depression overcame him.

It lasted as he talked with his sisters as they prepared food to take to the fields. Romesh listened how they stumbled with words, how they found it difficult to express themselves. He thought how regretful it was that they couldn't go to school. He widened the thought and embraced all the children in the village, growing up with such little care, running naked in the mud with a piece of *roti* in their hands, missing out on all the things that life should stand for.

But when the food was ready and they set off for the fields, with the sun in their eyes making them blind, he felt better. He would try to be happy with them, while he was here. No more preaching. No more voicing of opinion on this or that.

Other girls joined his sisters as they walked, all carrying food. When they saw Romesh they blushed and tittered, and he wondered what they were whispering about among themselves.

There were no effusive greetings. Sweating as they were, their clothes black with the soot of burnt canes, their bodies in the motions of their work, they just shouted out, and Romesh shouted back. Then Ramlal dropped the reins and jumped down from his cart. He curved his hand like a boomerang and swept it over his face. The soot from his sleeves smeared his face as he wiped away the sweat.

Rookmin came up and opened tired arms to Romesh. "*Beta,*" she cried as she felt his strong head on her breast. She would have liked to stay like that, drawing his strength and vitality into her weakened body, and closing her eyes so her emotion wouldn't show.

"*Beta,*" his father said, "you getting big, you looking strong." They sat down to eat on the grass. Romesh was the only one who appeared cool, the others were flushed, the veins standing out on their foreheads and arms.

Romesh asked if it was a good crop.

"Yes *Beta,*" Ramlal said, "Is a good crop, and plenty of work for everybody. But this year harder than last year, because rain begin to fall early, and if we don't hurry up with the work, it will be too much trouble for all of us. The overseer come yesterday, and he say a big bonus for the man who do the most work. So everybody working hard for that bonus. Two of my mules sick, but I have to work them, I can't help. We trying to get the bonus."

After eating Ramlal fished a cigarette out from his pocket and lit it carefully. First greetings over, he had nothing more to tell his son, for the time being anyway.

Romesh knew they were all remembering his last visit, and the things he had said then. This time he wasn't going to say anything, he was just going to have a holiday and enjoy it, and return to school in the city refreshed.

He said, "Hari, I bet I could cut more canes than you."

Hari laughed. "Even though I work the whole morning already is a good bet. You must forget to use *poya*, your hands so soft and white now."

That is the way life is, Ramlal thought as Romesh took his cutlass. Education, school, *chut!* It was only work put in a *roti* in your belly, only work that brought money. The marriage would soon change Romesh. And he felt a pride in his heart as his son spat on the blade.

The young men went to a patch of burnt canes. The girls came too, standing by to pile the fallen stalks of sweet juice into heaps, so that they could be loaded quickly and easily on to the carts and raced to the weighing bridge.

Cane fell as if a machine were at work. The blades swung in the air, glistened for a moment in the sunlight, and descended on the stalks near the roots. Though the work had been started as a test of speed, neither of them moved ahead of the other. Sometimes Romesh paused until Hari came abreast, and sometimes Hari waited a few canes for Romesh. Once they looked at each other and laughed, the sweat on their faces getting into their mouths. There was no more enmity on Hari's part: seeing his brother like this, working, was like the old days when they worked side by side at all the chores which filled the day.

Everybody turned to in the field striving to outwork the others, for each wanted the bonus as desperately as his neighbour. Sometimes the women and the girls laughed or made jokes to one another, but the men worked silently. And the crane on the weighing bridge creaked and took load after load. The labourer manipulating it grumbled: there was no bonus for him, though his wage was more than that of the cane-cutters.

When the sun set all stopped work as if by signal. And in Ramlal's hut that night there was laughter and song. Everything was all right, they thought. Romesh was his natural self again, the way he swung that cutlass! His younger sisters and brother had never really held anything against him, and now that Hari seemed pleased, they dropped all embarrassment and made fun. "See *bhai*, I make *meetai* especially for you," his sister said, offering the sweetmeat.

"He work hard, he deserve it," Hari agreed, and he looked at his brother, almost with admiration.

Afterwards, when Ramlal was smoking and Rookmin was searching in the youngest girl's head for lice ("put pitch-oil, that will kill them," Ramlal advised), Romesh said he was going to pay Doolsie a visit.

There was a sudden silence. Rookmin shut her eyes, the children stopped playing, and Ramlal coughed over his pipe.

"Well what is the matter?" Romesh asked, looking at their faces.

"Well, now," Ramlal began, and stopped to clear his throat. "Well now, you know that is our custom, that a man shouldn't go to pay a visit to the girl he getting married..."

"What!" Romesh looked from face to face. The children shuffled their feet and began to get embarrassed at the stranger's presence once more.

Ramlal spoke angrily. "Remember this is your father's house! Remember the smaller ones! Careful what you say, you must give respect! You not expect to get married one day, eh? Is a good match we make, boy, you will get good dowry, and you could live in village and forget them funny things you learning in the city."

"So it has all been arranged," Romesh said slowly. "That is why everybody looked at me in such a strange way in the fields. My life already planned for me, my path pointed out—cane, labour, boy children, and the familiar village of Cross Crossing." His voice had dropped lower, as if he had been speaking to himself, but it rose again as he addressed his mother: "And you, *mai*, you have helped them to do this to me? You whose idea it was to give me an education?"

Rookmin shut her eyes and spoke. "Is the way of our people, is we custom from long time. And you is Indian? The city fool your brains, but you will get back accustom after you married and have children."

Ramlal got up from where he was squatting on the floor, and faced Romesh. "You have to do what we say," he said loudly. "Ever since you in the city, we notice how you change. You forgetting custom and how we Indian people does live. And too besides, money getting short. We want help on the estate. The garden want attention, and nobody here to see about cattle and them. And no work after crop, too besides."

"Then I can go to school in San Fernando," Romesh said desperately. "If there is no money to pay the bus, I will walk. The government schools are free, you do not have to pay to learn."

"You will be married and have boy children," Ramlal said, "and you will stop answering your *bap*..."

"*Hai! Hai!*" Drivers urged their carts in the morning sun, and whips cracked crisply on the air. Dew still clung to the grass as workers took to the fields to do as much as they could before the heat of the sun began to tell.

Romesh was still asleep when the others left. No one woke him; they moved about the hut in silence. No one spoke. The boys went to harness the mules, one of the girls to milk the cows and the other was busy in the kitchen.

When Romesh got up he opened his eyes in full awareness. He could have started the argument again as if no time had elapsed, the night had made no difference.

He went into the kitchen to wash his face. He gargled noisily, scraped his tongue with his teeth. Then he remembered his toothbrush and toothpaste in his suitcase. As he cleaned his teeth his sister stood watching him. She never used a toothbrush: they broke a twig and chewed it to clean their mouths.

"You going away, *bhai*?" she asked him timidly.

He nodded, with froth in his mouth.

"If you stay, you could teach we what you know," the girl said.

Romesh washed his mouth and said, "*Baihin*, there are many things I have yet to learn."

"But what will happen to us?"

"Don't ask me questions little sister," he said crossly.

After he had eaten he left the hut and sulked about the village, walking slowly with his hands in his pockets. He wasn't quite sure what he was going to do. He kept telling himself that he would go away and never return, but bonds he had refused to think about surrounded him. The smell of burnt cane was strong on the wind. He went to the pond, where he and Hari used to bathe the mules. What to do? His mind was in a turmoil.

Suddenly he turned and went home. He got his cutlass—it was sharp and clean, even though unused for such a long time, Ramlal never allowed any of his tools to get rusty.

He went out into the fields, swinging the cutlass in the air, as if with each stroke he swept a problem away.

Hari said: "Is time you come. Other people start work long time, we have to work extra to catch up with them."

There was no friendliness in his voice now.

Romesh said nothing, but he hacked savagely at the canes, and in half an hour he was bathed in sweat and his skin scratched from contact with the cane.

Ramlal came up in the mule cart and called out, "Work faster! We a whole cartload behind!" Then he saw Romesh and he came down from the cart and walked rapidly across. "So you come! Is a good thing you make up your mind!"

Romesh wiped his face. "I am not going to stay, *bap*." It was funny how the decision came, he hadn't known himself what he was going to do. "I will help with the crop, you shall get the bonus if I have to work alone in the night. But I am not going to get married. I am going away after the crop."

"You are mad, you will do as I say." Ramlal spoke loudly, and other workers in the field stopped to listen.

The decision was so clear in Romesh's mind that he did not say anything more. He swung the cutlass tirelessly at the cane and knew that when the crop was finished, it would be time to leave his family and the village. His mind got that far, and he didn't worry about after that...

As the wind whispered in the cane, it carried the news of Romesh's revolt against his parents' wishes, against tradition and custom.

Doolsie, working a short distance away, turned her brown face from the wind. But women and girls working near to her whispered among themselves and laughed. Then one of the bolder women, already married, said, "Well girl, is a good thing in a way. Some of these men too bad. They does beat their wife too much—look at Dulcie husband, he does be drunk all the time, and she does catch hell with him."

But Doolsie bundled the canes together and kept silent.

"She too young yet," another said. "Look, she breasts not even form yet!"

Doolsie did not have any memories to share with Romesh, and her mind was young enough to bend under any weight. But the way her friends were laughing made her angry, and in her mind she too had revolted against the marriage.

"All-you too stupid!" she said, lifting her head with a childish pride so that her sari fell on her shoulder. "You wouldn't say Romesh is the only boy in the village! And too besides, I wasn't going to married him if he think he too great for me."

The wind rustled through the cane. Overhead, the sun burned like a furnace.

baghi: spinach; *baihin*: sister; *bap*: father; *beta*: son; *beti*: young girl or sister; *bhai*: brother; *creole*: a native descendant of a European or African settler in the West Indies as opposed to those of Indian heritage; *mai*: mother; *poya*: cutlass used in harvesting sugar cane; *roti*: baked flour cake

ENTRY POINTS

1. Why does Ramlal view his son's education with suspicion? How does Rookmin's view differ from that of her husband? Evaluate their points of view.

2. "See how he has changed." How has Romesh changed? Why does *he* think change is necessary? Do you agree? Explain.

3. Is Romesh unappreciative and irresponsible or is he individualistic and far-sighted? As sons and daughters, what do we owe our parents? What do our parents owe to us? Share your responses with your group.

4. The story, "Skipper" (page 28), set in New Brunswick, and this story, set in Trinidad, are both essentially about decisions that a young man must make amidst conflicts with his family.
   (a) How are the conflicts similar?
   (b) How are they different?
   (c) Who makes the better decision ultimately, Skipper or Romesh? Evaluate their decisions in terms of their characters and the probable consequences on their lives.
   (d) Compare the characteristics and motivation of the two fathers, Rupert and Ramlal.
   (e) Compare the roles and desires of the two mothers, Ethel and Rookmin, in the two stories. Pay particular attention to their

relationships to their husbands and sons. How have mothers' roles and attitudes changed in the twentieth century?

5 Adapt this story into a script with a partner in which a son argues with his father about the value of education and change. Act out the script in front of your class or on video.

6 For other views on alienation, read Samuel Selvon's novel, *The Lonely Londoners* (1956), and his collection of short stories, *Ways of Sunlight* (1958). For other coming-of-age material set in the West Indies, read Michael Anthony's *Green Days by the River* (1967), set in Trinidad, and Olive Senior's *Summer Lightning and Other Stories* (1986), set in Jamaica. Write a book review.

7 Write your own story in which a teenager must make an important decision which will affect the rest of his/her life.

8 Write a personal essay in which you reveal how *your* education has changed you, and if that change has created conflict with other members of your family or with your childhood friends.

ON THE SHOOTING OF A BEAVER

GEORGE KENNY

Joe Rivers stood in front of an irregular line of spruce. He rubbed his leather mitted hands together. The air was still quite cold. The sun of spring in early April had not yet begun to melt the snows of the winter past, here in this region of Northwestern Ontario.

Joe's brown deep-set eyes scanned to his left and right as he faced a hole in the frozen creek surface. Careful not to move too much, he removed the leather covering of his new Olympus OM-1. He wanted to get a photograph of any creature, likely a beaver or a muskrat, that might crawl out of that watery opening.

His father, a trapper, had positioned him in this spot so that Joe might be able to shoot any furry animal using this hole to get a look at the above-water surroundings of its habitat. The elder Rivers had left Joe a Winchester 30:30 for this purpose.

Joe, who had spent most of his twenty-one years in town going to various schools, had not been too eager to act on his father's wish. Maybe it was because he never had to depend upon trapping and hunting in order to live, Joe reasoned, consenting nonetheless to follow his father's instructions.

What a contrast, being a bushman compared to life in the town of Dryden. Where did he belong, really, he wondered.

If the education counsellor from the Department of Indian Affairs had had his way, Joe, a grade twelve graduate should have gone to college and worked at getting some "real education." Though he had not been an outstanding student, he had the marks to go on.

He had decided, however, to work, and he had worked at the Dryden Paper mill ever since.

Joe shook a lock of hair out of his eyes. He began to feel his leather-booted feet getting cramped as well as cold. Maybe living in town had its advantages, he thought ruefully, as he shifted his hundred and seventy pounds; then again, it was really something out here.

He took his eyes away from the watery hole and gazed around. To his left, the snowy shoreline could not totally conceal golden strands of bulrushes, nor hide the broken pieces of aged trees lying down in natural death. Across the frozen stream a wall of balsam, cedar, and birch trees stood in uniform—nature's vanguard, he thought. To his right, the curve of shoreline ended at a shrub-tipped point. Beyond it lay the wide expanse of Moose Lake, across which he and his father had come on snowshoes. Squinting his eyes, he looked up at the sun, a round saucer coloured bright yellow in the empty blue sky.

The breeze rippled the water of the opening, making Joe's heart seem to bob up to his throat; but as no furry animal appeared, he slowly exhaled and found that he was relaxing muscles of his body. Come on, you dumb beaver, he thought, and then smiled at the idea of a beaver hurrying out to be shot.

His legs sore from standing, Joe sat back on his haunches as he thought of where he was.

He was by a small stream, deep in a forest somewhere to the northwest of Dryden, Ontario. Town life had gotten to be too much for him. Joe had gone to the foreman in the finishing room of the plant and had asked for a leave of absence for a couple of months. His boss, he first thought, would be disgusted, but instead had broken into a grin and said, go ahead, but come back if you still want to work. He seemed to understand this need that Joe, and others before him, had had. Joe began to feel a sense of freedom he had never experienced before.

For three years, he had visited his father along the shores of Moose Lake. On his visits, during winter weekends, he had used a friend's snowmobile, roaring up the forty miles or so, on old logging trails. His father, a small and tough Indian, had never ceased to fish, trap, and hunt, as so many of the men from the reserve had done. Joe recalled those days and nights of his weekends off when he and his father would drink tea brewed in a cast-iron pot, munch on fried bannock, and talk in the comfort of the well-insulated log cabin. Measuring no more than eight by twelve, the cabin was warmed by the heat of an old oil drum stove. Ah, those were the days, he thought, his chest aching with the memory of his father. On those occasions his father had hinted how nice it would be if his only son would come to share his few remaining years. Joe had wanted that. Yet, he had been too dependent upon living in electrically heated homes with their flush toilets, the town's offerings of a library, picture shows, a coffee and talk in the small Chinese-owned restaurants. Sighing, Joe gazed blindly at the hole, remembering his father's gladness and smile when Joe told him that he had come to stay with the elder Rivers for at least a couple of months. And so wrapped in his thoughts was he, that Joe didn't see...

A brown, furry head with a black nose peeking from the water, its button eyes sliding around in a circling watch, its rounded ears pointing to the other shore. The head of the beaver was barely above the water level, when with a catch of breath, Joe became aware of it. Apparently satisfied no danger was near, the large rodent put its front paws on the far edge of the ice, and slowly started to climb onto the ice.

With a sudden throbbing of his temples, Joe instinctively recovered from his initial surprise; bending swiftly, he exchanged items. For one long drawn out moment he held his breath, focusing, as the large beaver swung around to face him, droplets of moisture rolling down its glistening fur. Joe seemed to see sudden shock in the beaver's eyes as he fired, and then a red spurt of liquid came from just above the animal's right temple, as it fell backward onto the icy surface. Feeling sick instantly, Joe watched, frozen, as the large adult beaver spat out scarlet, its heated breath substance coming into the cold air as steam. Its wide flat tail pounded hard, then gradually stilled as the animal thrashed out its death throes.

Bending down, Joe picked up the expensive camera he had so quickly forsaken. I really only wanted a picture, he thought. What does this say about me? The first cloud of the coming spring day seemed to chill the sun as he swung both the camera and the Winchester over one shoulder. With his hands he picked up the now-still creature. One man, he knew, would be pleased with his choice.

ENTRY POINTS

1 "Where did he belong, really, he wondered." Why does Joe wonder about this question? Where do you think he now belongs? Where do *you* belong?

2 How has town life and education changed Joe? How is education changing you? Read Samuel Selvon's story, "Cane Is Bitter" (page 33).

3 Even though his father never appears in this story, he is a dominant force in Joe Rivers's thoughts. Why? Explain with specific references to the text.

4 The preceding two stories (page 28 to page 44) were, in part, about father-son relationships. Compare those relationships with that in this story.

5 (a) Why did Joe shoot the beaver with his Winchester 30:30 instead of with his new Olympus OM-1? What is his reaction to his killing, instead of only photographing, the beaver? "What does this say about me?" he asks. What does this say about Joe?

(b) Write about a "turning point" in your own life when you suddenly understood something new about yourself or your relationships with family members. As you do, think about this question: "What does this say about you?"

6 (a) Imagine you are an animal rights activist. Write a short article on your reaction to Joe's killing of the beaver.

(b) Imagine you are an aboriginal person dependent on hunting for your living. Write about your reaction to Joe's killing of the beaver.

7 Read George Orwell's classic essay, "Shooting an Elephant" (1950), and compare Orwell's reaction to the shooting of an animal in Burma to Joe's reaction to a similar act in Northwestern Ontario.

THE STOLEN PARTY

LILIANA HEKER

As soon as she arrived she went straight to the kitchen to see if the monkey was there. It was: what a relief! She wouldn't have liked to admit that her mother had been right. *Monkeys at a birthday?* her mother had sneered. *Get away with you, believing any nonsense you're told!* She was cross, but not because of the monkey, the girl thought; it's just because of the party.

"I don't like you going," she told her. "It's a rich people's party."

"Rich people go to Heaven too," said the girl, who studied religion at school.

"Get away with Heaven," said the mother. "The problem with you, young lady, is that you like to fart higher than your ass."

The girl didn't approve of the way her mother spoke. She was barely nine, and one of the best in her class.

"I'm going because I've been invited," she said. "And I've been invited because Luciana is my friend. So there."

"Ah yes, your friend," her mother grumbled. She paused. "Listen, Rosaura," she said at last. "That one's not your friend. You know what you are to them? The maid's daughter, that's what."

Rosaura blinked hard: she wasn't going to cry. Then she yelled: "Shut up! You know nothing about being friends!"

Every afternoon she used to go to Luciana's house and they would both finish their homework while Rosaura's mother did the cleaning.

They had their tea in the kitchen and they told each other secrets. Rosaura loved everything in the big house, and she also loved the people who lived there.

"I'm going because it will be the most lovely party in the whole world, Luciana told me it would. There will be a magician, and he will bring a monkey and everything."

The mother swung around to take a good look at her child, and pompously put her hands on her hips.

"Monkeys at a birthday?" she said. "Get away with you, believing any nonsense you're told!"

Rosaura was deeply offended. She thought it unfair of her mother to accuse other people of being liars simply because they were rich. Rosaura too wanted to be rich, of course. If one day she managed to live in a beautiful palace, would her mother stop loving her? She felt very sad. She wanted to go to that party more than anything else in the world.

"I'll die if I don't go," she whispered, almost without moving her lips.

And she wasn't sure whether she had been heard, but on the morning of the party she discovered that her mother had starched her Christmas dress. And in the afternoon, after washing her hair, her mother rinsed it in apple vinegar so that it would be all nice and shiny. Before going out, Rosaura admired herself in the mirror, with her white dress and glossy hair, and thought she looked terribly pretty.

Señora Ines also seemed to notice. As soon as she saw her, she said: "How lovely you look today, Rosaura."

Rosaura gave her starched skirt a slight toss with her hands and walked into the party with a firm step. She said hello to Luciana and asked about the monkey. Luciana put on a secretive look and whispered into Rosaura's ear: "He's in the kitchen. But don't tell anyone, because it's a surprise."

Rosaura wanted to make sure. Carefully she entered the kitchen and there she saw it: deep in thought, inside its cage. It looked so funny that the girl stood there for a while, watching it, and later, every so often, she would slip out of the party unseen and go and admire it. Rosaura was the only one allowed into the kitchen. Señora Ines had said, "You yes, but not the others, they're much too boisterous, they might break something." Rosaura had never broken anything. She even managed the jug of orange juice, carrying it from the kitchen into the dining-room. She held it carefully and didn't spill a single drop. And Señora Ines had said: "Are you sure you can manage a jug as big as that?" Of course she could manage. She wasn't a butterfingers, like the others. Like that blonde girl with the bow in her hair. As soon as she saw Rosaura, the girl with the bow had said:

"And you? Who are you?"

"I'm a friend of Luciana," said Rosaura.

"No," said the girl with the bow, "you are not a friend of Luciana because I'm her cousin and I know all her friends. And I don't know you."

"So what," said Rosaura. "I come here every afternoon with my mother and we do our homework together."

"You and your mother do your homework together?" asked the girl, laughing.

"I and Luciana do our homework together," said Rosaura, very seriously.

The girl with the bow shrugged her shoulders.

"That's not being friends," she said. "Do you go to school together?"

"No."

"So where do you know her from?" said the girl, getting impatient.

Rosaura remembered her mother's words perfectly. She took a deep breath.

"I'm the daughter of the employee," she said.

Her mother had said very clearly: "If someone asks, you say you're the daughter of the employee; that's all." She also told her to add: "And proud of it." But Rosaura thought that never in her life would she dare say something of the sort.

"What employee?" said the girl with the bow. "Employee in a shop?"

"No," said Rosaura angrily. "My mother doesn't sell anything in any shop, so there."

"So how come she's an employee?" said the girl with the bow.

Just then Señora Ines arrived saying *shh shh*, and asked Rosaura if she wouldn't mind helping serve out the hot-dogs, as she knew the house so much better than the others.

"See?" said Rosaura to the girl with the bow, and when no one was looking she kicked her in the shin.

Apart from the girl with the bow, all the others were delightful. The one she liked best was Luciana, with her golden birthday crown; and then the boys. Rosaura won the sack race, and nobody managed to catch her when they played tag. When they split into two teams to play charades, all the boys wanted her for their side. Rosaura felt she had never been so happy in all her life.

But the best was still to come. The best came after Luciana blew out the candles. First the cake. Señora Ines had asked her to help pass the cake around, and Rosaura had enjoyed the task immensely, because everyone called out to her, shouting "Me, me!" Rosaura remembered a story in which there was a queen who had the power of life or death over her subjects. She had always loved that, having the power of life or death. To Luciana and the boys she gave the largest pieces, and to the girl with the bow she gave a slice so thin one could see through it.

After the cake came the magician, tall and bony, with a fine red cape. A true magician: he could untie handkerchiefs by blowing on them and make a chain with links that had no openings. He could guess what cards were pulled out from a pack, and the monkey was his assistant. He called the monkey "partner." "Let's see here, partner," he would say, "turn over a card." And, "Don't run away, partner: time to work now."

The final trick was wonderful. One of the children had to hold the monkey in his arms and the magician said he would make him disappear.

"What, the boy?" they all shouted.

"No, the monkey!" shouted back the magician.

Rosaura thought that this was truly the most amusing party in the whole world.

The magician asked a small fat boy to come and help, but the small fat boy got frightened almost at once and dropped the monkey on the floor. The magician picked him up carefully, whispered something in his ear, and the monkey nodded almost as if he understood.

"You mustn't be so unmanly, my friend," the magician said to the fat boy.

"What's unmanly?" said the fat boy.

The magician turned around as if to look for spies.

"A sissy," said the magician. "Go sit down."

Then he stared at all the faces, one by one. Rosaura felt her heart tremble.

"You, with the Spanish eyes," said the magician. And everyone saw that he was pointing at her.

She wasn't afraid. Neither holding the monkey, nor when the magician made him vanish; not even when, at the end, the magician flung his red cape over Rosaura's head and uttered a few magic words...and the monkey reappeared, chattering happily, in her arms. The children clapped furiously. And before Rosaura returned to her seat, the magician said:

"Thank you very much, my little countess."

She was so pleased with the compliment that a while later, when her mother came to fetch her, that was the first thing she told her.

"I helped the magician and he said to me, 'Thank you very much, my little countess.'"

It was strange because up to then Rosaura had thought that she was angry with her mother. All along Rosaura had imagined that she would say to her: "See that the monkey wasn't a lie?" But instead she was so thrilled that she told her mother all about the wonderful magician.

Her mother tapped her on the head and said: "So now we're a countess!"

But one could see that she was beaming.

And now they both stood in the entrance, because a moment ago Señora Ines, smiling, had said: "Please wait here a second."

Her mother suddenly seemed worried.

"What is it?" she asked Rosaura.

"What is what?" said Rosaura. "It's nothing; she just wants to get the presents for those who are leaving, see?"

She pointed at the fat boy and at a girl with pigtails who were also waiting there, next to their mothers. And she explained about the presents. She knew, because she had been watching those who left before her. When one of the girls was about to leave, Señora Ines would give her a bracelet. When a boy left, Señora Ines gave him a yo-yo. Rosaura preferred the yo-yo because it sparkled, but she didn't mention that to her mother. Her mother might have said: "So why don't you ask for one, you blockhead?" That's what her mother was like. Rosaura didn't feel like explaining that she'd be horribly ashamed to be the odd one out. Instead she said:

"I was the best-behaved at the party."

And she said no more because Señora Ines came out into the hall with two bags, one pink and one blue.

First she went up to the fat boy, gave him a yo-yo out of the blue bag, and the fat boy left with his mother. Then she went up to the girl and gave her a bracelet out of the pink bag, and the girl with the pigtails left as well.

Finally she came up to Rosaura and her mother. She had a big smile on her face and Rosaura liked that. Señora Ines looked down at her, then looked up at her mother, and then said something that made Rosaura proud:

"What a marvellous daughter you have, Herminia."

For an instant, Rosaura thought that she'd give her two presents: the bracelet and the yo-yo. Señora Ines bent down as if about to look for something. Rosaura also leaned forward, stretching out her arm. But she never completed the movement.

Señora Ines didn't look in the pink bag. Nor did she look in the blue bag. Instead she rummaged in her purse. In her hand appeared two bills.

"You really and truly earned this," she said handing them over. "Thank you for all your help, my pet."

Rosaura felt her arms stiffen, stick close to her body, and then she noticed her mother's hand on her shoulder. Instinctively she pressed herself against her mother's body. That was all. Except her eyes. Rosaura's eyes had a cold, clear look that fixed itself on Señora Ines's face.

Señora Ines, motionless, stood there with her hand outstretched. As if she didn't dare draw it back. As if the slightest change might shatter an infinitely delicate balance.

Translated by Alberto Manguel

1 "I don't like you going.... It's a rich people's party." Why does Rosaura's mother make this comment to her daughter? How does her daughter react to this statement? How is this a good example of foreshadowing?

2 Evaluate Rosaura's relationship with (a) her mother; (b) Luciana; and (c) Luciana's mother, Señora Ines.

3 Even though her mother disapproves of Rosaura going to the party, why does she relent and let her go?

4 Reread the last five paragraphs.
(a) Describe and analyze Rosaura's reaction to Señora Ines's "payment."
(b) Evaluate Señora Ines's attitudes and actions toward Rosaura.
(c) In your own words, articulate what the "infinitely delicate balance" is.
(d) Comment on the significance of the title.

5 Reread the notes on Latin American literature in question 1 following "The Ex-Magician from the Minhota Tavern" (page 17). What criticism is Heker levelling at her Argentinian society? Can the same criticism be levelled against Canadian society? Discuss with your group and make a brief report to the class.

6 Write a short sequel to this story. What happens next after Rosaura and Señora Ines stare motionlessly at each other at the end of "The Stolen Party"? How does Rosaura now view her mother? How does she view her "friendship" with Luciana? Perform your sequel as a two-person skit or as a dramatic monologue.

7 Write a diary item in the voice of Rosaura in which you relate your feelings about the party, Señora Ines, and your mother.

8 Write a realistic story in which the major character suffers loss and humiliation. Use some dialogue to reveal character.

STEREOTYPE

I'm a fullblooded
West Indian stereotype
See me straw hat?
Watch it good

I'm a fullblooded
West Indian stereotype
You ask
if I got riddum
in me blood
You going ask!
Man just beat de drum
and don't forget
to pour de rum

I'm a fullblooded
West Indian stereotype
You say
I suppose you can show
us the limbo, can't you?
How you know!
How you know!
You sure
you don't want me
sing you a calypso too
How about that

I'm a fullblooded
West Indian stereotype
You call me
happy-go-lucky
Yes that's me

dressing fancy
and chasing women
if you think ah lie
bring yuh sister

JOHN AGARD

I'm a fullblooded
West Indian stereotype
You wonder
where do you people
get such riddum
could it be the sunshine
My goodness
just listen to that steelband

Isn't here one thing
you forgot to ask
go on man ask ask
This native will answer anything
How about cricket?
I suppose you're good at it?
Hear this man
good at it!
Put de willow
in me hand
and watch me stripe
de boundary

Yes I'm a fullblooded
West Indian stereotype

that's why I
graduated from Oxford University
with a degree
in anthropology

1 "I'm a fullblooded / West Indian stereotype." Define "stereotype." Why does John Agard, a Caribbean writer, make this insulting remark about himself? What is his real purpose?

2 What "West Indian stereotypes" does Agard refer to? List them. What is your reaction to these stereotypes of people who live in the West Indies nations?

3 Define "dialect" and point out specific examples of the poet's use of dialect in his poem. Why do you think he uses dialect in some instances? Read the story, "Cane Is Bitter" (page 33), for purposes of comparison. Further, find and read W. O. Mitchell's *Jake and the Kid* stories to discover how dialect is used in fiction set in Canada.

4 How is this poem satirical? Comment on the final stanza.

5 (a) Write a poem in which you outline and then satirize "stereotypes" in your own school or community. Use the conversational tone and the rhetorical question technique that Agard employs to put across his criticism of stereotypical thinking and attitudes. You might want to experiment with: "I'm a fullblooded teen-age stereotype."

(b) Rehearse this poem orally at home and present it as a dramatic reading to your class. Tape your performance and play it back. Did your performance evoke the irony in the poem?

6 What stereotypes of Canadians do you think might be held by people from other countries who have *not* visited Canada? Have you ever encountered any of these stereotypical views while travelling outside the country or before you moved to Canada? How do American television shows and commercials portray Canadians? Write a poem or personal essay entitled "I'm a fullblooded Canadian stereotype."

THE BENCH

RICHARD RIVE

"We form an integral part of a complex society, a society complex in that a vast proportion of the population are denied the very basic privileges of existence, a society that condemns a man to an inferior position because he has the misfortune to be born black, a society that can only retain its precarious social and economic position at the expense of an enormous oppressed proletariat!"

Karlie's eyes shone as he watched the speaker. Those were great words, he thought, great words and true. The speaker paused for a moment and sipped some water from a glass. Karlie sweated. The hot October sun beat down mercilessly on the gathering. The trees on the Grand Parade afforded very little shelter and his handkerchief was already soaked where he had placed it between his neck and shirt collar. Karlie stared round him at the sea of faces. Every shade of colour was represented, from shiny ebony to the one or two whites in the crowd. He stared at the two detectives, who were busily making shorthand notes of the speeches, and then turned to stare back at the speaker.

"It is up to us to challenge the rights of any groups who wilfully and deliberately condemn a fellow group to a servile position. We must challenge the rights of any people who see fit to segregate human beings solely on grounds of pigmentation. Your children are denied the rights which are theirs by birth. They are segregated socially, economically...."

Ah, thought Karlie, that man knows what he is speaking about. He says I am as good as any other man, even a white man. That needs much thinking. I wonder if he thinks I have the right to go into any bioscope or eat in any restaurant, or that my children can go to any school? These are dangerous ideas and need much thinking; I wonder what Ou Klaas would say to this. Ou Klaas said God made the white man and the black man separately and the one must always be *"baas"* and the other *"jong."* But this man says different things and somehow they seem true.

Karlie's brow was knitted as he thought. On the platform were many speakers, both white and black, and they were behaving as if there were no difference of colour between them. There was a white woman in a blue dress offering a cigarette to Nxeli. That could never happen at Bietjiesvlei. Old Lategan at the store would have fainted if his Annatjie had offered Witbooi a cigarette. And Annatjie had no such pretty dress. These were new things, and he, Karlie, had to be careful before he accepted them. But why shouldn't he accept them? He was not coloured any more, he was a human being. The speaker had said so. He remembered seeing pictures in the newspaper of people who defied laws which relegated them to a particular class, and those people were smiling as they went to prison. This was a strange world.

The speaker continued and Karlie listened intently. His speech was obviously carefully prepared and he spoke slowly, choosing his words. This is a great man, Karlie thought.

The last speaker was the white lady in the blue dress, who asked them to challenge any discriminatory laws or measures in every possible manner. Why should she speak like that? thought Karlie. She could go to the best bioscopes, and swim at the best beaches. Why, she was even more beautiful that Annatjie Lategan. They had warned him in Bietjiesvlei about coming to the city. He had seen the *Skollies* in District Six and knew what to expect there. Hanover Street held no terrors for him. But no one had told him about this. This was new, this set one's mind thinking, yet he felt it was true. She said one should challenge. He would challenge. He, Karlie, would astound old Lategan and Balie at the dairy farm. They could do what they liked to him after that. He would smile like those people in the newspaper.

The meeting was almost over when Karlie threaded his way through the crowd. The words of the speakers were still milling through his head. It could never happen in Bietjiesvlei, he thought, or could it? The sudden screech of a car pulling to a hurried stop whirled him back to his senses. A white head was angrily thrust through the window. "Look where you're going, you black bastard!"

Karlie stared dazedly at him. Surely this white man had never heard what the speakers had said. He could never have seen the white woman offering Nxeli a cigarette. Karlie could never imagine the white lady shouting those words at him. It would be best to catch a train and think these things over.

He saw the station in a new light. Here was a mass of human beings, some black, some white, and some brown like himself. Here they mixed with one another, yet each mistrusted the other with an unnatural fear. Each treated the other with suspicion, each moved in a narrow, haunted pattern of its own manufacture. One must challenge these things the speaker had said…in one's own way. Yet how in one's own way? How was one to challenge? Slowly it dawned upon him. Here was his chance, *the bench*. The railway bench with the legend "Europeans Only" neatly painted on it in white. For one moment it symbolized all the misery of the plural South African society. Here was a challenge to his rights as a man. There it stood, a perfectly ordinary wooden railway bench, like hundreds of thousands of others in South Africa. His challenge. That bench, now, had concentrated in it all the evils of a system he could not understand. It was the obstacle between himself and humanity. If he sat on it he was a man. If he was afraid he denied himself membership as a human in a human society. He almost had visions of righting the pernicious system if only he sat on that bench. Here was his chance. He, Karlie, would challenge.

He seemed perfectly calm when he sat down on the bench, but inside his heart was thumping wildly. Two conflicting ideas now throbbed through him. The one said, "I have no right to sit on this bench"; the other said, "Why have I no right to sit on this bench?" The one voice spoke of the past, of the servile position he had occupied on the farms, of his father and his father's father who were born black, lived like blacks and died like oxen. The other voice spoke of the future and said, "Karlie, you are a man. You have dared what your father would not have dared. You will die like a man!"

Karlie took out a cigarette and smoked. Nobody seemed to notice his sitting there. This was an anti-climax. The world still pursued its monotonous way. No voice shouted "Karlie has conquered!" He was a normal human being sitting on a bench on a busy station, smoking a cigarette. Or was this his victory, the fact that he was a normal human being? A well-dressed white woman walked down the platform. Would she sit on the bench, Karlie wondered. And then that gnawing voice, "You should stand and let the white woman sit." Karlie narrowed his eyes and gripped tighter at his cigarette. She swept past him without the slightest twitch of an eyelid and walked on down the platform. Was she afraid to challenge, to challenge his right to be a human? Karlie now felt tired. A third conflicting emotion was now creeping in, a compensatory emotion which said, "You do not sit on this bench to challenge, you sit there because you are tired. You are tired; therefore you sit." He would not move because he was tired, or was it because he wanted to sit where he liked?

People were now pouring out of a train that had pulled into the station. There were so many people pushing and jostling one another that nobody noticed him. This was his train. It would be quite easy to step into the train and ride off home, but that would be giving in, suffering defeat, refusing the challenge, in fact admitting that he was not a human being. He sat on. Lazily he blew cigarette smoke into the air, thinking…his mind was far from the meeting and the bench, he was thinking of Bietjiesvlei and Ou Klaas, how he had insisted that Karlie should come to Cape Town. Ou Klaas could look so quizzically at one and suck at his pipe. He was wise to know and knew much. He had said one must go to Cape Town and learn the ways of the world. He would spit and wink slyly when he spoke of District Six and the women he knew in Hanover Street. Ou Klaas knew everything. He said God made us white or black and we must therefore keep our places.

"Get off this seat!"

Karlie did not hear the gruff voice. Ou Klaas would be on the land now, waiting for his tot of cheap wine.

"I said get off the bench, you swine!"

Karlie suddenly whipped back to reality. For a moment he was going to jump up, then he remembered who he was and why he was sitting there. Suddenly he felt very tired. He looked up slowly into a very red face that stared down at him.

"Get up! I said, there are benches down there for you!"

Karlie stared up and said nothing. He stared up into very sharp, cold grey eyes.

"Can't you hear me speaking to you, you black swine!"

Slowly and deliberately Karlie puffed at his cigarette. So this was his test. They both stared at each other, challenged with the eyes, like two boxers, each knowing that they must eventually trade blows yet each afraid to strike first.

"Must I dirty my hands on scum like you?"

Karlie said nothing. To speak would be to break the spell, the supremacy he felt he was slowly gaining. An uneasy silence. Then,

"I will call a policeman rather than kick a Hotnot like you! You can't even open your black jaw when a white man speaks to you!"

Karlie saw the weakness. The white youth was afraid to take action himself. He, Karlie, had won the first round of the bench dispute!

A crowd now collected. "Afrika!" shouted one joker. Karlie ignored the remark. People were now milling around, staring at the unusual sight of a black man sitting on a white man's bench. Karlie merely puffed on.

"Look at the black ape! That's the worst of giving these Kaffirs too much rope!"

"I can't understand it, they have their own benches!"

"Don't get up, you have every right to sit there!"

"He'll get hell when a policeman comes!"

"Mind you, I can't see why they shouldn't sit where they please!"

"I've said before, I've had a native servant, and a more imperti-
nent...."

Karlie sat and heard nothing. Irresolution had now turned to determination. Under no condition was he going to rise. They could do
what they liked.

"So this is the fellow, hey, get up there! Can't you read?" The policeman was towering over him. Karlie could see the crest on his buttons and the thin wrinkles on his neck.

"What is your name and address?"

Karlie still maintained his obstinate silence. It took the policeman
rather unawares. The crowd was growing every minute.

"You have no right to speak to this man in such a manner!" It was
the white lady in the blue dress.

"Mind your own business! I'll ask your help when I need it. It is
people like you who make Kaffirs think they're as good as white people!"

Then addressing Karlie, "Get up, you!"

"I insist that you treat him with proper respect!"

The policeman turned red. "This...this...." He was at a loss for
words.

"Kick up the Hotnot if he won't get up!" shouted a spectator. Rudely,
a white man laid hands on Karlie. "Get up you bloody bastard!"

Karlie turned to resist, to cling to the bench, his bench. There were
more than one man now pulling at him. He hit out wildly and then
felt a dull pain as somebody rammed a fist into his face. He was now
bleeding and wild-eyed. He would fight for it. The constable clapped a
pair of handcuffs around Karlie's wrists and tried to clear a way through
the crowds. Karlie was still struggling. A blow or two landed on him.
Suddenly he relaxed and slowly struggled to his feet. It was useless
fighting any longer. Now it was his turn to smile. He had challenged
and won. Who cared at the result?

"Come on, you swine!" said the policeman, forcing Karlie through
the crowd.

"Certainly," said Karlie for the first time, and stared at the policeman
with the arrogance of one who dared to sit on a "European" bench.

ENTRY POINTS

1 "They are segregated socially, economically...." Why does Rive begin
his story with a political speech? What is the speaker recommend-
ing that his audience do about South Africa's now-revoked policy of
apartheid, a racist policy based on the complete segregation of the
white and black peoples of that country?

2 What, specifically, is Karlie's initial reaction to the speaker's impassioned words? What are his ultimate reactions?

3 What does "the bench" at the train station come to symbolize for Karlie? Outline the reactions of different people at the station to Karlie's act of defiance. Analyze their attitudes and motivations with your group.

4 "He was not coloured any more, he was a human being." Why is Karlie now able to make this statement? How does he now see things differently? How has he broken free of his previous limitations?

5 Karlie is punched and arrested at the end of the story, but he feels "he [has] challenged and won." What exactly has he won? In your own words, describe your feelings about Karlie's "victory."

6 (a) In your library's vertical files, research the following: South Africa, apartheid, civil rights, and the co-winners of the 1993 Nobel Prize for Peace, Nelson Mandela and F. W. deKlerk. Report your findings to your group and relate them to "The Bench." To what extent have things changed since Rive wrote this story?

(b) Having done your research, write a political speech in which you protest injustice in Canada or in your own community and recommend political action and reform. Present your speech in a dramatic fashion to your class.

7 Write a short story in which your protagonist gains a personal victory against a perceived injustice. Use both interior monologue and external dialogue techniques.

8 Compare the victory of Karlie to that of Balthazar in the story set in Columbia, "Balthazar's Marvellous Afternoon" (page 254).

SO WHAT ARE YOU, ANYWAY?

LAWRENCE HILL

Carole settles in Seat 12A, beside the window, puts her doll on a vacant seat and snaps open her purse. She holds up a mirror. She looks into her own dark eyes. She examines her handful of freckles, which are tiny ink spots dotting her cheeks. She checks for pimples, but finds none. Only the clear complexion that her father sometimes calls "milk milk milk milk chocolate" as he burrows into her neck with kisses.

"This is yours, I believe." A big man with a sunburnt face is holding her doll upside down.

"May I have her, please?" Carole says.

He turns the doll right side up. "A black doll! I never saw such a thing!"

"Her name's Amy. May I have her, please?"

"Henry Norton!" cries the man's wife. "Give that doll back this instant!"

Carole tucks the doll close to the window.

The man sits beside Carole. The woman takes the aisle seat.

"Don't mind him," the woman says, leaning towards Carole. "By the way, I'm Betty Norton, and he's my husband, Henry."

The man next to Carole hogs the armrest. His feet sprawl onto her side. And he keeps looking at her.

The stewardess passes by, checking seat belts. "Everything okay?"

"May I go to the bathroom?" Carole asks.

"Do you think you could wait? We're about to take off."

"Okay."

Carole looks out the window, sees the Toronto airport buildings fall behind and wonders if her parents are watching. Say goodbye, she instructs Amy, waving the doll's hand, say goodbye to Mom and Dad. The engines charge to life. Her seat hums. They taxi down the runway. She feels a hollowness in her stomach when they lift into the air. Her ears plug and stay that way until the plane levels out over pillows of cotton. They burn as bright as the sun. So that is what the other side of clouds look like!

"Excuse me. *Excuse me!*" The man is talking to her. "You can go to the bathroom now, you know."

"No, that's all right," Carole says.

"Travelling all alone, are you?"

Carole swallows with difficulty.

"Where do you live?" he asks.

"Don Mills."

"Oh, really?" he says. "Were you born there?"

"Yes."

"And your parents?"

"My mother was born in Chicago and my father was born in Tucson."

"And you're going to visit your grandparents?"

She nods.

"And your parents let you travel alone!"

"It's only an airplane! And I'm a big girl."

The man lowers the back of his seat, chuckling. He whispers to his wife. "No!" Carole hears her whisper back, "*You* ask her!"

Carole yawns, holds Amy's hand and goes to sleep. The clinking of silverware wakens her, but she hears the man and woman talking about her, so she keeps her eyes shut.

"I don't know, Henry," says the woman. "Don't ask me. Ask *her*."

"I'm kind of curious," he says. "Aren't you?"

Carole can't make out the woman's answer. But then she hears her say:

"I just can't see it. It's not fair to children. I don't mind them mixed, but the world isn't ready for it. They're neither one thing nor the other. Henry, wake that child and see if she wants to eat."

When the man taps her shoulder, Carole opens her eyes. "I have to go to the bathroom," she says.

"But they're going to serve the meal," the man says.

"Henry! If she wants out, let her out. She's only a child."

Carole grimaces. She is definitely not a child. She is a young lady! She can identify Drambuie, Kahlua, and Grand Marnier by smell!

Once in the aisle, Carole realizes that she has forgotten Amy.

Henry Norton hands her the doll. "There you go. And don't fall out of the plane, now. There's a big hole down by the toilet."

"There is not!" Carole says. "There isn't any such thing!" She heads down the aisle with an eye out just in case there is a hole, after all.

Coming out of the toilet, Carole finds the stewardess. "Excuse me, miss. Could I sit somewhere else?"

The woman frowns. "Why?"

"I don't like the window."

"Is that it? Is that the only reason?"

"Well...yes."

"I'm sorry, but we don't have time to move you now. We're serving a meal. Ask me later, if you like."

After Carole has eaten and had her tray taken and been served a hot face towel, the man says: "What *are* you, anyway? My wife and I were wondering."

Carole blinks, sees the man's clear blue eyes and drops her head.

"What do you mean?" she says.

"You know, what are you? What race?"

Carole's mouth drops. Race? What is that? She doesn't understand. Yet she senses that the man is asking a bad question. It is as if he is asking her something dirty, or touching her in a bad place. She wishes her Mom and Dad were there. They could tell her what "race" meant.

"That doll of yours is black," Henry Norton says. "That's a Negro doll. That's race. Negro. What's your race?"

The question still confuses her.

"Put it this way," the man says. "What is your father?"

The question baffles her. What is her father? He is her Dad! He is her Dad and every Sunday morning he makes pancakes for the whole family and lets Carole pour hot syrup on them and afterwards he sits her on his lap and tells stories.

Mrs. Norton leans towards Carole. "Say you had a colouring book. What colour would you make your Dad?"

"I never use just one colour."

"Okay. What colour would you make his face?"

"Brown."

"And your mother?"

Carole imagines a blank page. What would she put in her mother's face? She has to put something in there. She can't just leave it blank. "I don't know."

"Sure you do," Mrs. Norton says. "How would you colour your mother's face?"

"Yellow."

Carole sees Mr. and Mrs. Norton look at each other.

"Is your mother Chinese?" Mrs. Norton asks.

"No."

"Are you sure you'd colour her yellow?"

"No."

"What else might you colour her?"

What else? Carole feels ashamed at her stupidity. A tear races down her cheek. "Red," she says, finally.

"Red! You can't colour a face red! Is your mother white? Is she like me? Her face! Is it the same colour as mine?"

"Yes."

"And your father's brown?"

Carole nods.

"When you say brown, do you mean he is a Negro?"

"Yes." Of course her father is a Negro. If Mrs. Norton wanted to know all along if her Dad was a Negro, why didn't she just ask?

"So you're mixed?" Mrs. Norton says. "You're a mulatto!"

Carole's lip quivers. What is mulatto? Why do they keep asking her what she is? She isn't anything!

"So is that it? You're a mulatto? You know what a mulatto is, don't you? Haven't your parents taught you that word?"

Approaching with a cart of juice, the stewardess looks up and smiles at Carole. That gives her a rush of courage.

"Leave me alone!" she screams at Mrs. Norton.

Passengers stare. The stewardess spills a drink. Mrs. Norton sits back hard in her seat, her hands raised, fingers spread. Carole sees people watching.

"Why do you keep asking me if my Dad is Negro? Yes, he's a Negro! Okay? OKAY? Negro Negro Negro!"

"Calm down," Mrs. Norton says, reaching over.

"Don't touch her," the stewardess says.

"Who are these people?" someone says from across the aisle. "Imagine, talking to a child like that, and in 1970!"

One woman sitting in front of Carole stands up and turns around.

"Would you like to come and sit with me, little girl?"

"No!" Carole shouts. "I don't like all these questions. She keeps asking me how I would colour my parents in a colouring book! Why do you keep asking me that?"

Mrs. Norton pleads with Carole to stop.

"How would you like it if that happened to you?" Carole says. "So what are you, anyway? What are your parents? How would you colour them? Well, I don't care! I don't even care!"

"How would you like to come and sit with me?" the stewardess says, smiling. "I'll make you a special drink. Have you ever had a Shirley Temple?"

Carole nods enthusiastically. Already she feels better. Clutching Amy, she passes by the Nortons, who swing their legs to let her out.

"My God," Carole hears Mrs. Norton tell her husband, "talk about sensitive."

1. Why do you think Henry Norton and his wife behave the way they do to Carole? Discuss within your group and share your thoughts with your class.

2. "What *are* you, anyway?"
   (a) Outline and analyze Carole's reaction to this question from the Nortons.
   (b) Characterize the Nortons. What are *they*, anyway? Are the Nortons themselves portrayed in a stereotypical way? Explain your response.
   (c) Do you think much has changed in relation to stereotypical attitudes in Canadian society since 1970? Explain your response. Read the poem, "Stereotype" (page 55).

3. Unlike South Africa's former policy of apartheid, Canadians cannot discriminate legally against anyone because of race. Our Charter of Rights outlaws racist behaviour. With reference to this story and others you may have read, show how racism amongst some individuals may still exist in Canada. Characterize this racism.

4. Imagine you are Carole. Write a letter to your parents telling them about your experience on the plane trip from Toronto.

5. In role as Carole's parents, try to explain to her about the kinds of racism she may encounter during her life.

6. So what are *you*, anyway? Answer this question about yourself in your own words. Use whatever tone you think appropriate and/or persuasive. Assess your assumptions about yourself.

7. With your group, discuss the differences between overt, obvious bigotry and subtle or "polite" discrimination. Think of specific examples of each. Share your ideas with your class.

THE MIDDLE GROUND

GENNI GUNN

They came to live in Vancouver after her husband died: Rosalba and her small son, Claudio—her son who, in spite of her husband's persistent teachings, grew more Canadian each year. When he was born, Giulio had made her promise to speak only Italian to the boy—a rule she insisted upon even now that he was almost six. But the boy grew more Canadian each year. He would sit on her lap and listen attentively to stories (in Italian, always in Italian) about her parents. "*Il nonno e la nonna,*" Rosalba had taught him to say. But he had no grandparents here, no olive trees and no watermelons to hug. Claudio told her the other children laughed when he told them these stories. The boy had never been to Italy. His imagined homeland was no different to him than Canada had been to Rosalba before she came. It was not his fault that he could not remember the taste of prickly-pears, persimmons and fresh fruit.

In Vancouver, Rosalba bought persimmons in a little Chinese store on Commercial Drive. But they had been picked too soon and she could not find the right words to describe to Claudio their real taste.

She'd been in Canada almost ten years, had come at nineteen to live in Victoria where Giulio taught Italian Studies at the University. But Rosalba had always loved Vancouver, its mountains and ocean so close together she could almost smell the Adriatic Sea: Trieste leaning lazy against low-slung mountains, rooftops baked ruddy in the hot summers. From the viewpoint up near the Conservatory in Queen Elizabeth

Park, she could almost imagine herself sitting on the stone wall of the old castle that overlooked Trieste. Only the cobblestones were missing and the long steep hills and curved narrow roads leading to the university. In Vancouver, a different beauty: the clumps of evergreens, cedar-shake roofs and coloured houses. Then the downtown high-rises jutting into the sky, dwarfed by the backdrop of mountains.

She came to Vancouver to teach Italian at a school set in Little Italy and filled with Italian teenagers, both first and second generation. It had been the natural thing for her to do, now that Giulio was gone. Many of the students came from small villages in southern Italy and spoke only dialects. Most had never learned proper Italian grammar. Strange that she should be the one to recreate with patience a language and a culture for strangers' children—she, who could not keep her own son from becoming Canadian.

The changes had been subtle. Like the night he'd asked her to read him a story in English, although she always read to him from *Il Tesoro*. She had been raised on it herself. The thick red volume with gold-embossed printing on the cover, the fairy-tales and jokes and pictures— all part of her childhood. She could almost recite each word by heart. She'd said "no," of course, and read him his favourite story. But the next day, seized with unbearable guilt, she'd gone to a book store and bought *Peter Pan*, in English.

And another evening, when he'd asked if they could order pizza with pineapple on top, she'd said, "absolutely not, that's not real pizza," and had made him one at home, the way her mother had taught her. But later, she'd opened a can of pineapple chunks and let him put them on top of his. She was trying to keep him Italian, but the boy grew more Canadian each year.

In the area around Commercial Drive, a new Italy had been established long before she came. Here, families lived the traditional roles of their homeland. Some women were still clad in dark dresses that reached to below their knees, their elbows covered with shawls and cardigans. It made Rosalba think of Goya's *Disasters of War*. All that black—black skirts, black hair, black eyes. Only the shop windows on Commercial Drive twinkled with vibrant colours. Mannequins sporting the newest fashions from Rome smiled into the street, eyes vacant, smooth blond bobs and turned-up noses. Rosalba wished they didn't look so *American*. She'd always said *America* when she was in Italy, even though she'd been speaking of Canada. From across the ocean, there had been only one continent, no differentiation between countries. She supposed it was the same for Italy. Canadians thought of Italians as one people—all born of the same fat little dark-haired Italian Mother Earth. But she had only to think of her youth, of the many provinces and dialects, of the animosity between North and South, water and mountains.

She had chosen Vancouver, when her husband died, because of Commercial Drive, because of the mountains and the ocean. When the insurance money came, she went house-hunting with Claudio. At first, they looked in the Italian district. Rosalba tip-toed politely from house to house. "The bathroom counters are all marble. My husband had it sent direct from Italy, you know." Windows shuttered, floors glistening, Madonnas mounted on corner altars in the hall. "And that couch belonged to my grandmother. But we're going back. I'll sell it, if you're interested." Plaster busts of Roman Emperors; outdoors, lions guarding a driveway and at the back, a clothesline to the hydro pole. "These dryers make clothes yellow." And the neighbours peering from doorsteps. "And where are you from, Signora?" All so *Italian*. After the fifth house, Rosalba hurried Claudio into the car seat and drove back to their rented apartment. Inside, she took a deep breath and leaned back on the couch. She had panicked back there, among icons and idols; she felt she might be absorbed into their darkness, their familiarity. She waited a few days, then contacted a real-estate firm. She asked the school secretary to call for her. "It's my accent," she explained apologetically. "They think I'm stupid."

The real-estate lady showed her houses on the West Side, tall beautiful wooden houses made of bleached grey cedar and nicked with skylights that captured the dawn. She loved these monolithic structures, the white inner walls and the echo of her heels on the hardwood floors. Although she longed to live in one of these houses, she settled finally on a sturdy, squat bungalow with precise rectangular windows with nine panes in each. She bought it because of its cream stucco exterior that reminded her of the white stone of her parents' house. She bought it because it seemed more *Italian*, and this was her concession for not buying one within the Italian district.

She enrolled Claudio in first grade at the elementary school just two blocks away from their new home and made arrangements to have a babysitter take him there in the mornings and pick him up at the end of the day. She had to leave much earlier than he did, to drive across town and be settled into the classroom before her students arrived.

"Now don't you let anyone call you anything but *Claudio*," she said on the first morning, squeezing him to her and wishing she could go with him. "Repeat it slowly if they say it wrong." Rosalba hated the way people here pronounced her name "Rozelba" or "Ruzolba," as if there were no such thing as a soft *r* or *s*. Often, she tried to break it down phonetically: "Ross-al-ba," or "Row-sal-ba, like rosary," she'd say. But they forgot too soon.

At her school, she noticed Peppi Armano immediately. He had a physical disability and always entered her ninth grade class after all the other students were seated. He had large eyes—round white saucers with pupils swimming in the middle, which followed her around the classroom.

He walked slowly, painfully, his small hands grasping the combination locks on the lockers that lined the hallways. Her classroom was upstairs, and she grew accustomed to the shuffling of feet after the bell had rung. At times, she watched Peppi make his way up or down the stairs, one foot at a time on each step. She wanted to help him, to take his free hand, the one which was not so tightly clasped to the bannister, and walk down with him, but she was afraid to show her concern because Peppi kept his head down and stared only at his feet. At the end of the first week, he stayed after class and stood in front of her desk until she prompted him, "Is there something I can do?" He blushed and for a moment let go of her desk with both hands, trying to stand up straight as he spoke. "About my being late," he said in a muffled, quiet voice, "I have to wait until the others have gone. It's easier when I can hold on to the lockers. My legs...," he stopped and leaned against the desk and Rosalba felt tears sting in her eyes.

"I understand," she said. But she didn't, and later, asked the Principal about it.

"Friedreich's ataxia," the Principal told her. "His parents want to buy him a wheelchair, but he won't hear of it. He's a very stubborn boy. We've talked to him on many occasions."

After that, it seemed her ears were attuned to the sound of Peppi's small feet as they dragged through the halls. She could hear lock after lock swinging on its gate after he'd passed. She imagined she could count the lockers by his steps, by his hands which clung to the round black dials. She asked the Principal if she could have a room on the bottom floor. But he said it was impossible to reroute the school for Peppi. There were too many classes, too many students, too many timetables. "We have to do what's best for the majority," he said. And Rosalba lay in bed at night and tried to think of ways to help one small boy.

She noticed that Peppi remained reserved and always a little apart from the rest of the students. On one occasion, when she organized an after-school trip to the Italian Cultural Centre to see an Italian film, Peppi did not come. She waited for him until one of the students told her that his brother had taken him home at the usual time.

Rosalba went to see Mrs. Crombie, the school counsellor, to ask about Peppi's family.

"As far as we can tell," Mrs. Crombie said, "the parents are over-protective. The boy has no friends—in fact, goes nowhere without either one of his parents or his brother. If only he'd agree to use a wheelchair." She paused. "Has he talked to you about it?"

Rosalba shook her head.

"Poor kid. Last year, we tried talking to the parents...but you know how it is with these families. They believe they're doing what's best for him." She tapped her pen on her desk for a moment, then looked up at Rosalba. "Why don't *you* talk to them? They might listen to you, if you spoke in their language."

Their language. Rosalba noticed the choice of words. Mrs. Crombie had not said, *your language. Their language,* as if *they* were somehow different from her. She said, "It's *my* language too."

And Mrs. Crombie smiled. "Yes, but you're different."

Strange the concept of foreigners. And how cultures could be massed under one umbrella. Yet individuals were considered separate. She wanted to shout, "I'm Italian." But she shook her head instead and said nothing. When she was still in Italy and the tourist season began, she had thought of all Americans in the same way. She had never considered each person as separate and distinct, but rather had seen Americans as a collective of brash, loud, forward peoples, with bermuda shorts and cameras. And when she'd had occasion to meet one, she too had thought that one person was different. The prejudice, then, came out of ignorance, out of the stereotypes they all accepted.

"What is a Wop?" Claudio asked.

Rosalba said, "Schoolchildren often give names to things they don't understand. You are *Italian.*"

"I don't want to be Italian," Claudio said, "because Italians are Wops. And I don't want to be a Wop."

The first few weeks of school passed quickly. She was busy with marking papers, remembering names, preparing a five-minute skit in Italian to be performed for the school. I must do something about Peppi, Rosalba thought, just as soon as I'm more settled. She became aware that Claudio had started to speak English to her at home. At first, he began with a sentence here and there that she asked him to repeat in Italian, as if she couldn't understand.

Two months into the school year, Claudio announced, "I'm not going to speak Italian at home any more."

Rosalba pleaded with him (in Italian), "You'll forget the language," she said. Then, "If your father were alive, he'd be heartbroken."

But Claudio was obstinate. "I don't want to," he said. "What's the use of it, anyway? Nobody in my school speaks Italian."

And Rosalba went to bed feeling guilty and thought about what Giulio would have done in this case. Giulio would have enrolled the boy in a school in the Italian district, where he would be with other Italian children. Each day, he grew more Canadian. And she was afraid to draw him back, to make him live a life he'd never known. She noticed that her students at school were distressed, secretive, trying to cope with the mixture of cultures—their survival dependent on the separation rather than the integration of the two. Was it fair, she thought, to force them to abide by rules that made no sense here, rules which had been implemented for a different culture in a different time?

What startled her the most was that the majority of the Italians she'd met adhered to strict oppressive customs to which she had not been exposed even in Italy. They had brought with them a culture several decades old. Things changed, times changed even in Italy, but these people insisted on remaining the same. "If you stand still, you go backward." She'd read that somewhere, and now the words appeared to make much more sense.

Rosalba asked Peppi to come and see her after school.

"I'll have to phone my brother and tell him what time to pick me up."

"I'll call him," Rosalba said, "and tell him not to come."

He looked at her doubtfully. "Oh, he'll come anyway."

Peppi arrived at 4:00 p.m., after the school halls had thinned out. He stood at her desk and when she told him to sit down, he reluctantly did so. She thought that if he could have managed it, he would have run out of the room, so much did he resemble a trapped animal.

She stared at the papers on her desk and tried to find opening words. "Peppi," she finally began. "I had a talk with Mrs. Crombie."

"It's about the wheelchair, isn't it? Why does everyone talk behind my back?"

"No one is talking behind your back. We're all very concerned about you. Your parents—"

"I'm tired of their concern." His voice rose in pitch. "They always decide everything for me. Nobody asks me what I want."

She stared at him for a moment, then asked softly, "What do *you* want, then?"

"I want to—be myself," he said. "I want to do things myself. They treat me like I can't even think."

"Maybe they're trying to do what's best for you." She paused. "If you can think for yourself, then surely you must realize that a wheelchair would help you tremendously."

"I can manage just fine on my own."

She said nothing, waiting, noting the tremor in his words. "And besides, if I get the stupid wheelchair, they'll never let me out of their sight. I don't want it!"

"You know," Rosalba said after a moment. "It might not be at all how you think. With a wheelchair, you'd be able to get around on your own a lot easier. For instance, you wouldn't need anyone to take you to or from school."

"Oh sure. As if they'd let me go alone." He sat, quiet, staring at his hands. "I'm not even allowed to go to a movie by myself. Not unless Papa drives me. It's *embarrassing*. Being watched all the time. If it wasn't for the law here, I bet I wouldn't even be allowed to go to school; they'd keep me at home always."

"Do you want me to talk to them?" she asked.

He shrugged. "I don't think it would do any good."

A few days later, Rosalba called Peppi's parents and asked them to come to the school to speak to her. She distinctly said she wanted to see them both.

They came a little past six. She'd asked the babysitter to stay late, even though Claudio had insisted that he was old enough to be left alone for a few hours. Mr. Armano was short and round and Rosalba could see that the boy's beauty came from his mother. She was dressed much older than her years. She could not have been much more than thirty, yet she carried herself like an old woman. Her hair was smoothed back into a bun at the nape of her neck, tight and shiny, making her eyes— Peppi's eyes—appear even larger and rounder than they were. Mrs. Armano kept wringing her hands. "Is something wrong?" Mr. Armano said in English as soon as he walked into the room. "Peppi did something bad? We teach him in the house. We give him the manners—"

"No," Rosalba interrupted, and spoke in Italian. "He's done nothing wrong. He's a very good student." The Armanos looked at her, puzzled. "Then why did you want us to come if there's nothing wrong?"

Rosalba made them sit in two of the desks of the classroom. She explained to them that Peppi was growing up, that he needed to spend time with people his own age. She asked them why Peppi had not come to see the film with the class.

Mrs. Armano clenched and unclenched her hands on her lap. "He's sick," she said.

"He has a *physical* disability," Rosalba said more sharply than she'd meant to, "but this doesn't mean he can't do a lot of things other boys his age do."

Mrs. Armano looked away. "But he might hurt himself—"

"Mrs. Armano, it's part of growing up. You know that. You've raised another boy."

"Yes, but Peppi is different," she said solemnly.

"Perhaps you're trying to keep him different," Rosalba concluded.

And that night, after she tucked Claudio into bed, she thought about the Armanos, about the fine line between protectiveness and suffocation, about Peppi's symbolic stand against it. She heard Claudio's voice a few days earlier:

"Mamma, don't hold my hand when we're out."

"But why not?"

"I'm too old and Jimmy says only babies hold their mother's hand."

She had told him about her family—her brothers and sisters—and how they still held hands even as adults. But he'd slipped his fingers out of hers as she talked and hooked them into the opening of his pocket. Claudio becoming more Canadian—was she, too, trying to keep him different?

She acted as mediary between Peppi and his parents, spoke to them twice more over the next month, and was finally able to convince them to agree to a compromise: they would allow Peppi to come to school alone if he used the wheelchair. It was only a small concession, but for Peppi, the first triumph of a new independence.

She watched him anxiously that first day, his hands caressing the chrome of the large new wheels. He smiled shyly at her at the end of the day, when he left her classroom with the other teens.

She sat at her desk, long after they'd all gone, and thought about Claudio and herself. She too was trying to do what was best for him. She thought of Giulio, his smile there in Trieste. He'd preserved laughter and bittersweet memories like pressed flowers of intense moments with his family and friends. He had not been rigid. He had embraced the new way of life and enriched it with the old. Rosalba remained in her classroom, thinking, until the janitor asked her to leave so he could lock up the school.

When she arrived home, she saw Claudio sitting at his little table, drawing a picture for her. "I missed you," he said in Italian and buried his face in her skirt. "I missed you too, Claudio," she answered in English. Then she took him onto her lap and told him stories of Italy.

ENTRY POINTS

1 "But the boy grew more Canadian each year."
  (a) What does the above statement mean to you?
  (b) Define "assimilation." Why does Rosalba resist assimilation for her young son, Claudio? Discuss the pro's and con's of assimilation with your group. Keep in mind your own social and cultural perspective.
  (c) How does Rosalba try to "remain Italian" in a pluralistic city like Vancouver? Describe the multicultural elements in Vancouver as detailed in this story.
  (d) Why does Claudio wish to be "Canadianized"? What does this mean to you? Is this process inevitable?
  (e) How is Rosalba being "Canadianized" by her young son? Reread the last two paragraphs.

2 "Canadians thought of Italians as one people...." Is this true, or is Rosalba herself promoting a stereotype? Debate this question with your group and share your responses with your class. How, according to Rosalba, is Italy itself a country of "differences"?

3 Why does Gunn include Rosalba's relationship with Peppi Armano in the story? What does Rosalba learn about herself and her son as a result of Peppi's problems? How are Peppi's problems resolved? For another view of the physically challenged, read "The Wheelchair" by Gabrielle Roy (page 124).

4 "Yes, but you're different." How is Rosalba different from the Armanos in the principal's eyes? How is she similar to them? What do you think of the principal's comments and behaviour?

5 "If you stand still, you go backward." Explain this apparent paradox with specific references to the story and to the concept of "culture" within a multicultural community. For another view, read the poem, "Multiculturalism" (page 87).

6 In this conflict of living between two worlds, can or should there be a "middle ground"? Explain. Discuss with your group and share your thoughts with your class. Compare the "middle ground" Rosalba tries to find in this story with the "middle ground" in which the mother and son find themselves in "Borders" (page 77).

7 How is this a story of triumph for those who see themselves as marginalized from mainstream society? Read the two stories preceding "The Middle Ground."

8 Adapt this story into a script in which various students role-play Rosalba, Claudio, Peppi, Peppi's parents, and Mrs. Crombie.

9 For other views of Italians in Canada, read the novels, *The Italians* by F. G. Paci, and *In a Glass House* by Nino Ricci, and the anthology, *Italian Canadian Voices*, edited by Caroline Morgan DiGiovanni. Write a review of one of these books and share your assessment with the class.

BORDERS

THOMAS KING

When I was twelve, maybe thirteen, my mother announced that we were going to go to Salt Lake City to visit my sister who had left the reserve, moved across the line, and found a job. Laetitia had not left home with my mother's blessing, but over time my mother had come to be proud of the fact that Laetitia had done all of this on her own.

"She did real good," my mother would say.

Then there were the fine points to Laetitia's going. She had not, as my mother liked to tell Mrs. Manyfingers, gone floating after some man like a balloon on a string. She hadn't snuck out of the house, either, and gone to Vancouver or Edmonton or Toronto to chase rainbows down alleys. And she hadn't been pregnant.

"She did real good."

I was seven or eight when Laetitia left home. She was seventeen. Our father was from Rocky Boy on the American side.

"Dad's American," Laetitia told my mother, "so I can go and come as I please."

"Send us a postcard."

Laetitia packed her things, and we headed for the border. Just outside of Milk River, Laetitia told us to watch for the water tower.

"Over the next rise. It's the first thing you see."

"We got a water tower on the reserve," my mother said. "There's a big one in Lethbridge, too."

"You'll be able to see the tops of the flagpoles, too. That's where the border is."

When we got to Coutts, my mother stopped at the convenience store and bought her and Laetitia a cup of coffee. I got an Orange Crush.

"This is real lousy coffee."

"You're just angry because I want to see the world."

"It's the water. From here on down, they got lousy water."

"I can catch the bus from Sweetgrass. You don't have to lift a finger."

"You're going to have to buy your water in bottles if you want good coffee."

There was an old wooden building about a block away, with a tall sign in the yard that said "Museum." Most of the roof had been blown away. Mom told me to go and see when the place was open. There were boards over the windows and doors. You could tell that the place was closed, and I told Mom so, but she said to go and check anyway. Mom and Laetitia stayed by the car. Neither one of them moved. I sat down on the steps of the museum and watched them, and I don't know that they ever said anything to each other. Finally, Laetitia got her bag out of the trunk and gave Mom a hug.

I wandered back to the car. The wind had come up, and it blew Laetitia's hair across her face. Mom reached out and pulled the strands out of Laetitia's eyes, and Laetitia let her.

"You can still see the mountain from here," my mother told Laetitia in Blackfoot.

"Lots of mountains in Salt Lake," Laetitia told her in English.

"The place is closed," I said. "Just like I told you."

Laetitia tucked her hair into her jacket and dragged her bag down the road to the brick building with the American flag flapping on a pole. When she got to where the guards were waiting, she turned, put the bag down, and waved to us. We waved back. Then my mother turned the car around, and we came home.

We got postcards from Laetitia regular, and, if she wasn't spreading jelly on the truth, she was happy. She found a good job and rented an apartment with a pool.

"And she can't even swim," my mother told Mrs. Manyfingers.

Most of the postcards said we should come down and see the city, but whenever I mentioned this, my mother would stiffen up.

So I was surprised when she bought two new tires for the car and put on her blue dress with the green and yellow flowers. I had to dress up, too, for my mother did not want us crossing the border looking like Americans. We made sandwiches and put them in a big box with pop and potato chips and some apples and bananas and a big jar of water.

"But we can stop at one of those restaurants, too, right?"

"We maybe should take some blankets in case you get sleepy."

"But we can stop at one of those restaurants, too, right?"

The border was actually two towns, though neither one was big enough to amount to anything. Coutts was on the Canadian side and consisted of the convenience store and gas station, the museum that was closed and boarded up, and a motel. Sweetgrass was on the American side, but all you could see was an overpass that arched across the highway and disappeared into the prairies. Just hearing the names of these towns, you would expect that Sweetgrass, which is a nice name and sounds like it is related to other places such as Medicine Hat and Moose Jaw and Kicking Horse Pass, would be on the Canadian side, and that Coutts, which sounds abrupt and rude, would be on the American side. But this was not the case.

Between the two borders was a duty-free shop where you could buy cigarettes and liquor and flags. Stuff like that.

We left the reserve in the morning and drove until we got to Coutts.

"Last time we stopped here," my mother said, "you had an Orange Crush. You remember that?"

"Sure," I said. "That was when Laetitia took off."

"You want another Orange Crush?"

"That means we're not going to stop at a restaurant, right?"

My mother got a coffee at the convenience store, and we stood around and watched the prairies move in the sunlight. Then we climbed back in the car. My mother straightened the dress across her thighs, leaned against the wheel, and drove all the way to the border in first gear, slowly, as if she were trying to see through a bad storm or riding high on black ice.

The border guard was an old guy. As he walked to the car, he swayed from side to side, his feet set wide apart, the holster on his hip pitching up and down. He leaned into the window, looked into the back seat, and looked at my mother and me.

"Morning, ma'am."

"Good morning."

"Where you heading?"

"Salt Lake City."

"Purpose of your visit?"

"Visit my daughter."

"Citizenship."

"Blackfoot," my mother told him.

"Ma'am?"

"Blackfoot," my mother repeated.

"Canadian?"

"Blackfoot."

It would have been easier if my mother had just said "Canadian" and been done with it, but I could see she wasn't going to do that. The guard wasn't angry or anything. He smiled and looked towards the building. Then he turned back and nodded.

"Morning, ma'am."

"Good morning."

"Any firearms or tobacco?"

"No."

"Citizenship?"

"Blackfoot."

He told us to sit in the car and wait, and we did. In about five minutes, another guard came out with the first man. They were talking as they came, both men swaying back and forth like two cowboys headed for a bar or a gunfight.

"Morning, ma'am."

"Good morning."

"Cecil tells me you and the boy are Blackfoot."

"That's right."

"Now, I know that we got Blackfeet on the American side and the Canadians got Blackfeet on their side. Just so we can keep our records straight, what side do you come from?"

I knew exactly what my mother was going to say, and I could have told them if they had asked me.

"Canadian side or American side?" asked the guard.

"Blackfoot side," she said.

It didn't take them long to lose their sense of humour, I can tell you that. The one guard stopped smiling altogether and told us to park our car at the side of the building and come in.

We sat on a wood bench for about an hour before anyone came over to talk to us. This time it was a woman. She had a gun, too.

"Hi," she said. "I'm Inspector Pratt. I understand there is a little misunderstanding."

"I'm going to visit my daughter in Salt Lake City," my mother told her, "We don't have any guns or beer."

"It's a legal technicality, that's all."

"My daughter's Blackfoot, too."

The woman opened a briefcase and took out a couple of forms and began to write on one of them. "Everyone who crosses our border has to declare their citizenship. Even Americans. It helps us keep track of the visitors we get from the various countries."

She went on like that for maybe fifteen minutes, and a lot of the stuff she told us was interesting.

"I can understand how you feel about having to tell us your citizenship, and here's what I'll do. You tell me, and I won't put it down on the form. No-one will know but you and me."

Her gun was silver. There were several chips in the wood handle and the name "Stella" was scratched into the metal butt.

We were in the border office for about four hours, and we talked to almost everyone there. One of the men bought me a Coke. My mother brought a couple of sandwiches in from the car. I offered a part of mine to Stella, but she said she wasn't hungry.

I told Stella that we were Blackfoot and Canadian, but she said that that didn't count because I was a minor. In the end, she told us that if my mother didn't declare her citizenship, we would have to go back where we came from. My mother stood up and thanked Stella for her time. Then we got back in the car and drove to the Canadian border, which was only about a hundred yards away.

I was disappointed. I hadn't seen Laetitia for a long time, and I had never been to Salt Lake City. When she was still at home, Laetitia would go on and on about Salt Lake City. She had never been there, but her boyfriend Lester Tallbull had spent a year in Salt Lake at a technical school.

"It's a great place," Lester would say. "Nothing but blondes in the whole state."

Whenever he said that, Laetitia would slug him on his shoulder hard enough to make him flinch. He had some brochures on Salt Lake and some maps, and every so often the two of them would spread them out on the table.

"That's the temple. It's right downtown. You got to have a pass to get in."

"Charlotte says anyone can go in and look around."

"When was Charlotte in Salt Lake? Just when the hell was Charlotte in Salt Lake?"

"Last year."

"This is Liberty Park. It's got a zoo. There's good skiing in the mountains."

"Got all the skiing we can use," my mother would say. "People come from all over the world to ski at Banff. Cardston's got a temple, if you like those kinds of things."

"Oh, this one is real big," Lester would say. "They got armed guards and everything."

"Not what Charlotte says."

"What does she know?"

Lester and Laetitia broke up, but I guess the idea of Salt Lake stuck in her mind.

The Canadian border guard was a young woman, and she seemed happy to see us.

"Hi," she said. "You folks sure have a great day for a trip. Where are you coming from?"

"Standoff."

"Is that in Montana?"

"No."

"Where are you going?"

"Standoff."

The woman's name was Carol and I don't guess she was any older than Laetitia. "Wow, you both Canadians?"

"Blackfoot."

"Really? I have a friend I went to school with who is Blackfoot. Do you know Mike Harley?"

"No."

"He went to school in Lethbridge, but he's really from Browning."

It was a nice conversation and there were no cars behind us, so there was no rush.

"You're not bringing any liquor back, are you?"

"No."

"Any cigarettes or plants or stuff like that?"

"No."

"Citizenship?"

"Blackfoot."

"I know," said the woman, "and I'd be proud of being Blackfoot if I were Blackfoot. But you have to be American or Canadian."

When Laetitia and Lester broke up, Lester took his brochures and maps with him, so Laetitia wrote to someone in Salt Lake City, and, about a month later, she got a big envelope of stuff. We sat at the table and opened up all the brochures, and Laetitia read each one out loud.

"Salt Lake City is the gateway to some of the world's most magnificent skiing."

"Salt Lake City is the home of one of the newest professional basketball franchises, the Utah Jazz."

"The Great Salt Lake is one of the natural wonders of the world."

It was kind of exciting seeing all those colour brochures on the table and listening to Laetitia read all about how Salt Lake City was one of the best places in the entire world.

"That Salt Lake City place sounds too good to be true," my mother told her.

"It has everything."

"We got everything right here."

"It's boring here."

"People in Salt Lake City are probably sending away for brochures of Calgary and Lethbridge and Pincher Creek right now."

In the end, my mother would say that maybe Laetitia should go to Salt Lake City, and Laetitia would say that maybe she would.

We parked the car to the side of the building and Carol led us into a small room on the second floor. I found a comfortable spot on the couch and flipped through some back issues of *Saturday Night* and *Alberta Report*.

When I woke up, my mother was just coming out of another office. She didn't say a word to me. I followed her down the stairs and out to the car. I thought we were going home, but she turned the car around and drove back towards the American border, which made me think we were going to visit Laetitia in Salt Lake City after all. Instead she pulled into the parking lot of the duty-free store and stopped.

"We going to see Laetitia?"

"No."

"We going home?"

Pride is a good thing to have, you know. Laetitia had a lot of pride, and so did my mother. I figured that someday, I'd have it, too.

"So where are we going?"

Most of that day, we wandered around the duty-free store, which wasn't very large. The manager had a name tag with a tiny American flag on one side and tiny Canadian flag on the other. His name was Mel. Towards evening, he began suggesting that we should be on our way. I told him we had nowhere to go, that neither the Americans nor the Canadians would let us in. He laughed at that and told us that we should buy something or leave.

The car was not very comfortable, but we did have all that food and it was April, so even if it did snow as it sometimes does on the prairies, we wouldn't freeze. The next morning my mother drove to the American border.

It was a different guard this time, but the questions were the same. We didn't spend as much time in the office as we had the day before. By noon, we were back at the Canadian border. By two we were back in the duty-free shop parking lot.

The second night in the car was not as much fun as the first, but my mother seemed in good spirits, and, all in all, it was as much an adventure as an inconvenience. There wasn't much food left and that was a problem, but we had lots of water as there was a faucet at the side of the duty-free shop.

One Sunday, Laetitia and I were watching television. Mom was over at Mrs. Manyfingers's. Right in the middle of the programme, Laetitia turned off the set and said she was going to Salt Lake City, that life around here was too boring. I had wanted to see the rest of the programme and really didn't care if Laetitia went to Salt Lake City or not. When Mom got home, I told her what Laetitia had said.

What surprised me was how angry Laetitia got when she found out that I had told Mom.

"You got a big mouth."

"That's what you said."

"What I said is none of your business."

"I didn't say anything."

"Well, I'm going for sure, now."

That weekend, Laetitia packed her bags, and we drove her to the border.

Mel turned out to be friendly. When he closed up for the night and found us still parked in the lot, he came over and asked us if our car was broken down or something. My mother thanked him for his concern and told him that we were fine, that things would get straightened out in the morning.

"You're kidding," said Mel. "You'd think they could handle the simple things."

"We got some apples and a banana," I said, "but we're all out of ham sandwiches."

"You know, you read about these things, but you just don't believe it. You just don't believe it."

"Hamburgers would be even better because they got more stuff for energy."

My mother slept in the back seat. I slept in the front because I was smaller and could lie under the steering wheel. Late that night, I heard my mother open the car door. I found her sitting on her blanket leaning against the bumper of the car.

"You see all those stars," she said. "When I was a little girl, my grandmother used to take me and my sisters out on the prairies and tell us stories about all the stars."

"Do you think Mel is going to bring us any hamburgers?"

"Every one of those stars has a story. You see that bunch of stars over there that look like a fish?"

"He didn't say no."

"Coyote went fishing, one day. That's how it all started." We sat out under the stars that night, and my mother told me all sorts of stories. She was serious about it, too. She'd tell them slow, repeating parts as she went, as if she expected me to remember each one.

Early the next morning, the television vans began to arrive, and guys in suits and women in dresses came trotting over to us, dragging microphones and cameras and lights behind them. One of the vans had a table set up with orange juice and sandwiches and fruit. It was for the crew, but when I told them we hadn't eaten for a while, a really skinny blonde woman told us we could eat as much as we wanted.

They mostly talked to my mother. Every so often one of the reporters would come over and ask me questions about how it felt to be an Indian without a country. I told them we had a nice house on the reserve and that my cousins had a couple of horses we rode when we went fishing. Some of the television people went over to the American border, and then they went to the Canadian border.

Around noon, a good-looking guy in a dark blue suit and an orange tie with little ducks on it drove up in a fancy car. He talked to my mother for a while, and, after they were done talking, my mother called me over, and we got into our car. Just as my mother started the engine, Mel came over and gave us a bag of peanut brittle and told us that justice was a damn hard thing to get, but that we shouldn't give up.

I would have preferred lemon drops, but it was nice of Mel anyway.

"Where are we going now?"

"Going to visit Laetitia."

The guard who came out to our car was all smiles. The television lights were so bright they hurt my eyes, and, if you tried to look through the windshield in certain directions, you couldn't see a thing.

"Morning, ma'am."

"Good morning."

"Where you heading?"

"Salt Lake City."

"Purpose of your visit?"

"Visit my daughter."

"Any tobacco, liquor, or firearms?"

"Don't smoke."

"Any plants or fruit?"

"Not any more."

"Citizenship?"

"Blackfoot."

The guard rocked back on his heels and jammed his thumbs into his gun belt. "Thank you," he said, his fingers patting the butt of the revolver. "Have a pleasant trip."

My mother rolled the car forward, and the television people had to scramble out of the way. They ran alongside the car as we pulled away from the border, and, when they couldn't run any farther, they stood in the middle of the highway and waved and waved and waved.

We got to Salt Lake City the next day. Laetitia was happy to see us, and, that first night, she took us out to a restaurant that made really good soups. The list of pies took up a whole page. I had cherry. Mom had chocolate. Laetitia said that she saw us on television the night before and, during the meal, she had us tell her the story over and over again.

Laetitia took us everywhere. We went to a fancy ski resort. We went to the temple. We got to go shopping in a couple of large malls, but they weren't as large as the one in Edmonton, and Mom said so.

After a week or so, I got bored and wasn't at all sad when my mother said we should be heading back home. Laetitia wanted us to stay longer, but Mom said no, that she had things to do back home and that, next time, Laetitia should come up and visit. Laetitia said she was thinking about moving back, and Mom told her to do as she pleased, and Laetitia said that she would.

On the way home, we stopped at the duty-free shop, and my mother gave Mel a green hat that said "Salt Lake" across the front. Mel was a funny guy. He took the hat and blew his nose and told my mother that she was an inspiration to us all. He gave us some more peanut brittle and came out into the parking lot and waved at us all the way to the Canadian border.

It was almost evening when we left Coutts. I watched the border through the rear window until all you could see were the tops of the flagpoles and the blue water tower, and then they rolled over a hill and disappeared.

1 "It would have been easier if my mother had just said 'Canadian' and been done with it, but I could see she wasn't going to do that."
   (a) Why doesn't the mother do the "easier" thing? Why does she feel that she *must* identify her citizenship as "Blackfoot"?
   (b) What are the border guards' reactions to her response? Why?
   (c) How does the child react to his mother's stand? Why?
   (d) To what extent do *you* agree with the mother's stand? Discuss and debate within your group. Read Richard Rive's "The Bench" (page 57). Are there similarities?

2 What kinds of differences does the boy observe between the two border towns: Coutts, Alberta, and Sweetgrass, Montana? What comment do you think King is making about Canadian and American cultures? Do you agree with his point of view? Why or why not?

3 Compare the question of identity in "The Middle Ground" with that in this story. Are there similarities? Are there differences? Support your view with specific references to both texts. (You might want to read about both authors in the biographies which begin on page 268.)

4 As news reporters, role-play and videotape the events at the border. Interview the participants and provide news commentary (an editorial) on the news event.

5 Write a lead editorial for your school newspaper on "Aboriginal Rights" and "Identity Within a Pluralistic Nation." Explore your library's vertical files for information. For further insights into Canada's First Peoples from their own voices and perspectives, read the anthologies, *Our Bit of Truth* (ed. Agnes Grant, 1990), *An Anthology of Canadian Native Literature in English* (ed. D. D. Moses and T. Goldie, 1992), and *All My Relations* (ed. Thomas King, 1992).

6 Invite a local First Nations speaker to visit your class to discuss the ideas, questions, and issues raised in "Borders." You might add to your discussion any issues that emerged from activity 5.

MULTICULTURALISM

CYRIL DABYDEEN

I continue to sing of other loves,
Places...moments when I am furious;
When you are pale and I am strong—
As we come one to another.

The ethnics at our door
Malingering with heritage,
My solid breath—like stones breaking;
At a railway station making much ado about much,
This boulder and Rocky Mountain,
CPR heaving with a head tax
As I am Chinese in a crowd,
Japanese at the camps,
It is also World War II.
Panting, I am out of breath.

So I keep on talking
With blood coursing through my veins,
The heart's call for employment equity,
The rhapsody of police shootings in Toronto,
This gathering of the stars one by one, codifying them
And calling them planets, one country, really...

Or galaxies of province after province,
A distinct society too:
Québec or Newfoundland; the Territories...
How far we make a map out of our solitudes
As we are still Europe, Asia,
Africa; and the Aborigine in me
Suggests love above all else—
The bear's configuration in the sky;
Other places, events; a turbanned RCMP,
These miracles—

My heritage and quest, heart throbbing;
Voices telling me how much I love you.
YOU LOVE ME; and we're always springing surprises,
Like vandalism at a Jewish cemetery
Or Nelson Mandela's visit to Ottawa
As I raise a banner high on Parliament Hill
Crying "Welcome!"—we are, you are—
OH CANADA!

ENTRY POINTS

1 Born in Guyana, South America, Dabydeen has lived in Canada since 1970 and served as Poet Laureate of Ottawa from 1984 to 1987. How has his personal history influenced his view of Canada as articulated in this poem? Point to specific images and attitudes.

2 How do you interpret his first stanza? Why does he "continue to sing of other loves"?

3 *How far we make a map out of our solitudes*
As we are still Europe, Asia,
Africa; and the Aborigine in me

Interpret these lines. How are *we* Europe, Asia, Africa, and Aborigine? Can we be all these things *and* Canadian too? Explain fully.

4 What is the poet's "heritage and quest" as put forward in this poem? What is *your* heritage and quest as a young Canadian? Discuss fully with your group.

5 Write a poem using images of the diversity of peoples' heritages and geography within Canada to evoke a sense of *your* vision of Canada.

6 Debate: "Multiculturalism *ultimately* promotes harmony and understanding."

7 Debate: "Assimilation means the act of gaining a new identity while losing your old one." Read "The Middle Ground" and "Borders" for reference points (page 68 and page 77).

8 Research in your library's vertical files and write an editorial on one of the following: (a) anti-racist education, (b) employment equity, (c) racism and race relations, (d) multiculturalism, (e) inclusive curriculum.

9 For various views of the effects of the multicultural policy in Canada, read the collection, *Twenty Years of Multiculturalism: Successes and Failures* (ed. Stella Hryniuk, 1992), and the collection, *Multiculturalism and "The Politics of Recognition"* (ed. Charles Taylor, 1992). Write a report summarizing the thoughts of one of the articles. Share your information with the class.

EVERYONE TALKED LOUDLY IN CHINATOWN

ANNE JEW

Lately I have been walking home from school in the sunshine with Todd. It's October and the leaves have turned, though the temperature hasn't changed since the end of August. My father says the reason for this is there were two Junes in the Chinese calendar this year. I wonder if that makes this year thirteen months long or if one month is left out to fit it into the regular calendar. But I don't ask. He would launch into a long, boring explanation of the history of the Chinese calendar and say it was superior to the Western calendar. If it was anyone else, I would probably ask.

Todd is very good looking. All the girls at school think so, and it makes me feel good when they turn to look at us walk down the hall together. Sometimes on our walk home we stop at the park to sit on the swings and talk. Actually Todd talks a lot and I listen. He usually describes his daily visit to the vice principal, the cars he wants, and the bands he likes. There is a Led Zeppelin logo drawn onto the back of his jean jacket in black felt pen which kind of bothers me.

"Have you ever really listened to their lyrics? They just make so much sense." It's his favourite band.

I try hard to stay interested in what he says and ask him questions, but mostly I end up nodding my head and saying, "Uh huh, uh huh." He doesn't seem to mind my quietness though. His eyes are clear blue, almost like glass, and it's hard to describe the feeling I get when he looks at me. My whole body feels like it's melting to the ground, and I'm always surprised to see that it hasn't.

Today Todd walks me to the beginning of my block as usual and then crosses the street to go on. My mother would start to ask questions if she saw us together.

As I enter the house, I pass my grandmother's room to go upstairs. She is lying in there dying. I throw my bag into my room and head into the kitchen. I take out a bag of chips from the cupboard and pour a glass of orange juice and join my brother in the living room where he is watching a rerun of "The Brady Bunch." It's the one where Jan refuses to wear her glasses and smashes into the family portrait with her bike. After a while I forget about the Bradys and start to daydream about Todd.

The next thing I know, my mother is waking me up to feed my grandmother, whose hands shake all the time so she can't do it herself. My brother and I take turns every night.

I stand by the window in the kitchen waiting for my mother to put the food onto the dinner tray. I draw hearts encircling Todd's initials and mine on the steamed glass.

"Hey, what are you doing?" she asks. I quickly wipe away the evidence.

"Nothing."

Her dinner is basically the same every night—soup, rice with water, steamed vegetables, salted fish and a thermos of tea. When I go into the room, she is sleeping with the quilt drawn up to her chin, which is usually how I find her now. Before, my mother would move her to an armchair by the window where she could watch people walk by or she would watch the new television set my father bought for her. Her favourite shows were "The Roadrunner" and "The Beverly Hillbillies," both which I couldn't stand. She would point and laugh and mumble something in Chinese. She didn't understand them, but I think she liked their movements. Now she stays in bed, too weak to get up.

She looks really old. I think she's almost eighty-four, but no one knows for sure. They didn't have birth certificates in China then, and she had to lie about her age when she came over to Canada. Her skin is bunched up like fabric and it just kind of hangs from her cheekbones. But it feels thin and soft. I touched it once when she was asleep. Her hair is grey and white and oily. It's combed back, making her forehead look like a shiny grapefruit. The lobes of her ears have been stretched by the weight of gold earrings I have never seen her take off. She is hardly moving. She almost looks as if she were dead already.

"Grandmother, it's time to eat rice."

She briefly opens her eyes and then closes them again.

"Grandmother, it's time to eat rice," I repeat a little louder.

She opens her eyes again, and I bring the tray closer for her to see. She starts to sit up, and I put down the tray to help her. After I prop her up onto some pillows, I tuck a paper napkin into the neck of her pyjamas and begin to feed her. I really hate doing it and I always want it to be over as soon as possible. Luckily she has been eating less and less. I have been begging my mother to do it instead, but so far she hasn't given in.

"You're not the one who has to bathe her and change the sheets. Don't be so bad. You are the only one she has treated well. She is going to die soon anyway."

My mother can't wait for my grandmother to die. She is always telling my brother and me how she was treated like a slave by Grandmother when she first married my father.

"Why didn't you stand up for yourself?" I ask.

"Oh, you don't know what it was like then."

We start with the soup. The spoon makes a clanging noise as it knocks against her teeth, sending a shiver through me. She still has all of them, which is amazing since my mother already has false front teeth. She doesn't chew the food very much though. It stays in her mouth a while, and then she makes a great effort to swallow. I try to show her how to chew by making exaggerated movements with my mouth, but she just ignores me. She finishes the soup, and we start on the rice in water. Some of it dribbles out of her mouth, so I have to scrape it off her chin and spoon it back in like I'm feeding a baby. I feel disgusted and guilty and I don't know why. I also feel guilty for not spending more time with her and for not wanting to spend more time with her. Todd would die if he knew I had to do this.

She is a grown-up who has always taken care of me, but now I have to take care of her. It bothers me. She used to be different.

When I was little, she would take me to Chinatown every weekend. We would go to a small pastry shop at the corner of Pender and Gore. I would have a Coke and a coconut bun while she had tea with the owners. I had to call them Uncle and Auntie although they weren't related to us. They spoke to each other about the people they knew: who was dying, who was dead, whose daughter-in-law was lazy. They drew out their words into sighs and shook their heads at the misfortunes of others. Sometimes they would comment on me, looking at me as if I couldn't see or hear them.

"Look at that high nose. She doesn't look Chinese."

"She is such a shy cute girl."

I usually watched the customers, the bell tinkling above the door as they came and went. Most were short, chubby women with unmade faces and hair. They always looked tired and reminded me of my mother. They carried plastic shopping bags with different shop logos on them in Chinese characters, and their children would run around them as they tried to order. They would scream out their orders and at their children at the same time.

There were also old stooping men with brown spots on their faces and the odd gold front tooth, and old women with straight grey hair pinned back over their ears. The old people were always buried under layers of clothing no matter what season it was.

Each time we left, the owners would give me a box of barbecued pork buns to take home.

"Lin, thank Uncle and Auntie."

"Thank you Uncle and Auntie."

"What a cute girl."

My grandmother was very popular in Chinatown. While we shopped we would be stopped every few feet by her acquaintances. Everyone talked loudly and waved their arms. I couldn't understand why they had to be so loud. It seemed uncivilized. She also took me to visit her friends and I would occupy myself with extra game pieces while they played mah jong.

But as I started to grow up, I stopped going to Chinatown with her, where it was too loud, and then I stopped spending time with her altogether. I started to play with friends who weren't loud and who weren't Chinese. This upset my mother. She was suspicious of all other cultures. My best friend for a long time was a German girl who lived up the block. Everything was neat and orderly at her house, and her mother was a quiet, pleasant woman who offered me green apples from their tree. My mother only bought red ones in Chinatown.

Grandmother eats the rest of the rice and some vegetables and then motions me to stop. I wipe her mouth and chin and help her to lie down again. She closes her eyes, and I turn out the light and climb the stairs to my own dinner.

On our walk home from school the next day, Todd asks me to see a movie with him. I lie to my parents and tell them I am going with my girlfriend Sandra. She swears not to say anything to anyone. Todd pays for the movie and the popcorn, and we sit in the back row of the theatre. He puts one arm around me, balances the bucket of popcorn on his knee, holds his drink between his legs, and eats and drinks with his other hand. I am impressed. I usually gorge myself on popcorn, but I feel compelled to eat one kernel at a time.

Halfway through *The Great Santini* and after we've finished the popcorn, Todd offers me a Certs. Then after a while he turns to me and kisses me on the lips. He opens his mouth on mine, and not knowing what to do, I open my mouth. I feel his tongue moving around in my mouth, so I move my tongue around in his. He still tastes faintly of popcorn under the flavour of the Certs. Just as I'm becoming used to the new sensation, he stops and kisses me on the lips and turns back to the movie. I can feel saliva clinging to the edges of my mouth, and not wanting to wipe it away with my hand, I press my face into his shoulder, hoping his shirt will absorb the moisture. It works.

As we leave the theatre, Todd takes hold of my hand. I am quickly beginning to fall in love.

"Now that was a great movie. That Robert Duvall guy is one harsh dude. What'd you think? Did you like it?"

"Yeah, I thought it was quite good."

"Yeah, it was great."

My hand feels good in his, but his strides are twice as long as mine, so our mismatched rhythms make us bounce along instead of walk. By now I am truly in love and I let him take me all the way home. Only the living room light is on, so we sit in the darkness of the carport in the back. Todd kisses me again and we move our tongues around. I am lost in the kissing until a car's headlights shine at us as it pulls into the driveway.

"Oh my God! It's my mother!"

I grab Todd's arm, and we run to the front of the house.

"Go! Hurry up!" He quickly kisses me and runs up the block. I stand around debating whether to go inside or escape to Sandra's house. I finally decide to go in. My mother and father are standing in the living room.

"How can you be so fearless! Going out with a white boy!" screams my mother.

My father walks up to me, his eyes wide with anger, and slaps me on the face. Automatically, I slap him back. He is stunned and I take the opportunity to run into my room. I expect him to come charging after me, but I am left alone for the rest of the night. It is only when the last light is turned out that I start to cry.

When I wake up hours later, my eyelashes are clumped together with dried tears. I didn't draw the curtains, so the moon shines into my room. Everything looks calm and quiet covered in moonlight. It comforts me. Todd, my father—it seemed to happen so long ago.

Only the hum of the fridge can be heard as I creep out into the hallway. I slowly climb down the stairs to my grandmother's bedroom. I imagine the sound of movement as I enter, but I stop and there is nothing. It is dark, so I feel my way over to the window and draw the curtains back a little. She is so still in the moonlight. I go to her and touch her face. It is soft, but cool. The shadows make it look almost ghostly. I take her hand, bony and fragile, and find she has no pulse. I drop it instantly and stand back to look at her. She is dead, I think. I stare at her face expecting it to move, but somehow it looks peaceful. I take her hand again, kneel beside the bed, and rest my head against her. Soon I am asleep.

1 Describe and analyze the young narrator's attitude to her family's Chinese home culture. How does her home culture differ from the culture of her community and her school? How is living within the broader North American culture affecting her and her family?

2 Explore with your group her relationship with her grandmother, her parents, and her boyfriend, Todd. Do you sympathize with her perceived inner conflicts or do you find her selfish and egocentric? Explain with a persuasive argument.

3 " 'How can you be so fearless! Going out with a white boy!' screams my mother." Define "reverse discrimination" and apply it to this story of intergenerational conflict within a multicultural city (Vancouver) and country.

4 What is your reaction to the "slapping" scene near the end? With your group, suggest other ways that this situation could have been handled and resolved.

5 Compare the family conflict in this story to those found in Alden Nowlan's "Skipper" (page 28), and Samuel Selvon's "Cane Is Bitter" (page 33). How do children attempt to resolve being caught in two different worlds?

6 Imagine you are the young narrator. Write a diary item in which you express your feelings about Todd, your parents' expectations and, finally, your grandmother's death.

7 With your group, adapt this story into a script with three to four distinctive scenes and then act it out in front of your class. Videotape your production for future showings.

8 Compare the romantic plot in this story with that found in William Shakespeare's *Romeo and Juliet*. Note the influence of family and social restrictions.

9 In his *Culture of Complaint*, Robert Hughes stated, "In the world that is coming, if you can't navigate difference, you've had it." In reference to this story and other items in this anthology, discuss Hughes's statement. To what extent is his projection valid?

LAND OF NO DELIGHT

HAROLD MARSHALL

He was standing on the street corner in the lightly falling snow feeling his displacement. It was a displacement that was real because he was different. He felt his exclusion because of his colour. He looked into the night with weighted eyes and tried to swallow his feelings of anger and impotence. He wondered at the gentleness of the falling snow and not for the first time questioned his existence as he experienced the nausea of feeling inferior.

He was black in a white night, and in the cold he felt an indifferent passion. He lived on a street which seemed doomed by the sameness of the design of the small, close-packed houses which went on and on, where there was dust and dimness in the yellow light, and stale smells, where bodies crouched in different postures and where different people of endless mutations of one colour unravelled their lives in skeins of time inside the peeling walls.

He saw surreal, blue shadows caused by the mercury street lights warping and throwing back images in irresolute, silhouette shapes on the narrow, unplowed sidewalk, tapering to black where there was no light. In the long, deep, shadows the snow seemed to be black. An opaque black that absorbed everything and reflected nothing. Just like he did.

He tried not to think of his blackness and his separation but he could not prevent the seething rage from kindling inside his soul. It was ongoing. It was kindred to his being and he lived with it day and night. It was not something he wanted to explain, even if he could. He knew he was angry because he had long since come to think of himself as a some kind of primitive living like an alien in forced exile. He saw the colours of his human feelings in tears, pain, hurt, humiliation and futile dreams all draped in impenetrable black, like mourning, with no contours to give definition to its character.

In his early life, his was a black innocence which had lain dormant inside a veil of white consciousness. It seemed as if his soul had been stored within his body and ignored and with discovery came the sudden trauma from which it had never recovered.

As he became aware of his displacement and difference it seemed as if his colour had agitated and distilled itself into a constant threat which seeped into his senses, making a mockery of what he believed himself to be. He wanted to love himself and to fill his consciousness, to feel good and to affirm his existence, but he felt he did not belong to himself. His life was not his own. His birthright had been stolen and replaced with something which was counterfeit.

Standing shivering on the corner he saw people muffled against the evening wind and the winter cold, some with parcels and others with small children trudging to their low-income apartments with tired footsteps. The noise of cars ebbed and flowed around him like tidal water curling around a rock in the sea.

He was just about to go towards the house where he lived with his parents when he recognised his father by his lumbering walk, and hunched over, coming towards him. His father was carrying a lunch bucket in one hand and a laden shopping bag in another. His shapeless fedora was pulled low over his face and a scarf was wrapped thickly around his neck.

He turned and walked away to escape from his father. He would have to wait sometime before he went home. He did not want to face his father just then. He was not sure that he wanted to go home at all. He was afraid and resentful of the man who tried to hide behind his high, broad face bones, flared nostrils and thick lips, whose crooked teeth were white against the dark tan of his skin. His father was a wrathful man whose black eyes could emit a profound sadness but often seared, and whose tongue would lash the world in unremitting distrust and whose senses seemed to focus inwardly on the slow corrosion of his life. It was a life far different from the one his father had dreamed it would be when he first left the island.

"It is for the better," he remembered his father saying to his mother at the time. "It is for the future. We have to give the children a chance. There's nothing here for them."

Those were the dreams which were made in the bright tropical sun only to be shattered in the dark and cold of a dingy street.

He had felt important then. He was part of a family plan. He was six years old when they first arrived. Now ten years later everything had changed. He recalled the first outbursts from his father that would stun him and split the serenity of the house. It became impossible to please his father.

He remembered his father raging at his sister Janice, who was two years younger than he was, when she arrived home late from school one evening and explained that she was chosen to be a cheer leader.

"A what? Cheer leader? What is that? Where we come from they don't have no cheer leaders. You think I working as a orderly at the hospital and cleaning bed pans so you can prance around at a basketball game. No missie, you get your tail in here right after school and study your books. There is no future in a cheer leader," his father had thundered at Janice and sent her to her room in tears.

"Selwyn, why you so hard on the children all the time?" his mother had asked.

"Don't you get at me," his father warned his mother. "You know why we come here in the first place."

"Quarreling and shouting at the children isn't helping them, you know," his mother had said, but retreated, as she usually did when his father glared at her.

"I know what is good for them," his father had responded. A surly silence had surged angrily through the house making it difficult to breathe in the angered air.

It was even worse when one of Janice's white classmates had called for her one day. His father had answered the doorbell and when he saw who it was he told the boy never to come near his daughter again, and told Janice she could not go out for a month.

Joylessness settled like an amorphous cloud over them.

But it wasn't just his father. The exile which he felt was a coil to his freedom. Once he had become aware of who he was, his life was not simple or separate. He found it difficult to make decisions. He did not know what he wanted to do with his life and there was really nobody he could talk to. He might have talked to his mother but there was not a whole lot she could do. She always seemed so tired from working at the two jobs she had, as a cleaner in the evenings and as a short-order cook at a friend's small Caribbean restaurant on weekends, and she was overwhelmed by the war of words from her husband.

"What it is you want to do in life, boy?" his father asked him not long ago, after pursuing him with other words.

"I don't know what I want," he said.

He really didn't want to talk to his father because the experience was one-sided and belaboured and always left him fatigued.

"That is the blasted trouble with you. You don't know what you want. These people over here not people like us. They really don't want people like you and me polluting up their country. In this place you have to try double hard. And you don't seem to be trying to get somewhere in life. Is a lot of sacrifice I make, Y'better pay attention to what I saying. You have to have something to keep y' head up so's these people can't push you around. You get what I saying, boy?" his father said.

His father's voice was like a net which was flung wide to trap everything in its reach.

"You don't understand, dad. It isn't easy. In fact it is impossible."

His voice sounded lame, even to his ears. His protest was a faint incredulous cry. He called from the dim confusion of his mind and it had a quality of numbness in it. His father ignored him.

"You think I don't know. I know everything that is good for you. Why you think I left home to come here?" his father asked unyielding. "It seems I wasting time. I just treading water. Soon's I can put by enough for the piece o' land back on the island, I gone from this place."

His father chafed at the street in which he lived and the people in it, but he seemed to have been overcome by the restriction as he never went anywhere.

He wanted to talk to his father about his displacement. It was his exclusion too. But he could not. He was too bruised inside and too spent for anger. He had never considered his father to be a friend, not even when he was younger. Now he knew he would never see him as a friend.

He could not speak of an invisible landfall in the darkness which his life had become. He had no direction. His life was lost, like blood.

At school he was no good at sports and he found reading to be difficult. Not so much difficult as it was the way he heard things and comprehended them. He had given up trying to hear what people were saying. It was useless and it only added to the pain. The cumulative hurt. It wasn't that he was slow. It was because he wasn't interested. There was no affinity. There was no reason for him to be involved. All he wanted to do was draw things. All kinds of things, but his father didn't see the benefit of a son as an artist.

"Only lazy people want to write and draw. They don't want to do real work," his father said.

Last week he had gone to a dance. The first he had ever attended. He had bought a ticket because the girl had asked him to. She knew he would buy one from her, that is why she asked him. He had never bought one before. He had got the money from his mother and when she asked him what he wanted it for and he told her, she had given him a quizzical look and walked away from him.

The girl was the only person he talked to and she was not a friend. She was in his art class. He was attracted to her and watched her from a distance. He thought she knew that he watched her because sometimes she would smile at him with her eyes which were large and blue with long eyelashes, but her mouth remained in a straight line. It was her eyes which were warm, unsurprised and unequivocal that made him want to be near to her. He marvelled at the transparent whiteness of her skin and he wanted to touch it. But he was careful not to make a fool of himself. He was conscious of his difference and felt his displacement even as he went towards her when she was alone for a moment, and separated from her friends.

His thoughts became a racing jumble of impressions which he could not fathom when she shook her head, even as her eyes smiled, and told him she was sorry when he asked her to dance. She did not give a reason. She just said she was sorry. That was all. Her voice was flat and nasal. Without intonation, as if it had been rehearsed.

Sorry? Sorry for what? What did it mean?

He didn't feel crushed. He just felt weary.

He had left the dance immediately afterwards. He saw her the next day in art class and she smiled at him with her eyes.

He was thinking about the girl when the police car drove alongside him slowly. He discovered he had walked quite a distance and was alone on a deserted street. The car stopped and one of the policeman got out and came towards him.

He panicked and started to run. "Stop," he heard the policeman shout.

He kept on running. Black in a white night.

ENTRY POINTS

1 "…he experiences the nausea of feeling inferior."
   (a) Why does this teenager feel inferior? Can you understand and empathize with his feelings? Discuss thoroughly with your group, keeping in mind your own perspective or "difference."
   (b) To what degree do you feel his feelings of inferiority and displacement result from his home life, and to what degree do they result from his experiences and conflicts with society? Discuss and assess thoroughly with your group.

2 Why did his father leave his Caribbean island home to immigrate to Canada? What were his dreams? How and why did they change? What events might have occurred in his life to change his opinion of Canada?

3 "What it is you want to do in life, boy?"
   (a) Why doesn't the young man know what he wants to do? To what extent is his indecision very different from other teenagers

his age? What factors seem to be complicating his decision?

(b) Assess his father's reaction to his son's indecision. How could he have responded in a more productive way?

(c) What is it that *you* want to do in life? Elaborate.

4 Why wasn't the teenager "interested" in high school? Assess his reasoning. With your group, make recommendations for helping him become more interested and involved in school and share your ideas with your class.

5 Compare the father-son relationships in "Skipper" (page 28), "Cane Is Bitter" (page 33), and "Goalie" (page 238) with this story. Is it possible to create more positive relationships using the techniques explored in "The Kid Nobody Could Handle" (page 243)? Discuss with your group.

6 Define "xenophobia." With your group, examine and compare the xenophobia exhibited by the father in this story, the Armanos in "The Middle Ground" (page 68), the parents in "Everyone Talked Loudly in Chinatown" (page 90), and Costa in "A Proper Goodbye" (page 194). How can this phenomenon be minimized? Present recommendations.

7 What does the teenager do after he stops running, "Black in a white night"? Write a short sequel to this story.

8 Adapt this story into a short script of about five scenes. Externalize the teenager's interior monologues into brief soliloquies—or create a chorus. Videotape your production.

9 Susan Aglukark, a Canadian Inuit singer, said: "People are people from the inside out, not from the outside in." Relate this message of hope to this story and write a personal essay which emphasizes appreciating people "from the inside out."

10 For more ideas and insights into the Black experience in Canada, read the following books: *Other Voices: Writings by Blacks in Canada* (ed. Lorris Elliott, 1985); *A Shapely Fire* (ed. Cyril Dabydeen, 1987); *Voices: Canadian Writers of African Descent* (ed. Ayanna Black, 1992); *The Black Experience in Manitoba: A Collection of Memoirs* (ed. Pat Graham and Darryl Stevenson, 1993); *Fiery Spirits: Canadian Writers of African Descent* (ed. Ayanna Black, 1994). Write a brief report on one of these books and share your thoughts with your class.

TELEPHONE CONVERSATION

The price seemed reasonable, location
Indifferent. The landlady swore she lived
Off premises. Nothing remained
But self-confession. "Madam," I warned,
"I hate a wasted journey—I am African."
Silence. Silenced transmission of
Pressurized good-breeding. Voice, when it came,
Lipstick-coated, long gold-rolled
Cigarette-holder pipped. Caught I was, foully.

"HOW DARK?"...I had not misheard..."ARE YOU LIGHT
"OR VERY DARK?" Button B. Button A. Stench
Of rancid breath of public hide-and-speak.
Red booth. Red pillar-box. Red double-tiered
Omnibus squelching tar. It was real! Shamed
By ill-mannered silence, surrender
Pushed dumbfoundment to beg simplification.
Considerate she was, varying the emphasis—

"ARE YOU DARK? OR VERY LIGHT?" Revelation came.
"You mean—like plain or milk chocolate?"
Her assent was clinical, crushing in its light
Impersonality. Rapidly, wavelength adjusted,
I chose, "West African sepia"—and as an afterthought,
"Down in my passport." Silence for spectroscopic
Flight of fancy, till truthfulness clanged her accent
Hard on the mouthpiece "WHAT'S THAT?", conceding,
"DON'T KNOW WHAT THAT IS." "Like brunette."

WOLE SOYINKA

"THAT'S DARK, ISN'T IT?" "Not altogether."
"Facially, I am brunette, but madam, you should see
"The rest of me. Palm of my hand, soles of my feet
"Are a peroxide blonde. Friction, caused—
"Foolishly, madam—by sitting down, has turned
"My bottom raven black—One moment madam!"—sensing

Her receiver rearing on the thunder-clap
About my ears—"Madam," I pleaded, "wouldn't you rather
"See for yourself?"

1 Why does the speaker feel he must state to the landlady in England that he is African? What is her reaction to his revelation?

2 "ARE YOU DARK? OR VERY LIGHT?"
(a) How would you characterize the landlady?
(b) Why does she think she has the right to ask such a question?
(c) Evaluate the speaker's response to her question.
(d) Role-play the two characters in a dramatic reconstruction of the poem. Perform for your class.

3 In many ways, this is a very humorous poem. Do you think that the issue of racism should ever be treated humorously or lightly? Look up "satire" in a glossary of literary terms. Evaluate Soyinka's use of humour in this poem given the nature of satire throughout history. Read John Agard's poem "Stereotype" (page 55).

4 Imagine you own a house. You want to rent it for six months and then move back into it. What would you want to know about a prospective tenant? How do you think you would find out? Research landlord and tenant law in your province to find out what your rights and your tenant's rights would be.

5 Write a poem in which you juxtapose and comment on fragments of a telephone conversation. Tape-record your poem.

6 Write a satirical short story about a character who must deal with and resolve an act of social injustice or discrimination. Read the story, "The Bench" by Richard Rive (page 57).

7 Winner of the Nobel Prize for Literature, Wole Soyinka is also a Professor of Comparative Literature at the University of Ife in Nigeria. For an interesting insight into his critical thinking, read his work, *Myth, Literature and the African World* (1976; republished 1990) in which he reveals the African world and its literature as a cultural entity different from European-based culture and literature.

THE GROUND RULES

EUNICE SCARFE

When I wake up I pretend.

I pretend I'm at home in my own bed and I pretend that my father has come back in the night. I pretend the white outside my window is snow falling and not the wall of an apartment block filled with tatami mats. I pretend my mother isn't outside on the balcony staring towards the skyscrapers of Shinjuku and I pretend she isn't listening for sirens, her hands pressed into the concrete, waiting to feel the first tremor. I pretend my mother is sleeping and I pretend earthquakes occur only in the dim light of dreams.

They say an earthquake is not a matter of whether but when. They say the Izu Peninsula is shaking like a leaf. They say the earth hasn't trembled so much since all of Tokyo fell down in 1923. Every sixty years, they say, a big earthquake comes. This is the year, people say. When some people say this, they smile.

When the earthquake comes, my mother will see the signs first. She knows them all. She analyses cloud formations and watches for red locusts. A barking dog paralyses her. If we had catfish she'd be watching them too. She scrutinizes the moon as if she were reading a palm. A sudden stillness fills her with dread. Unnatural light in the sky makes her tremble.

Last week we received a brochure from the Earthquake Institute. "In the event of an earthquake," we read, "the Institute will inform the Prime Minister who will convene a committee."

"A committee!" my mother shouted. "What good would that do?"

Every day since my father went away we feel the earth trembling. The first time I wanted it to last forever. I was rocked in my bed while my wardrobe door banged against the wall. I wasn't afraid but my mother was. "Get under the table," she cried in the dark. But by the time I got there, the rocking had stopped. We watched the overhead light swing back and forth while we listened to crows shrieking in the tree-tops just outside our windows.

"I wish they'd crow *before* it happens," my mother said.

That morning she dismantled my top bunk and left it outside in the hall.

At night my mother uses one of her shoes to keep our apartment door open. "We don't want the door jammed shut," she says. "We can't jump from the sixth floor."

We can't cook anything because she's turned the gas off. "More people die from fire than from falling objects," she says, quoting from the Earthquake Institute brochure. Every evening she sends me to buy supper from the fast food counter at Sukinokea.

"I'm tired of yakatori," she says. "Get something new."

"I don't know the names of anything else at Sukinokea," I say.

"Just point," she says. "It doesn't matter if you don't know what it's called." It does matter. I want to know the names of the food I eat.

In our apartment are both kinds of helmets. Yellow hard hats for falling objects and silver quilted hoods for fire. We sleep with the hoods under our pillows and the helmets on the floor beside our beds.

My mother fills the tea kettle every night. When the earthquake comes, she says, we'll need a supply of fresh water.

I miss my father. He is a scientist and he uses instruments to measure things, not clouds or catfish and locusts. He speaks Japanese and he knows the names of things. He says we have to laugh at the earth's efforts to intimidate us. She doesn't need to try so hard, he says. Laugh when the earth moves beneath your feet, he says. Laugh when the volcanoes blow, when the seas rise, when the glaciers give way. The earth is moving out of joy. Or pride. Or passion, he says, looking at my mother. But she tells him to hush. When the earth moves the earth is angry, she answers him, angry, unpredictable and cruel.

But my father is not here. He has flown to Iceland to observe a glacier which is melting at a remarkable rate, warmed by the heat of volcanic activity. Scientists from all over the world have gone to watch. He is travelling in a helicopter, beyond roads or even a map. He said he'd call as soon as he could. My mother won't leave the apartment until he does. "I want to talk to him," she says. "Don't you understand? He speaks to me in English." And then she starts to cry.

I do understand. She won't leave the apartment because she is terrified. Her skin is cold, even though every day the temperature rises to forty degrees Celsius before noon. She hasn't laughed since my father left. She hasn't changed her clothes since the tremors began. She hasn't washed or combed her hair and she smells of sweat. Out on the balcony she'll be wearing a black tank top, white wide-bottomed shorts, no bra and no shoes. She even sleeps in those clothes. "In case we have to evacuate," she says.

I have stopped changing my clothes too. I sleep in shorts and a shirt just like she does. When we evacuate I will be ready.

"Couldn't we go to the baths?" I have asked her. "Just for awhile?"

In the baths she would stop watching for signs.

In the baths she would relax.

In the baths we wash according to the rules. We squat on low stools which face the wall of faucets and mirrors. We rub long cloths back and forth across our shoulders and shampoo our hair until it squeaks.

In the baths we watch the other women and stare at them in the steamed glass: grannies and mothers and toddlers whose hands reach for every nipple they see.

In the baths we know the rules. We do it just right. No one monitors us anymore. No one guards the edges of the room-size bath to make sure we scrub every bit of our bodies before we step in. They know we'll remember to wear plastic slippers and to replace the wooden buckets in stacks by the door. We don't splash in the bath, or try to swim. The women, nodding approval, watch us lower ourselves inch by inch into the scalding water until only our chins show. They smile at our discomfort and would prevent us if we tried to add even one drop of cold water.

Sitting in the baths my mother's head would not tower above the others. Our hair could be black under the thick plastic caps. In the baths we don't need to know or understand Japanese.

In the baths we belong.

"Please come to the baths," I say to my mother. Doesn't she know I'm frightened too?

But she won't leave the apartment. My father might call. The sirens might ring. The earth might open.

If we were home in Canada we could hike up Mill Creek Ravine or go swimming in Queen Elizabeth Park on a day like today. In Canada my mother is never frightened. But if perhaps she were, if perhaps I found her lying in bed with her eyes wide open seeing nothing, not even me, I would call her friend and I would say 'please could you come for tea?' and I would put the kettle on and pour milk into thin china cups. We would sit on the porch and I would listen to them talk while I watched green leaves polish the glass of the long windows and they would laugh and my mother would forget she was frightened and everything would be as it should be—or as it was before we came to Tokyo.

My mother sends me for the English papers every day, the minute I wake up, all the way to Rappongi station. "It's the only way we'll know your father's safe," she says. "No news is good news, you know."

The first day I got the papers we read that all of Tokyo had practiced an earthquake drill the day before. "What do they mean?" my mother said. "*All* of Tokyo? All of Japanese Tokyo. Do they think an earthquake won't affect foreigners? Why didn't anyone tell the *gaijin*?"

In the drill, we read, subway trains and traffic had slowed down, children had worn helmets, and buildings had been rated for safety. Fire fighting equipment had been tested. In every ward sirens had practiced their warning blasts.

"And we didn't know what was happening," my mother said. "We didn't know a damn thing."

She wouldn't say 'damn' in front of the Japanese. She says we are visitors here, by invitation, and we must be polite and follow the rules. "Does that mean I have to bow?" I ask.

"No," she hesitates. "Just nod your head. We'd never get the bowing right."

I have to cycle almost a mile for the papers. I buy the *Japan Times*, the *Asahi Press* and the *Mainichi Express*. "Go easy," my mother says. "But hurry. You can't ride your bike in the street, no matter how crowded the sidewalks are. Remember an accident is more complicated if a *gaijin* causes it. Carry your alien card, just in case. Say *gomenasai* when you ring your bell and *arigato* when you overtake someone. Walk your bike past the food stalls—and at the intersections. Can you remember all that?" Of course I can. I know the rules as well as she does. I always follow them all. It's the only way to feel safe.

We live in a lodge for foreigners who are guests of the government of Japan. Almost everyone else is on 'home leave' because of the heat, but we can't go until my father gets back.

Yesterday we went down to the lobby. The man at the desk is supposed to be fluent in English. My mother says never expect anyone to speak English. "Why should they speak English if we don't speak Japanese?" she says.

The man at the desk says 'hello' and smiles at us warily. "Naito," my mother says loudly. "Are we safe on the sixth floor? What should we do when the earthquake comes? Should we go under the table or down to the basement? What are the rules?"

"Good question," Naito says. "Very good question. What do you want to know?"

"Naito," she repeats, louder. "What should we do when the earthquake comes?"

"Table is safe," he says. "Basement is safe." His mouth is smiling but his eyes are not. "Outside is not so safe."

"It's only safe in Canada," my mother says to me.

"Yes," Naito says, eagerly. "There's no place like home."

My mother looks at him and starts to cry.

"Thank you, Naito," I say. "*Arigato.*" I don't know if I should say 'Mr. Naito'. Is Naito his last name or his first? I don't know if I should bow. I nod. If my mother bowed her breasts would show, hanging loose beneath her shirt.

Standing in the lobby is a man, a foreigner like us. "There is nothing you can do," he says. "When nature wants to move, she will. An earthquake is like war or making love—" his voice goes very low, "a necessary purge." My mother does not answer or even look at him. I nod, and then pretend I didn't. The elevator is out of order again. Even a tiny tremor makes it jam. We walk up the six flights of stairs to our apartment.

On Monday when I went to Sukinokea for our supper there was a table of emergency supplies in front of the shop: flashlights and bottled water and helmets; charcoal grills and first aid kits. No one was buying any. On the street was a small van with one side removed. Every five minutes it began shaking violently and a demonstrator showed what to do when an earthquake began. Children begged to be in the van during the demonstration. They laughed as they tried to stay on their feet. The man showed them how to kneel on the floor like they were bowing to a god, their heads bent low between their knees. No one stopped to watch. The attendant motioned to me but I shook my head and hurried away.

I bought my mother some roses after I paid for the *udon*. They were selling bunches by the dozen for as little as we'd pay for pussy willows back home. I bought two bottles of Fuji water and pushed my bike slowly up the hill through a continuous wave of people. None of them looked worried. They were going into restaurants, choosing rice, riding cycles, bowing to each other, waiting for the bus, chatting outside the coffee shop. If only my mother would come out, I thought. She would see no one else is frightened. "Of course they're not frightened," she has said. "They have a different attitude toward death."

Over the temple wall just below our lodge I saw a priest disappear through a door and saw a man ringing the bell before he bowed his head. I pretended I was Japanese and prayed to their gods to make the earth be still.

The tinkle of a bicycle bell echoes from the sidewalk. I open my eyes and squint at the sun bouncing off the concrete balcony wall. White washing is flapping on the roof across the street from us. The sky is so blue I think it has been dipped in dye, stripped of the clouds that spread across it at sunset last night.

Last night.

I lie there and remember.

The foreign man had stopped with two bottles of Suntory beer, cold, and had drunk them with my mother on our balcony. "The danger's over," he had said. "The tremors are shifting to Nagano. Tokyo is out of danger now."

"How do you know?" my mother had asked. She had reached out and actually touched his hand. He was from the Earthquake Institute he said, and had flown from Poland just to help monitor and analyse the data.

"You scientists are playing hopscotch," my mother had said. "My husband's off in Iceland monitoring glaciers." And then she had laughed, the first time I had heard her laugh since my father went away. She sent me out for yakatori, all I wanted, and more beer. "This is the last time you'll have to go alone," she said. "Tomorrow I'll come with you."

"To the baths?" I asked. "Please."

"Why not? What a good idea."

When I got back she had showered, had shaved her legs and put on perfume and her nails were painted pink. She kept taking deep breaths and smiling and saying how silly she had been. She put clean sheets on our beds and rubbed her feet and elbows with cream. I was glad for her. I couldn't tell her then.

Tell her what? I sit up in bed and hug myself hard. Against the white wall of my bedroom I can see again the black print of the newspaper headline: "Flash flood in Iceland: hundreds feared dead." The story gave no details, only that an ice dam had given way and a tidal-wave torrent of water had swept down the mountain valley, more sudden and swift than a *tsunami*.

Yesterday I told my mother the *Japan Times* was sold out. It was a lie. I pretended it was sold out. I pretended I hadn't read the headline. I threw away the paper before I reached the lodge.

I see my father standing on the shale, gazing at the blue glacier when an avalanche of water rushes at him. Has he been swept downstream? Buried under debris? Drowned? Frozen in glacial ice? Thrown into the brush? Or is he now safely on a plane flying first to Moscow and then to us? I reach out my hand to my father, pull him out of the torrents of water, away from the shards of ice, far from the tons of gravel.

My hand comes away cold and empty.

I get up and walk slowly to the balcony door. My feet are as heavy as boulders. The air is already humid and intense. At the other end of the balcony the glass doors of my mother's room are open. Will she be awake, like I have often seen her, eyes staring at the ceiling, her body paralysed?

She is sitting up, her back a wall of white to me, her hair like soft hands resting on her shoulders. I cannot see his face, but I can hear his voice, low, speaking words I can't understand. His hands are wide around her hips. She is as still and smooth as a sheet of ice. Then something like a tremor shakes her body and I hear her laugh: deep and soft and slow.

"Out of my way, get out of my way!" I shout as I careen down our hill, fast, my bicycle a sword cutting through the sidewalk crowds. Blue business suits and children's sun hats and white kimono aprons and bent grandmothers shuffle swiftly to one side. I can hear *'gaijin, gaijin, gaijin'* echo down the street as if they are playing pass the parcel.

I don't walk my bike when I pass the vegetable lady's stall. Her boxes of onions and oranges and apple pears pour into the street. I don't slow down a bit. I ring my bell constantly. "You blinkered Buddhists. You little people—you can't even speak English." I head straight into the busy street at the bottom of the hill. Cars screech to a halt. Just let them hit me. Let them hit a foreigner. Let them kill a Canadian. They'll have hell to pay.

I pull up in front of the baths, lean my bike against a tree and push through the curtain. I ignore the plastic sandals, holler 'pay ya later' to the attendant, and burst into the women's room where sun slants through the misted windows.

The eyes of the women submerged up to their necks in steaming water open in surprise. I toss off my clothes, leave them in a heap, and slide into the bath, sweaty, dirty and unwashed. It is scorching hot. I grab a wooden bucket and slosh the hot water from my corner onto the floor. For every bucket emptied I fill a bucket of cold water and pour it in the bath. The women and children slide away from my corner. They huddle at the far end. They are talking nonstop; so am I. "You don't know the earth is opening up?" I shout. "You think you can escape in the baths? You think it matters if you're clean before you die?"

I hear *'gaijin, gaijin, gaijin'* echo in the bath chamber. They sound like crows after an earthquake. "Earthquake. That's what I said. It's starting. A *big* one. Tokyo's going to be swallowed. We're all going to slip into the centre of the earth, dirty and clean, we the *gaijin* and you the Japanese. All of us. Dead. When nature wants to move, she will!"

I am shouting when I finish. I bow my head, buried up to my neck in swirling water, shaking, trembling. They can't see my tears. They can't see the signs. But I can feel the earth heaving, shifting, rumbling, soon going to break apart, soon going to crack, angrily tensing her body, ready to throw all of us over.

ENTRY POINTS

1. This is a story of displacement, in this case of Canadians in Japan. How does the young narrator cope with her displacement away from the safe, familiar surroundings of her homeland? Analyze and discuss her attitudes and emotions with your group. Have you ever been a "foreigner in a strange land"? What were *your* reactions?

2 What differences do you perceive in the attitudes of the Japanese citizens and the Canadian visitors towards the potential earthquakes? With whom do you sympathize? Elaborate.

3 What is the young narrator's father's attitude to the earthquakes? Characterize her relationship to him. Comment on the title of the story as part of your response.

4 "In the baths we belong." Why?

5 "It's only safe in Canada." Why does the mother make such a vast generalization? To what extent does her daughter agree? Explore their nostalgic dreams and thoughts about Canada.

6 "Out of my way, get out of my way!" Why is the girl behaving in such an erratic and rude way at the end of the story? Explore and comment on her final outburst and feelings at the Tokyo baths. What is the real target of her frustration and anger? Why hasn't she expressed her true feelings?

7 In what ways do the mother's and daughter's feelings of fear and loneliness lead them to develop stereotyped and sometimes hostile attitudes towards Japanese people? With your group, recommend steps they might take to feel more comfortable in Tokyo.

8 To a large extent, this story reverses the situation found in other stories in this anthology wherein "foreigners" have had to cope with the demands and unfamiliarity of *their* new country, Canada. Read and compare this story to the following: "The Middle Ground" (page 68), "Everyone Talked Loudly in Chinatown" (page 90), and "Land of No Delight" (page 96). Rethink questions of assimilation, integration, racism, reverse discrimination, and multiculturalism.

9 Write a diary item in which you imagine yourself as the young girl commenting on her mother's behaviour and her reaction to it, or in which you are a Japanese citizen observing the mother and daughter's behaviour.

10 Write a story in which your protagonist is a stranger in a strange land. Explore his/her feelings as he/she tries to cope with unfamiliar customs and foreign language.

LEAVING

M.G. VASSANJI

Kichwele Street was now Uhuru Street. My two sisters had completed school and got married and Mother missed them sometimes. Mehroon, after a succession of wooers, had settled for a former opening batsman of our school team and was in town. Razia was a wealthy housewife in Tanga, the coastal town north of Dar. Firoz dropped out in his last year at school, and everyone said that it was a wonder he had reached that far. He was assistant bookkeeper at Oriental Emporium, and brought home stationery sometimes.

Mother had placed her hopes on the youngest two of us, Aloo and me, and she didn't want us distracted by the chores that always needed doing around the store. One evening she secured for the last time the half a dozen assorted padlocks on the sturdy panelled doors and sold the store. This was exactly one week after the wedding party had driven off with a tearful Razia, leaving behind a distraught mother in the stirred-up dust of Uhuru Street.

We moved to the residential area of Upanga. After the bustle of Uhuru Street, our new neighbourhood seemed quiet. Instead of the racket of buses, bicycles and cars on the road, we now heard the croaking of frogs and the chirping of insects. Nights were haunting, lonely and desolate and took some getting used to. Upanga Road emptied after seven in the evening and the sidestreets became pitch dark, with no illumination. Much of the area was as yet uninhabited and behind the housing developments there were overgrown bushes, large, scary baobab trees, and mango and coconut groves.

Sometimes in the evenings, when Mother felt sad, Aloo and I would play two-three-five with her, a variation of whist for three people. I had entered the University by then and came back at weekends. Aloo was in his last year at school. He had turned out to be exceptionally bright in his studies—more so than we realised.

That year Mr. Datoo, a former teacher from our school who was also a former student, returned from America for a visit. Mr. Datoo had been a favourite with the boys. When he came he received a tumultuous welcome. For the next few days he toured the town like the Pied Piper followed by a horde of adulating students, one of whom was Aloo.

The exciting event inspired in Aloo the hope that not only might he be admitted to an American university, but he could also win a scholarship to go there. Throughout the rest of the year, therefore, he wrote to numerous universities, culling their names from books at the USIS, often simply at random or even only by the sounds of their names.

Mother's response to all these efforts was to humour him. She would smile. "Your uncles in America will pay thousands of shillings just to send you to college," she would say. Evidently she felt he was wasting his time, but he would never be able to say that he did not have all the support she could give him.

Responses to his enquiries started coming within weeks and a handful of them were guardedly encouraging. Gradually Aloo found out which were the better places, and which among them the truly famous. Soon a few catalogues arrived, all looking impressive. It seemed that the more involved he became with the application process, the more tantalizing was the prospect of going to an American university. Even the famous places did not discourage him. He learnt of subjects he had never heard of before: genetics, cosmology, artificial intelligence: a whole universe was out there waiting for him if only he could reach it. He was not sure if he could, if he was good enough. He suffered periods of intense hope and hopeless despair.

Of course, Aloo was entitled to a place at the local university. At the end of the year, when the selections were announced in the papers, his name was on the list. But some bureaucratic hand, probably also corrupt, dealt out a future prospect for him that came as a shock. He had applied to study medicine, he was given a place in agriculture. An agricultural officer in a rural district somewhere was not what he wanted to become however patriotic he felt. He had never left the city except to go to the national parks once on a school trip.

When Aloo received a letter from the California Institute of Technology offering him a place with a scholarship, he was stupefied at first. He read and reread the letter, not believing what it seemed to be saying, afraid that he might be reading something into it. He asked me to read it for him. When he was convinced there was no possibility of a mistake he became elated.

"The hell I'll do agriculture!" he grinned.

But first he had to contend with Mother.

Mother was incredulous. "Go, go," she said, "don't you eat my head, don't tease me!"

"But it's true!" he protested. "They're giving me a scholarship!"

We were at the table—the three of us—and had just poured tea from the thermos. Mother sitting across from me stared at her saucer for a while then she looked up.

"Is it true?" she asked me.

"Yes, it's true," I said. "All he needs is to take 400 dollars pocket money with him."

"How many shillings would that make?" she asked.

"About three thousand."

"And how are we going to raise this three thousand shillings? Have you bought a lottery? And what about the ticket? Are they going to send you a ticket too?"

As she said this Aloo's prospects seemed to get dimmer. She was right, it was not a little money that he needed.

"Can't we raise a loan?" he asked. "I'll work there. Yes, I'll work as a waiter. A waiter!—I know you can do it, I'll send the money back!"

"You may have uncles in America who would help you," Mother told him, "but no one here will."

Aloo's shoulders sagged and he sat there toying with his cup, close to tears. Mother sat drinking from her sauce and frowning. The evening light came in from the window behind me and gave a glint to her spectacles. Finally she set her saucer down. She was angry.

"And why do you want to go away, so far from us? Is this what I raised you for—so you could leave me and go away to a foreign place? Won't you miss us, where you want to go? Do we mean so little to you? If something happens..."

Aloo was crying. A tear fell into his cup, his nose was running. "So many kids go and return, and nothing happens to them.... Why did you mislead me, then? Why did you let me apply if you didn't want me to go...why did you raise my hopes if only to dash them?" He raised his voice to her, the first time I saw him do it, and he was shaking.

He did not bring up the question again and he prepared himself for the agricultural college, waiting for the term to begin. At home he would slump on the sofa putting away a novel a day.

If the unknown bureaucrat at the Ministry of Education had been less arbitrary, Aloo would not have been so broken and Mother would not have felt compelled to try and do something for him.

A few days later, on a Sunday morning, she looked up from her sewing machine and said to the two of us: "Let's go and show this letter to Mr. Velji. He is experienced in these matters. Let's take his advice."

Mr. Velji was a former administrator of our school. He had a large egg-shaped head and a small compact body. With his large forehead and big black spectacles he looked the caricature of the archetypal wise man. He also had the bearing of one. The three of us were settled in his sitting-room chairs staring about us and waiting expectantly when he walked in stiffly, like a toy soldier, to welcome us.

"How are you, sister?" he said. "What can I do for you?"

Aloo and I stood up respectfully as he sat down.

"We have come to you for advice..." Mother began.

"Speak then," he said jovially and sat back, joining his hands behind his head.

She began by giving him her history. She told him which family she was born in, which she had married into, how she had raised her kids when our father died. Common relations were discovered between our families. "Now this one here," she pointed at me, "goes to university here, and *that* one wants to go to America. Show him the documents," she commanded Aloo.

As if with an effort, Aloo pushed himself out of the sofa and slowly made his way to place the documents in Mr. Velji's hands. Before he looked at them Mr. Velji asked Aloo his result in the final exam.

At Aloo's answer, his eyes widened. "Henh?" he said, "All A's?"

"Yes," replied Aloo, a little too meekly.

Mr. Velji flipped the papers one by one, cursorily at first. Then he went over them more carefully. He looked at the long visa form with the carbon copies neatly bound behind the original; he read over the friendly letter from the Foreign Student Adviser; he was charmed by the letters of invitation from the fraternities. Finally he looked up, a little humbled.

"The boy is right," he said. "The university is good, and they are giving him a bursary. I congratulate you."

"But what should I do?" asked Mother anxiously. "What is your advice? Tell us what we should do."

"Well," said Mr. Velji, "it would be good for his education." He raised his hand to clear his throat. Then he said, a little slowly: "But if you send him, you will lose your son.

"It's a far place, America," he concluded, wiping his hands briskly at the finished business. "Now what will you have—tea? orange squash?"

His wife appeared magically to take orders.

"All the rich kids go every year and they are not lost," muttered Aloo bitterly as we walked back home. Mother was silent.

That night she was at the sewing machine and Aloo was on the couch, reading. The radio was turned low and through the open front door a gentle breeze blew in to cool the sitting room. I was standing at the door. The banana tree and its offspring rustled outside, a car zoomed on the road, throwing shadows on neighbouring houses. A couple out for a stroll, murmuring, came into sight over the uneven hedge; groups of boys or girls chattered before dispersing for the night. The intermittent buzz of an electric motor escaped from mother's sewing machine. It was a little darker where she sat at the other end of the room from us.

Presently she looked up and said a little nonchalantly, "At least show me what this university looks like—bring that book, will you?"

Mother had never seen the catalogue. She had always dismissed it, had never shown the least bit of curiosity about the place Aloo wanted so badly to visit. Now the three of us crowded around the glossy pages, pausing at pictures of the neoclassic façades and domes, columns towering over humans, students rushing about in a dither of activity, classes held on lush lawns in ample shade. It all looked so awesome and yet inviting.

"It's something, isn't it?" whispered Aloo, hardly able to hold back his excitement. "They teach hundreds of courses there," he said. "They send rockets into space…to other worlds…to the moon—"

"If you go away to the moon, my son, what will become of me?" she said humorously, her eyes gleaming as she looked up at us.

Aloo went back to his book and Mother to her sewing.

A little later I looked up and saw Mother deep in thought, brooding, and as she often did at such times she was picking her chin absentmindedly. It was, I think, the first time I saw her as a person and not only as our mother. I thought of what she must be going through in her mind, what she had gone through in bringing us up. She had been thirty-three when Father died, and she had refused several offers of marriage because they would all have entailed one thing: sending us all to the "boarding"—the orphanage. Pictures of her before his death showed her smiling and in full bloom: plump but not excessively fat, hair puffed fashionably, wearing high heels and make-up. There was one picture, posed at a studio, which Father had had touched up and enhanced, which now hung beside his. In it she stood against a black background, holding a book stylishly, the nylon pachedi painted a light green, the folds falling gracefully down, the borders decorated with sequins. I had never seen her like that. All I had seen of her was the stern face getting sterner with time as the lines set permanently and the hair thinned, the body turned squat, the voice thickened.

I recalled how Aloo and I would take turns sleeping with her at night on her big bed; how she would squeeze me in her chubby arms, drawing me up closer to her breast until I could hardly breathe—and I would control myself and hope she would soon release me and let me breathe.

She looked at me looking at her and said, not to me, "Promise me…promise me that if I let you go, you will not marry a white woman."

"Oh Mother, you know I won't!" said Aloo.

"And promise me that you will not smoke or drink."

"You know I promise!" He was close to tears.

Aloo's first letter came a week after he left, from London where he'd stopped over to see a former classmate. It flowed over with excitement. "How can I describe it," he wrote, "the sight from the plane...mile upon mile of carefully tilled fields, the earth divided into neat green squares...even the mountains are clean and civilised. And London...Oh London! It seemed that it would never end...blocks and blocks of houses, squares, parks, monuments...could any city be larger? How many of our Dar es Salaams would fit here, in this one gorgeous city...?"

A bird flapping its wings: Mr. Velji nodding wisely in his chair, Mother staring into the distance.

ENTRY POINTS

1 "Kichwele Street was now Uhuru Street." This story is set in Dar es Salaam, a city on the east coast of Africa, which formed part of the trade route visited by Arabians, Indians, and Europeans. Significantly, "Uhuru" means "independence."
   (a) Outline the significant characteristics and activities of Dar es Salaam. What is the author's attitude towards this city?
   (b) Given the meaning of "Uhuru," relate it to the title and to Aloo.

2 Why does Aloo want to enrol in an American university instead of his local one? Are his dreams and expectations ones with which you sympathize? Do *you* want to go to university or college? If so, why? Discuss with your group.

3 Why does Aloo's mother initially discourage Aloo from going to an American university? Do you sympathize with her feelings and concerns?

4 "But if you send him, you will lose your son." What does Mr. Velji mean by this statement? Do you agree with his pronouncement? Read Samuel Selvon's "Cane Is Bitter" (page 33), and then rethink your response. Given Mr. Velji's statement, why does Aloo's mother ultimately agree to send Aloo away to university?

5 "A bird flapping its wings...." Comment on this final image and relate it to Aloo's first letter from London, England.

6 This story deals with a "leaving," but it also deals with a "letting go." Explore these concepts with specific references to this story. What are the emotional and psychological consequences on Aloo and his mother as a result of his momentous decision to leave his homeland?

7 (a) As Aloo, write another letter to your mother describing your feelings and hopes after your first month at university. Mention, too, any new worries or concerns that you might have.

(b) Exchange your letter with a partner, then, as Aloo's mother, respond to your son's letter, expressing both encouragement and your own honest feelings about his absence from your home.

8 Read the essay, "Redrawing the Map of African Literature," by the Lagos writer, Chinweizur, found in *Voices from Twentieth-Century Africa* (Faber and Faber, 1988), to obtain a different point of view on the importance of an African-centred curriculum, education, and literature as opposed to a Eurocentric perspective. Rethink your own cultural assumptions and perspective.

9 For more stories from the African continent, read *African Short Stories* (ed. Chinua Achebe and C. L. Innes, 1985), an anthology that groups writers geographically in four different sections: Western, Eastern, Northern, and Southern African. Write a report on one of the stories and share your information with your class.

10 Read M. G. Vassanji's *The Book of Secrets* (1994) to gain further insights into how European wars changed colonial East Africa. Write a book report in which you critically examine the European impact on African society and summarize the changes that occurred. Share these ideas with your class.

HISTORY LESSON

Out of the belly of Christopher's ship
a mob bursts
Running in all directions
Pulling furs off animals
Shooting buffalo
Shooting each other
left and right

Father mean well
waves his makeshift wand
forgives saucer-eyed Indians

Red coated knights
gallop across the prairie
to get their men
and to build a new world

Pioneers and traders
bring gifts
Smallpox, Seagrams
and Rice Krispies

Civilization has reached
the promised land.

Between the snap crackle pop
of smoke stacks
and multi-coloured rivers
swelling with flower powered zee
are farmers sowing skulls and bones
and miners
pulling from gaping holes
green paper faces
of smiling English lady

The colossi
in which they trust
while burying
breathing forests and fields
beneath concrete and steel
stand shaking fists
waiting to mutilate
whole civilizations
ten generations at a blow.

Somewhere among the remains
of skinless animals
is the termination
to a long journey
and unholy search
for the power
glimpsed in a garden
forever closed
forever lost.

JEANNETTE C. ARMSTRONG

1 What is Armstrong's view of the European explorers and their descendants who exist "to build a new world"? How do you feel about her images and observations? Discuss your observations with your group.

2 Compare Armstrong's views on the impact of contact between Europeans and aboriginal peoples to the views expressed in Oodgeroo Noonuccal's poem "Civilisation" (page 122). For further insights into the impact of this contact over the last five centuries, read the non-fiction work, *Stolen Continents: The "New World" Through Indian Eyes* (1992), by Ronald Wright. Write a report on Wright's ideas about how American Indians "discovered" Europe. Share these ideas with your class.

3 Explain the following lines:

for the power
glimpsed in a garden
forever closed
forever lost.

4 Comment on Armstrong's use of symbolism and metaphor. How could farmers be "sowing skulls and bones"? What are "the colossi/ in which we trust"? Which of Armstrong's other images did you particularly like or dislike? Elaborate.

5 Write a letter to an editor in which you present an argument about why it is important for North Americans to listen to the concerns and ideas of the First Peoples. This is the way Antonine Maillet, an Acadian author living in Montreal, has put it: "People come to a country—Canada—that has learned to deal with differences, to be flexible and subtle, confident and yet not arrogant. The one weak spot is in our ignorance of the native peoples who came before us. We have a treasure in those centuries of native history. If we could learn to incorporate their experience into mainstream culture, imagine the result. It would only add to the mix that has made this country so unique."

6 Write a story in which our world has been "discovered" by beings from another planet. How are we affected by the contact? How are the aliens affected? You might want to read A. C. Clarke's science fiction novel, *Childhood's End*, for added insights into the possible impact of alien contact with earthlings.

CIVILISATION

We who came late to civilisation,
Missing a gap of centuries,
When you came we marvelled and admired,
But with foreboding.
We had so little but we had happiness,
Each day a holiday,
For we were people before we were citizens,
Before we were ratepayers,
Tenants, customers, employees, parishioners.
How could we understand
White man's gradings, rigid and unquestioned,
Your sacred totems of Lord and Lady,
Highness and Holiness, Eminence, Majesty.
We could not understand
Your strange cult of uniformity,
This mass obedience to clocks, time-tables.
Puzzled, we wondered why
The importance to you, urgent and essential,
Of ties and gloves, shoe-polish, uniforms.
New to us were jails and orphanages,
Rents and taxes, banks and mortgages.
We who had so few things, the prime things,
We had no policemen, lawyers, middlemen,
Brokers, financiers, millionaires.
So they bewildered us, all the new wonders,
Stocks and shares, real estate,
Compound interest, sales and investments.
Oh, we have benefited, we have been lifted
With new knowledge, a new world opened.
Suddenly caught up in white man ways
Gladly and gratefully we accept,
And this is necessity.
But remember, white man, if life is for happiness,
You too, surely, have much to change.

OODGEROO NOONUCCAL (KATH WALKER)

1   (a) How does the poet view the life of her people, the Aborigines of Australia, *before* the arrival of the European explorers and settlers? Be specific in your details.

     (b) How does her view change *after* the arrival of the Europeans? What have the Aborigines become?

2 What are her specific critical perceptions of the European form of society and the settlers' ambitions and ideals? Are you sympathetic to or convinced of her complaints and perceptions? To what degree?

3 Define "irony." Apply this definition to the following lines in the context of the whole poem:

Oh, we have benefited, we have been lifted.
With new knowledge, a new world opened.

4   (a) Of the many aspects of "civilization" which Noonuccal lists, which ones would *you* most like to see changed? Why?

     (b) Within your group, argue the point that "if life is for happiness," the white man "[has] much to change."

5 Look up the word "civilization" (spelled here "civilisation"). Write a short composition in which you define "civilization" in your own terms. As Thomas More did in his famous novel, *Utopia*, how would you describe a "perfect" society?

THE WHEELCHAIR

GABRIELLE ROY

The people of the village had been warned to get ready for the package that was to be delivered by air. Such a big and cumbersome package! One could imagine how difficult it would be for a man to carry it on his back across the uneven tundra—a tundra so cut up by little lakes there was virtually one in every hollow of the ground.

The plane would not touch down. It would fly low over the village searching for a spot to let the package drop. Then it would be up to the villagers to catch it and take good care of it, since it was unlikely that such a package would ever come again to the Arctic.

And so it was that on a long, warm, summer's night in the little Eskimo community of Igavik, not far from the Bay of Ungava, there arrived from the sky a wheelchair, sent by a charitable society to Isaac who, since his seal-hunting accident last winter, has been transformed, so to speak, into a rock from his head to his feet.

Perhaps if he could have spoken with a fragment of his former liveliness Isaac would have first asked how it was that he had become so famous as to have been sent a chair from the other end of the world.

Taken from its crate and exposed against the naked sky the chair did at any rate make an extraordinary impression with its chrome armrests, a back, a padded seat and two large rubber-covered wheels, in short, more attention to comfort than one would have thought existed in the whole world.

The healthy people decided to try out the chair to see what it felt like to be an invalid. They began to laugh as they passed the chair amongst themselves and enjoyed imagining what it would be like to be incapable of walking and to have to be wheeled about for the rest of one's days.

Finally, however, they thought to show the chair to Isaac. Isaac was a changed man since the days when he used to maintain in every possible way that dying was not difficult; that you just had to let yourself go when the moment came; that in truth nothing was more simple, that you only had to do what his grandmother had done when she turned, one fine day, of her own will, to death. He himself never got there, though no doubt that was all he thought of, left alone as he was in the corner of the hut where, indeed, another woman in his family, his own sister Deborah, had succeeded in escaping. While he himself...

With his good eye he seemed to be examining the chair. To someone who during his whole life had sat only on the ground or when necessary on a hard church bench this curious chair must have seemed like a throne. If there remained in his old head any of the mischief of his former days he might have laughed inside to see all the trouble he had singlehandedly caused. But with one side of his face paralyzed and the other barely more alive, Isaac, who used to be so vital, now looked as though he were removed from everything, though perhaps this was not the case at all. Nor were the few sounds he succeeded in emitting from his throat of any use to him. No one could understand them, or they pretended not to understand so as not to renew the effort of having to listen so attentively. It was true that the people of the area had changed since the disappearance of Deborah and the investigation that followed; since the arrival of the men from the government who came by plane and who asked endless senseless questions: Did she seem discouraged? Did she still have her mental faculties about her? Why do you think she behaved this way? What is your opinion as to why she did this?

After that no one wanted to draw the world's attention to such willing and consenting deaths.

So just like everywhere else in the world pains were taken to keep people alive as long as possible, by will or by force. Death separated the Eskimos almost as much as it did the White people.

Isaac could obviously have refused to swallow the mouthfuls that his daughter-in-law Esmeralda put on his tongue, especially since they were not always the best tasting ones. It seems that he did try to refuse, one day. But was it from disgust with the food? Or with himself? Or with living? Esmeralda put the piece of meat back in his mouth and he swallowed it, either because in the end his appetite was stronger than his sorrow or because he simply could not do otherwise.

Despite his numbness, like always being on the edge of an extreme cold, perhaps he too could have given in to that great sleep if only this wonderful chair, in coming all the way to this little community, had not succeeded in putting into question everything: life, death, what one must do for or against it … and when to leave.

$$\boxed{\text{II}}$$

When the excitement caused by the delivery of the chair began to wane, other feelings came to the surface.

Having come out of her hideaway, Eleonara, an old cousin of Isaac's, circled the chair three times and finished by offering envious congratulations.

"Well, well. Someone was well thought of around here. All one needs to do is lose the use of one's legs and one gets everything else in exchange. There are some lucky people in this world…."

"Lucky!" replied Isaac, more or less distinctly from the corner of his mouth perhaps by way of protestation. Lucky is what most people heard, although it was really only "eeh, eeh."

But Alfreda, who was a little deaf, heard "happy, happy" and, dragging herself forward on her swollen legs, agreed in an ill-humoured way.

"I really believe you when you say you have reason to call yourself happy. If you weren't happy before…"

Then she went on to explain to everyone that it was surely only Isaac who needed such a chair and that such a chair could only therefore have been sent for him.

Esmeralda saw this happening and lost no time in setting things straight.

"This chair," she said to those gathered round, "has been sent to the old man by the friends of the Federation of the Disabled and while I'm around no one is going to take it from him and use it for an hour here or an hour there."

Those who had been carefully scrutinizing Isaac's face while Esmeralda came to his defence thought he looked pleased.

And so goodwill returned and everyone ran to pick Isaac up.

On the count of four, on the count of six, they lifted him up, bent his legs and seated him in the chair.

For the moment, because of his position, his wrinkled hands placed flat on the armrests, head held rigid, Isaac looked like an old reigning king. Almost everyone was struck by the new importance he had taken on.

Not waiting a moment longer they set out to take him about his rough countryside.

No other terrain could lend itself less well to such outings. Despite the illusion of smoothness given to it by the covering of caribou moss, the land was bumpy in the extreme. One could certainly not go quickly. Even chugging along slowly the chair pitched and reeled. At each turn of the wheels as they stumbled over the rough lichen, the paralytic jolted, his head shaking. He moved his lips. Was he trying to protest? Was he asking to be left in peace? Or was he rather woken up by this walk and looking to obtain details? He had been given details at the start like someone who was being taken on a tour. But now in the general turmoil and excitement, he had become somewhat forgotten. Making desperate attempts to speak, his lip hitched up, he really looked like he was laughing. To see him with such an expression, seated in his new chair which itself was so comical, incited the women to hysterical laughter, each setting off the other. Such laughter gave them at least enough strength to push the chair up the little inclines and made them laugh all the more. Finally they stopped midstream, unable to do anything else but chortle.

Some distance away, the men, seeing the women so done in with so little to show for it, suddenly broke into great fits of laughter themselves.

The women, however, tired fairly quickly of pushing the chair. Favourable terrain was nowhere to be found. Either there was the lake around which the poor huts were assembled, or there was the ground which was always spongy and bumpy. The big wheels of the chair could barely roll along the caribou moss which itself had the consistency of rubber. The women finally left the old man to the children who were waiting anxiously for such an opportunity.

Joyously they danced around the chair.

His eyes at an angle, worried at what he saw, Isaac watched the children as best he could, wondering no doubt what the children were thinking and what they were planning to do with him now that he was in their possession.

Actually it was nothing too terrible. They only wanted to take him where the women had been unable to, to the top of the closest knoll.

There were twelve of them who set themselves to the task, representing all the children of the village who were over the age of six.

Each helping the other to push, the hands of one pressing against the hips of the other in front of him, every child bent over in the same direction and none of them wasting energy to laugh, serious and careful in their efforts, they climbed inch by inch with the chair at the head, in a narrow procession like a line of ants working together, heading straight for their destination. Finally they arrived at the crest of the bare hill facing a sky which spread out to eternity. It was only then that they agreed to rest.

Here the breeze was broad and pure. In the distance one could see the silver line of the Glacial Ocean which today seemed less severe than usual. There were virtually no clouds and the sky was filled with a gentle clarity. The old man looked happy. Had the children guessed that this was precisely the spot that Isaac wanted to see again before dying? Did they already know perhaps in their small, keen minds that the sea is that which all good Eskimos want to contemplate before dying? Or had they simply wanted to come here to play today?

They seemed, at any rate, to understand the few sounds by which Isaac made known his desire to stay in this place. They braced the wheels of the chair with clods of moss just as their mothers had told them and, leaving the old man conspicuously in the middle of the horizon on the highest point in the area, they ran as fast as they could to play down below around a little lake that was on this side of the hill. For a long time they amused themselves by trying to catch fish with their bare hands and the joyous noise they created there at the bottom reached up to the old man who had been seated in the heart of the sky, completely immobilized except for his hair blowing in the wind. In his attentive pose, his eyes staring into infinity, he seemed to be listening to a sort of long, silent sermon coming from the sea, the horizon and the air.

The pure breeze cleansed him of all the odours of illness. He could even hear, when the children were quiet, the faint murmuring of the sea as it dashed against the distant shore.

One felt in those days, along with Isaac, a renewed taste for life.

III

The children would take him up there often, either because they sensed the happiness the old man felt when he was carried to the middle of the sky, or because they just had more fun playing on that side of the hill.

Sometimes, however, in their hurry to run towards some new discovery they would abandon Isaac in a dismal hollow where one could see neither quivering water nor faraway mysteries. Then the old Eskimo felt really weary of being in this world. Even those who declared, because of his puckered cheek, that he still felt like laughing, would never have dared to maintain such a notion if only they could have seen Isaac during those hours when he was forgotten by the children, in the hollows of the earth where neither wind nor sun could reach.

The children, when they finally decided to get him, did seem somewhat conscious of Isaac's distress and were afraid to look at him from the side of his good eye, afraid of the intensity of expression he still managed to fix there.

For his part the old man made illusory attempts at moving his fingers; lifting his hand to reach the fresh round cheeks of the children. He almost arrived at the suggestion of a gesture that could have been a caress in the emptiness.

One day, however, they forgot him on top of the knoll. The mothers did not notice immediately that the children had come back alone. They were so used to seeing them together, the old man and the swarm of children. Memory played a trick with the image it had often recorded and they thought they had seen all of them together as usual.

When dinner time came even Esmeralda had not yet noticed that Isaac was missing. She was in a lazy mood that day and had warned everyone around her to fend for themselves because she, for her part, intended to spend the day with her arms folded.

Still, by midnight, everyone having come home to sleep, it was impossible for Esmeralda not to notice that the old man was not there.

She ran out of the hut. The stars were pale and as yet uncertain in the sky, itself barely dark. Esmeralda began to shriek at the top of her voice, calling Isaac home. It was as though she had forgotten he could not open his mouth wide enough to reply. She turned towards a point in the vast deserted countryside and called, her head thrown back, and then she turned to the other side and did the same thing, a little like the way dogs howl, and indeed at that moment the dogs joined in, almost completely covering Esmeralda's voice. In spite of this hullabaloo the rest of the village continued to sleep peacefully. Perhaps Esmeralda was upset to discover she was apparently the only person who still worried about the old man. She began to cry, turned to the night sky, raising her voice in an attempt to be heard by those who had so little heart as to be sleeping through such a plight.

At that very moment, as she found herself looking toward the side of the big knoll to the right, she saw distinctly this time as the clouds separated, the old man, in profile, outlined against the sky in a dark limpidity, black on black, his hands on the armrests, a faint crescent of moon over his head making him look more than ever like an old king now dethroned.

She hurried to get him. In bringing him back she found the descent very difficult, the heavy chair wanting at any minute to fly off on its own. She could not help grumbling a little as if it were his own fault that Isaac had stayed out so long.

At any rate, she communicated to him, his outings were finished with. He was going to stay now under her watch, at home, and if sometimes she allowed him to sit in the wheelchair it would only be for staying put.

But not having much determination or force, another day when the children came back three or four times to ask if they could not 'have' the old man again, she gave in and said without perhaps really realizing it, exhausted by their swarming round her, "Take him then and let me be in peace."

And so it began again. They went up and down and all around the lake and beyond this side of the hill.

In all his adult life Isaac had probably never seen as many charming corners of the countryside as the children took him to that summer.

One morning the children caught a rare butterfly. Some whim of creation had sent this delicate creature, dressed in its evening clothes, to live and die in the desert of the Arctic. Not knowing what to do with it, they gave it to the old man.

They often put little flowers into his hands.

But alas they were only carefree children and they forgot him once again. That night Esmeralda had gone to bed and was sleeping like a log. Not even the rumbling of the storm woke her. Then everything exploded.

The rain poured onto the old man who was placed to receive it on the top of the knoll. The winds slapped him about from all sides. It was as though nature held a grudge against him for still being alive. Or was he misinterpreting its motives? Perhaps nature was finally showing clemency in working to remove him from the earth.

Flashes of lightning revealed from time to time in the midst of the darkness his inscrutable face. It had always been hard to know what Isaac was thinking even in the days when he gave of himself little, because of his peculiarly caustic and disconcerting way of speaking.

For example, one of his favourite sayings had been that one should die with as little fuss as possible. Now of course, he was denied even this dignity.

His dripping face, appearing at the base of the tormented sky, was obliterated as the whirling clouds returned to the horizon.

Was he rejoicing at having finally found help in the claws of the wind, in the cloudbursts, the bitterness of the elements which were tonight perhaps the allies of his weary soul? Or was he thinking instead of the others who were at this hour sheltered and warm?

The rain stopped. On the bare hilltop, crushed into his chair, Isaac looked like some vegetable creature which had been spoiled by too much water. But with the help of the wind a plant could at least shake itself a bit and begin to dry. He could not even shiver to help chase away the cold from his limbs.

But he was still alive when the village below was wakened by a clear summer's-end morning.

IV

What was the real reason why Esmeralda began to take care of him again? Compassion? Remorse? Or perhaps out of stubbornness, habit? Once acquired, it is hard to know how to give it up, although one day or another one must learn to deal with it. Esmeralda seemed to be taken up with the task. She wrapped Isaac in the warmest blanket. She moved him from one corner to another, wherever there was a bit of sunshine. She got some penicillin for him from a neighbour who had some left over from the dose given by the nurse on her last visit.

She did so much and did it so well that she succeeded, as she could boast, in 'saving' Isaac, from which she derived a curious mixture of pride and weariness and when all was said and done, embarrassment because even the 'saved' Isaac was not worth much.

He was at this point so withered and shrunken that his daughter-in-law could easily carry him in her arms from one corner of the hut to another when she felt like cleaning somewhere.

There were still a few warm days left. In the course of one of them Esmeralda caught Isaac staring at the wheelchair and she took pity. Poor old man—he still had a longing for his throne!

She carried him over to it, wrapped him up and wheeled him outside so that he could see a little of the lake and the sky. She could still keep him in sight from inside the hut and her lethargic daydreams. "It's over," she explained to him, "no more roaming about all over the place for you. You're going to stay right here in front of the door, father."

Did she think she saw a ray of defiance light up his tired stare? At any rate she went off to busy herself with this and that and then came back to reprimand him gently, "With the scares you gave us it's not going to start again."

When the children passed by they no longer stopped to ask if they could take the old man out. They had other games in mind and eventually the wheelchair's bizarre attraction wore out. No one really knows how it happened, step by step, but one day one had to face the fact: there was nothing more there than old, worn-out tires, just a pile of scrap metal, and yet the chair still made a sort of impression. It had become part of the landscape.

At the same time, bit by bit, Isaac too lost his former importance.

There was no one who came up to him with that mixture of friendly curiosity and fear except an old limping dog that one had put off destroying because he had once been so brave.

And so it was the dog who was there to receive the caress that Isaac had been practising in case the children came back to get him, when he could finally sketch it out. It was a pitiful dog who had never felt the hand of a man placed on his back in simple friendship. Surprised, he sat down, shaking, his eyes staring like a human's, and then he began to cry as though his entire dog life was suddenly reviewed before his eyes, gradually, one thing leading to another.

It was, in spite of everything, a good summer, but it came to an end. Nothing could be done except to go on to be cooped up in the cruel winter. Deciding to take him out one more time, at the last minute, Esmeralda warned him charitably, "This may be the last time."

From where Esmeralda set up the chair the lake was not far, only thirty steps away down a battered slope.

Isaac kept his eyes fixed on the water at his feet. With the frost coming on, the water was already heavy, congealing at the shore. Almost without moving, the water perfectly reflected the warm colour that lichens have before they die. They fringed the entire lake in a beautiful and minutely detailed even border. This was almost the most beautiful time of the year, good to reflect upon, invigorating, short and poignant. Beneath the cover placed on the old man's knees no one noticed that his hand tried without ceasing to turn the right wheel of the chair.

Suddenly he succeeded. Esmeralda raised her head just in time to see him start to roll. In one leap she caught the chair, two fingers from the water's edge. She was trembling with fear, annoyance, spite and no doubt in her agitation came a variety of other feelings, all of them mixing and contradicting each other.

"This is a fine thing to do!" she reproached.

Her eye searched for a solid piece of rock to wedge under the wheel and not being able to find one she grew angry. She would have liked to have taken him back and put him inside once and for all except that to make room for him in the cabin she would have had to take out a number of things for which she had had to find room once before. One was always, in this borderless country, short of space and shelter. Finally she propped up the chair with a stump of wood. In getting up, all out of breath, half triumphant at having once more succeeded, half beaten down at being stuck with the old man all the time, she saw in the depths of his dead face an expression that was still surprisingly lively, endowed with a personal willpower that cried out to her silently: "Why? But why, in the end?"

She had always known that if ever he were able to speak intelligibly, this is what he would ask her, but she had no ready answer. She knew no better than he why she looked to save him. She glanced across the naked and tragic horizon and believed she saw that it was in part due to the rest of the world.

She shivered as a rougher gust of wind came in from the depths of the northern deserts.

"Nothing stays just with us anymore," she said with a sort of bitterness mixed with wonder. "You saw Deborah. 'They' arrived with all their questions; 'they' asked why. 'They' made us feel ashamed."

She bent over him to arrange his blanket, threatening him ineffectually, without malice, "You have to live now..." and then ran brusquely back into the warmth of the hut.

Translated by Sherri Walsh

1 (a) How do the villagers in Igavik first react to the "big and cumbersome package" of the wheelchair?

(b) How do you think Isaac would have viewed the wheelchair before his seal-hunting accident? How does he now react?

2 Examine the views of death presented in Section I of the story. Note the perspective of the Inuit as opposed to that of the "White people" and comment in your groups.

3 "Isaac looked like an old reigning king."

(a) How do you think Isaac feels in his new possession?

(b) Is he happy at the "crest of the bare hill" where the children have pushed him? Why?

(c) On the night that the rains explode on Isaac, what conflicting thoughts go through his mind?

4 With your group, discuss fully the reasons why Isaac is so miserable beyond the fact of his physical limitations. Take into consideration the following:

(a) the actions of his family;

(b) the actions of the community—why do people begin to forget the old man and his "throne"?;

(c) the problem of his increasing isolation (Refer to William Shakespeare's *King Lear* and Margaret Laurence's *The Stone Angel*);

(d) the lack of support services for disabled people in his community.

5 Compare the message of this story to that found in the poems "History Lesson" (page 120), and "Civilisation" (page 122). To what extent do you agree with the Aboriginal point of view? Discuss with your group.

6 You are Isaac. Write an interior monologue in which you try to understand your physical limitations and potential. Answer the question, "Why? But why, in the end?"

7 For other interesting views on the effect of European culture on the First Peoples in North America, read Fred Bodsworth's novel, *The Sparrow's Fall*, Brian Moore's *The Black Robe*, M. T. Kelly's *A Dream Like Mine*, and Peter Such's *Riverrun*. Write a book review on one of these Canadian novels.

VOCATIONAL COUNSELLING

CHRISTA REINIG

I was still a child, "talked like a child, was bright like a child and had childlike notions." But as far as the state was concerned, I was finishing school and next year I would go out into the real world, into the state. We formed lines in front of the white doors, the boys and girls separately. We read the flyers which they had handed to us at the door:

> In the testing booth absolute silence must prevail. Concentrate!
> If you do not understand the question, press the blue button.
> You have one minute to formulate your answer. At the sound
> of the bell, get up and leave the room.

The fact that someone suddenly addressed me by the polite form was no comfort to me. It increased my fears. As I finally confronted "it," alone in a humming room, I was trembling and I pressed the red button—the red button on my left. But I did not get it at all that I had given myself away as being left-handed. I could not sit down properly. My child's behind was wiggling on the stool. I had to go to the bathroom. A minute later I had forgotten about it.

The computer talked in its guttural, electronic voice:

> Comrade Reinig! Do you remember when you consciously
> heard the word *work* for the first time and what emotions it
> evoked in you?

Reinig: I consciously heard the word for the first time in the expression "without work" and it evoked pleasant emotions in me.

Computer: What images can you remember?

Reinig: It was in Humboldt Park. The men were sitting close together on benches, folding chairs or on the borders of the lawn. In front of them, on their knees they had cigar boxes and shoe cartons full of little pictures from their cigarette packages. They visited each other and exchanged the pictures back and forth. One Greta Garbo for one Emil Jannings. One French fighter plane for one Focke-Wulf, one Chinese Mandarin for one Huron Warrior in ceremonial garb. The whole of Humboldt Park was one big market swarming with these men exchanging little pictures. Later they said that the nightmarish time of unemployment was over and we could all look to the future with joy. I said to myself these adults are nuts, and secretly I decided to be unemployed one day.

Computer: What are the dominating feelings when early in the morning the sound of an alarm clock tears you from your sleep?

Reinig: I feel a great sorrow in my heart.

Computer: During the course of the day, do you repeatedly feel a great sorrow in your heart?

Reinig: No, once I have managed to get out of bed, the worst part of the day is behind me.

Computer: What is your favorite occupation?

Reinig: Reading.

Computer: What do you like to read best?

Reinig: Karl May, John Kling, Billy Jenkins, Rolf Torring, Jorn Farrow, Tom Mix.

Computer: What is your favorite book?

Reinig: Olaf K. Abelsen, *At the Fires of Eternity*. I must have read it a dozen times and I can recite it from memory.

Computer: Give a short summary of the contents.

Reinig: Well, the group of travelers is being followed by gangsters. One does not know why, because it is a story in installments. The gangsters blow up the island. Because of that, the group of travelers gets under the earth into a dark volcanic landscape, weakly lighted by a distant fire. There are animals there, too—crocodiles, bats. These animals are blind, their eyes have atrophied because they have been living in darkness for so long. Then the travelers discover the remains of an ancient Mayan culture. As they are about to recover the treasures, someone shoots poisoned arrows at them. It is not the Indians, however, but the gangsters who are pursuing them. The fire of eternity changes, and there is a volcanic eruption. The travelers are blown up from the depths and thrown into the sea. There they find each other again while fighting the waves. That is the end. The next volume is missing, but I believe they are rescued.

Computer: Did you ever try to read a classical work by Schiller or Goethe?

Reinig: Yes, I once tried to read a sea adventure play by Goethe or Schiller.

The familiar humming sound stopped. Suddenly there was complete silence. Then there was a soft, hoarse little cough that did not stop. In a sense it had been quite pleasant until now. But then I realized that I had bared the lining of my heart, not to a sympathetic soul, but to a machine which must have cost at least many millions of dollar-rubles. And I had wrecked it. Worse, at any moment it would explode and tear me to pieces. That might be better; at least I would not have to pay for it. How many years would it take to pay for it by working it off? I would rather prepare myself for death. Then there was that humming again. Our Father—thank God.

Computer: Did you ever try to read a classical work by Goethe or Schiller?

Reinig: Torquato Tasso.

The crazier these exotic names are the better one can remember them. Schimborassotschomolungmakiliman-dscharo! Why doesn't he ask me something like that?

Computer: Describe the artistic impressions which you have received.

Reinig: The book got in with our furniture and junk in some way. It got lost there and surfaced now and then. Finally I felt sorry. I always read the last page first. They mentioned a ship's sinking. The hero, battling the waves, was trying to hold onto a cliff. Then, again, the sequel was also missing. Possibly he was rescued, for if the shipwrecked man gets too close to the cliffs, he is finished. He would simply be dashed to pieces. Then I read the beginning, too. It was about some people or other who were walking around in a museum and looking at figures. I quickly had enough of this, and how the shipwreck happened, I never did find out.

Computer: Your good marks in school are incompatible with your unreasonable reading. How do you explain this contradiction?

Reinig: My mother gave me a high school textbook for Christmas. But since I go to elementary school, the book was completely useless. It did not fit our course of studies at all and I never did use it. And therefore I read it anyway.

Computer: Do you have any special vocational plans?

Reinig: Originally I wanted to go to the Trojan War. But then I learned that it was already over and people thought there would be no more war. So then I switched over to the Odyssey. I got my facts confused and prepared myself mentally to discover America. With time I got smarter and realized that there are things which cannot happen because they have already happened. I concentrated on the Antarctic in case something would turn up for me there, since I am first in tobogganing. In travel descriptions I read that modern seafaring consists only of removing rust and painting with red lead. So I got myself into an identity crisis, which was strengthened because I slowly had to realize that I was indeed a girl, and with that all of my previous vocational plans were thwarted in any case. Luckily, a little later on I got a prescription for glasses. This solved all of my problems, including the problems of sex. For the boys really had me run the gauntlet and shouted with sadistic pleasure: "My last will for lasses, one with glasses!" Wherever I appeared, they started up. Then, however, winter came and the boys as usual pummeled all the girls with snowballs. Only I was spared. Wherever I appeared, they warned each other: "Watch out, not her, she has glasses." This gave me new courage and I decided to become a professor and to excavate Mayan pyramids. And to that thought I have actually stuck until today.

Computer: You will be a writer. Within two minutes you can register a protest, and, for this, press the green button.

Within two seconds I pressed the button.

Computer: Counterproposal?

Reinig: Oh, please, may I not at least become a politician? I could work my way up to becoming chancellor and become the highest servant of my people. I have always been able to speak well.

Computer: Laziness in combination with ambition would allow for both possibilities. On them a political as well as a literary career can be based. In your case only the second possibility can be considered because your intelligence is not sufficient for politics.

And then, it seemed to me as if I were suddenly hearing a human voice, loving, concerned and personal. But that cannot be true. It was and remained a machine. It must only be my grateful memory that falsified something.

Computer: And, moreover, I am responsible for your further well-being. If something unpleasant should happen to you, one would reproach me and maintain that I was programmed incorrectly.—Objection refused.

Thirty years later I had another encounter with a computer. I stepped into the testing booth and with cocky indifference pressed the red button on the—right side and sat down.

Computer: Comrade Reinig, why do you write?

Reinig: I write because Comrade Computer prescribed it for me.

The bell rang and I left the room.

VOCABULARY NOTES

Greta Garbo and Emil Jannings: famous pre-1950s film actors of German origin; **Focke-Wulf:** a German fighter plane; **Karl May, John Kling, Billy Jenkins, Rolf Torring, Jorn Farrow, Olaf K. Abelsen:** writers of popular mid-twentieth century adventure stories; **Tom Mix:** a popular early-twentieth century American movie cowboy; **Schiller and Goethe:** great German nineteenth century writers considered equal to Shakespeare in English; **Torquato Tasso:** a sixteenth century Italian writer of *Jerusalem Delivered*, an epic poem filled with adventure and romance

ENTRY POINTS

1 "Do you remember when you consciously heard the word *work* for the first time and what emotions it evoked in you?"
  (a) Analyze and discuss Reinig's response to the computer's initial question. Are you sympathetic to her response?
  (b) What emotions does the word "work" evoke in you? Elaborate on your response.
  (c) Have you found your "vocational counselling" in high school helpful? Why or why not? How could it have been improved?

2 Reading is Reinig's favourite occupation.
  (a) What does she enjoy reading?
  (b) What does her preference in reading reveal about her? How would *you* counsel her for a future vocation given her preferred activity?
  (c) How does the Computer respond to Reinig's answer? Is the Computer's final dictum to Reinig a satisfactory one? Is there anything wrong with it? Explain.

3 Does Reinig write because Comrade Computer prescribed it for her? Why do professional writers write? Why do *you* write?

4 Define "allusion." The first sentence of this story contains an allusion to 1 Corinthians 13:9-12. Read the whole passage and show its relevance to this modern story.

5 How would you characterize the Computer in this story? To what extent do you think that computers today are controlling our lives? Are we in danger of, increasingly, not thinking for ourselves? Discuss and debate in your groups.

6 (a) Read Yevgeny Yevtushenko's poem, "Lies" (page 1). Are the state and the school system lying to Reinig? Is there anything wrong with their process in forcing Reinig to make a decision on her vocation? Elaborate.

(b) What interest might the government of a country have in determining the occupations of its citizens? What benefits and problems might result if the government assigned jobs to everyone? For further ideas, you might want to read Plato's *Republic*, and Aldous Huxley's *Brave New World*.

7 Use a computer to write a story using the same structure Reinig uses in which *you* get a computer's "vocational counselling" or advice on some other topic such as a love relationship. Do you ultimately accept the "computer's wisdom"?

8 Improvise a skit in which one student role-plays a Computer and another role-plays an interviewee looking for advice.

9 Interview various adults and ask them how they chose their vocations. Share your responses with the class.

A BEAUTIFUL WOMAN

J.J. STEINFELD

Arlene, dressed in her well-worn gardening outfit, was kneeling at the back of the house, scooping soil with her hand spade. She imagined the garden in full bloom, supplying the ingredients for the elaborate salads she enjoyed making for her family.

This year—1982—she was going to add some new seeds: parsnips, Brussels sprouts, leeks. She marvelled at the process of planting, nurturing, growing, and eventually happily devouring what was once a simple seed. It was a mild afternoon and Arlene felt good. Lori, her youngest child, and the family's Saint Bernard played tug-of-war with an old shirt of her husband's, indifferent to Arlene's communing with nature.

When she heard her husband pull into the driveway, Arlene left her labour of love and walked to greet him. Rudy awkwardly slid out of the station wagon with two bouquets of flowers, a bottle of champagne, a small bow-adorned box, and his briefcase. He struggled with his load and Arlene rushed towards him, smiling at the sight of this well-organized, graceful executive reduced to a clumsy, overburdened delivery boy.

Suddenly Arlene's smile faded. She realized that Rudy had a big announcement to make—why else the gifts on an ordinary Wednesday afternoon. The armful of goodies was to cushion her, to prepare her for the next big plateau of *his* career. When he was transferred from

Vancouver, her childhood home, to Calgary, it was a dozen roses and a china figurine; Calgary to Regina was chrysanthemums and a bottle of expensive perfume; Regina to Toronto had been three dozen orchids and front-row seats to a musical comedy. She recalled how miserable she was during that play while Rudy laughed loudly at every joke.

Where to now, Arlene wondered. She attempted to determine the mileage by the value of the gifts: a bottle of Dom Perignon could indicate Timbuktu! Now, after almost four years in Toronto, she was used to it here. Didn't Rudy realize she was halfway through getting her degree in English, even if it was only part-time. She had always wanted a degree in literature and was even starting to make daydreaming plans for graduate school one day. She loved the rambling old house, her expanding garden, and the older children, Eddie and Jennifer, had never attended one school for so long. She was not eager to disrupt her routine.

"I love you, darling," Rudy said, and handed his wife first the bouquet of tulips, then the one of carnations. She inhaled each bouquet, the fragrances lost in her anxiety. She guessed Ottawa or Halifax, but it could be any place. Rudy's insurance company believed in keeping its employees moving. GROWTH THROUGH MOVEMENT was on all the company's brochures and stationery. Sometimes Arlene believed that her family would have more stability if Rudy worked for the Mafia. Their marriage, she helplessly thought, was destined to be a sea-to-sea extravaganza.

The dog, still holding the ragged shirt in its mouth, and Lori raced from the backyard and charged into Rudy. He reeled with good humour, regaining his balance, then leaned over and simultaneously kissed his daughter and patted Keynes. He handed Lori his briefcase to carry, her favourite task.

"You get more beautiful each day," he said to his excited daughter, her nutbrown pigtails jiggling with each turn of her head. His long fingers traced a loving message on her chin and soft cheeks.

"Like Mommy," Lori said, swinging her daddy's briefcase, trying to be the miniature executive.

"Exactly like Mommy," Rudy laughed with the satisfied self-assurance of a man in control of his destiny. All the components of his life and career seemed secure.

"I have something to discuss with you, Rudy," Arlene said before they had reached the kitchen door. Her blue eyes dimmed with apprehension. He paused and smiled at her, as though to say, "Don't worry, darling. I'll take care of everything." Before he announced the enforced move to Tasmania or the Arctic—the whole world needed insurance—before he boasted about the significant raise and sparkling prospects, she needed to talk to him about their oldest child. Once Jennifer came home from school and overwhelmed her father with kisses and beguiling embraces it would be too late.

"Can't it wait?" he said, giving Arlene the little box and champagne bottle. Not listening for her reaction, he lifted Lori and carried her into the sun-yellow kitchen. This kitchen is nicer than the ones in Vancouver, Calgary, or Regina, he had tried to console his wife, attempting in his problem-solving manner to ease the transition she had resisted. "I have a surprise myself to tell you about."

"Please," she said softly, too plaintively. She said "please" to him with a frequency that distressed her, but she couldn't break herself of the habit. It had been easier to housetrain Keynes.

"Fine, I defer to beauty," he said. That was all he deferred to, she thought. "How about a little drink to lubricate our conversation?" he added, spinning his delighted daughter, raising her even higher.

It was important that she talk to Rudy now. After supper he would retreat into his den to work and Arlene wouldn't see him again until she brought in his ten o'clock tea and Melba toast. Then another hour of work until he came to bed and read *The Financial Post* or a new book on the economy. He decided when the lights would be turned off or which nights they would make love.

"Lift me to the sky, always, Daddy," Lori said joyously, touching the ceiling with a triumphant squeal. "Promise."

"Only if you stay a Munchkin, Munchkin." She giggled and Rudy spun her around even quicker until dizziness forced him to put her down. "More, more," the child begged.

"I promise tomorrow I will twirl you until we both fall down, gorgeous." Lori performed a dance of appreciation around the spacious kitchen, Keynes attempting to accompany her like a bizarre parody of Fred Astaire and Ginger Rogers. Rudy signalled for the dancers to go play elsewhere and the duo exited.

"Well, what do you want to discuss?" he asked, taking a step towards the stove and inhaling the aromas of the cooking supper. He curiously lifted a pot lid and said, "Darling, where's my thank-you-for-the-hard-day-at-work drink?"

"Jennifer wants to enter the Miss Teen Toronto Contest," Arlene said uneasily.

"Terrific!"

"I told her no."

"No? It sounds marvellous. Like mother, like daughter."

"I was foolish in those days."

"You were a winner," he said with the enthusiasm of an exuberant hockey coach congratulating his best goal scorer.

Arlene placed her gifts on the kitchen table. She sought a few moments of solitary thought by retreating to the liquor cabinet in the dining room and mixing each of them a drink: slowly, deliberately, thoughtfully. A double. Why did such a simple decision about their daughter have to turn into a battle of wits and wills...like everything else in their household? The earlier backyard tug-of-war flashed through her mind.

"I'll bet a year's salary *and* bonuses she wins," Rudy said as Arlene reentered the kitchen. He was beaming, obviously having further relished the thought of his teenage daughter as a beauty queen.

"I don't find beauty contests acceptable anymore," she said, handing her husband his drink, hoping he didn't notice the slight quiver in her hand.

"It merely reinforces roles," she said almost as an afterthought. While gardening, Arlene had worked out a cogent speech, all the negative arguments against beauty contests and undue stress on impressionable teenagers; but the rehearsed speech dissolved in Rudy's executive presence. Even in her kitchen, he was in control. There was still soil under her fingernails and the sight momentarily comforted her. She drifted to the orderliness of her garden.

"And what is wrong with roles?" Rudy asked with the first hint of belligerence, thrusting his wife back into the kitchen reality. His body stiffened and he grew more alert, as though he had been challenged to a duel or a gruelling game of racquetball. He removed his tie, indicating that he was ready for a real bare-knuckled, knockdown bout. Arlene strained not to feel fainthearted.

"Beauty contests shouldn't be encouraged, that's all I'm saying. It wastes an incredible amount of energy working at being beautiful. You weren't behind the scenes, Rudy."

"You're a beautiful woman," he said softly, changing his tactics.

"That's not enough anymore." Whenever she indicated depression or was plagued with a domestic problem, he responded with "You're a beautiful woman." It was his oral medication for his wife; Arlene didn't even find the words an adequate placebo. Certainly she enjoyed being appreciated for her good looks—she was ageing without panic, more pleased with her natural appearance now than in her youthful modelling days—but not as a substitute for everything else.

"I swear, darling, you're starting to sound like Betty Friedan and Gloria Steinem and those *other women*," he said. You would think he was talking about an invasion force from outer space by the way he ground out his words and grimaced, she thought.

"They are admirable women," she said sincerely, seeming to defend trusted neighbours he had maligned unnecessarily. "What's wrong with them?"

"Nothing, except there is no crime in being beautiful and entering beauty contests. A girl can develop all sorts of useful skills in competition. It didn't ruin your life."

What could she answer Rudy? That as good as her life appeared to be, there was something missing. She couldn't even pinpoint what was lacking, couldn't list A, B and C for her logically minded husband. You have to define the problem precisely before you can solve it, he liked to say whenever she seemed confused or hinted at a vague irritation. Maybe if they stayed in one place she could have the feeling of root-edness and continuity she longed for. Moving about so often complicated everything for her.

"I won't allow Jennifer to enter."

"And I will," he rebutted forcefully. He stood unmoving, his gaze fixed on his wife as though he were trying to direct a laser beam to melt her stamina. She visualized Rudy as a waxwork at Madame Tussaud's—in the Chamber of Horrors section.

He always gets his way, she thought, but not this time. She clenched a fist in determination but he playfully uncurled her fingers, praising her beauty with each extended finger. He had a thousand ways to outflank and disarm his wife.

Seeking an escape hatch, Arlene buried her concentration in the dog as it wandered back into the kitchen. Rudy named the dog Keynes after his favourite economist. Their first dog had been good old Adam Smith the Beagle; their next dog would probably be Galbraith or whomever else he was reading at the time. She, after much argument, got to name the cockatoo: Garbo. He never addressed the bird by its name, only as "that noisy beast." It was the present the children had selected last year for her thirty-fifth birthday.

After finishing her drink, she got two vases and haphazardly placed the flowers in them, taking out her frustrations on the inanimate objects. The impulse to throw the vases, to make a statement Rudy couldn't ignore, jolted her. Why did he force her to go to extremes? He wanted ten children, wouldn't hear of any kind of birth control for either of them, so the only way she could stop at the three children she wanted was to have a tubal ligation after Lori. He was furious when she told him of the operation. What happens if the children are in a plane crash, what do we do then, was his only response.

"Like your flowers?" he asked, attempting to appease his wife. He didn't like to see Arlene angry; it simply didn't become her. Arlene was most beautiful when serene.

"I bet you'll like what's in the box better than the flowers," he continued, annoyed that Arlene wouldn't answer him.

She looked at the wrapped gift without curiosity. She wanted to drive her fist down on the small package, the bribe. "Jennifer will be home soon. Let's resolve this. I don't want to argue in front of her," she said.

"It is resolved. Jenny can try to be a beauty queen like her mother was—and is." He gazed at his wife admiringly over the rim of the glass as he sipped his drink. Arlene felt she was parading before the judges again, unblinking eyes assessing her worth, making her dread beauty. *"And the winner is...."*

Without warning or explanation, Rudy disappeared up the stairs and soon returned with two scrapbooks, both with singed covers. He had a conqueror's brazen, gloating smile on his face. To Arlene, at that tense moment, her handsome husband looked like an ugly stranger.

"Throw them away," she ordered, raising her voice only slightly, wanting to scream at the top of her lungs. She cursed her own ingrained self-control. "Little ladies don't shout or create a ruckus," her mother lectured after every battle Arlene had with her younger brother until she learned to deal with the vexatious brat through avoidance or silence.

"*You* never got rid of them," he accused. Why hadn't she? She had considered it for years. Twice she had even held the scrapbooks by the fireplace, had allowed the flames to lick the covers, but couldn't throw them in. The scrapbooks held the record of her various efforts in beauty contests, talent shows, amateur theatre, and modelling. When she married Rudy, already pregnant with Jennifer, she had willingly given up modelling and acting. Though she never told her husband, Arlene felt more secure in the home than on any stage.

Rudy held the scrapbooks, two bombs he could detonate at any second. He opened the thicker one and began to read the caption underneath a faded photograph from an old Vancouver newspaper: "Arlene Edwards charmed the audience with her tap dancing and singing and was crowned the junior princess of the summer festival...."

"I did it for my mother. She lived through me."

"A noble motivation," he said authoritatively. Such glib psychological insight she could do without. He turned several pages and resumed reading: "The vivacious young Miss Edwards includes dramatics, reading, cooking, and gardening as her leisure time activities...."

"Please, Rudy, no more." Was she ever *really* vivacious? Weren't the first twenty years of her life one long costume ball, a masquerade that pleased her mother and broke the hearts of little boys and men?

"...The daughter of Marsha and William Edwards has won many beauty contests in the past...." He read randomly from the scrapbooks, confronting his wife with unwanted memories, delivering the words like an incessant meteor shower. She wished she were Annie Oakley and could shoot the scrapbooks out of Rudy's hands. She wouldn't mind if the audience applauded her sharpshooting. All her former nervousness and anxiety and feelings of helplessness flooded over Arlene.

"Those beauty contests weren't beneficial for me."

"What are you missing, Arlene? Tell me."

Missing? You always dictate, never consult, she wanted to explain to her husband. She wanted to be heard, an equal voice: when they made love, where they lived...*important* decisions.

"We're like two children on a teeter-totter and I can never decide when I go up or down. You always decide for me. I'm missing choice, Rudy," she said with a growing anger.

"Choice? All right, you can have choice. Where do you want to vacation this year? It's completely your choice. The Bahamas, Miami Beach, perhaps Hawaii? Name it, darling."

"Mongolia," Arlene answered. Or Devil's Island or Alcatraz or the foot of any active volcano, she thought as her mood darkened.

"Beautiful, don't be ridiculous...."

At last it struck her, the problem. It wasn't a question of love or lack of love, of Rudy being a good husband or a bad husband. What she wanted to change were Rudy's attitudes. His attitudes towards women. Maybe she should try to change his height or brown eyes, it might be easier. Rudy's attitudes towards women had not shifted a fraction since they fell in love during high school. Her own attitudes towards herself and being a beautiful woman had. Like her cherished seeds, she had grown, but Rudy would not acknowledge that vital growth.

"Come on, what are you missing?" he demanded to know, losing his patience. "Name something real, Arlene."

He threw the scrapbooks to the floor, then clasped his wife's hand and began to lead her around the kitchen. Keynes fled the room. Rudy pointed emphatically to each and every convenience item in the kitchen—slow cooker, sixteen-speed blender, food processor, electric fondue, on and on—then opened drawers and removed gadgets and fancy devices she rarely used. He was acting like an overzealous TV game show host leading the bewildered contestant through a mazed paradise.

"Look what you have, darling.... Your beauty has gotten you so much."

His logic confounded her. He would tell a marathon runner who had broken his legs that he had wonderful arms. What could she say to him to open his eyes? Rudy didn't—or couldn't—understand what she needed.

"Open your present," he instructed, releasing her hand. "I guarantee you'll be ecstatic."

Just then Jennifer came through the kitchen door, school books in hand, smiling radiantly. When she smiled she looked so much like her mother, Rudy thought. She kissed her father and mother, then dramatically smelled the flowers, a young Sarah Bernhardt giving an inspired performance.

"What's in the box?"

"A present for your beautiful mother. But if she doesn't want it, I'm sure I could find another beautiful girl who does."

"Have you two been arguing?" Jennifer asked. Are we that obvious, Arlene thought.

"Nothing that drastic, Jenny. You mother has been talking to me about the beauty contest," he stated formally.

"Oh that," Jennifer said nonchalantly, waving the topic away. Rudy was certain she was attempting not to act too eager, to be the mature and sophisticated teenager. Fifteen, in her father's estimation, was an unfathomable, delightful age; she could stay this way forever if he had his way. He considered all three of his children at perfect ages. It only saddened him that there weren't more kids around the house.

Jennifer tossed her books down by the flowers and mysterious box and pulled out a mimeographed sheet of paper from a three-ring binder decorated with pictures of John Travolta and Wayne Gretzky, in a frozen face-off for her heart.

"Your mother used to worship Frankie Avalon and Elvis when she was around your age. I was hardly noticed because I couldn't sing or act. Your mother was the most beautiful homecoming queen in our school's history."

"And you were the third-string quarterback," Arlene said viciously. Caught off guard, Rudy turned angrily, poised to ward off more blows. He did have an Achilles' heel, Arlene realized. Where had the words come from? They both encouraged and frightened her.

Rudy had told the children that he had been a star quarterback, could have played professionally had he applied himself. If he was going to fight unfairly, so was she. He was accustomed to arguing and getting his way, working in a competitive, strenuous man's world all of his adult life. She had been competitive also, but the skills she relied on were different: an engaging smile, a heart-stopping sway, the lovely carriage; to excel and succeed had been instilled into him; into her, the belief that beauty speaks for itself and was its own worthwhile end.

Arlene looked into her husband's determined eyes and thought again that he always gets his way. Even the children's names were his selections. She had wanted literary names, after the authors she enjoyed. They would be Anaïs, Brendan and Virginia had he listened to her, yet he laughed at her choices, considered them sentimental and foolish. Once, when she reminded him of her preferences, he mocked that Wynken, Blynken and Nod would be better than her choices. Arlene was reduced to triumphing through a tubal ligation and naming a cockatoo after an actress who wanted to be alone.

"I need one of your signatures," Jennifer said, holding up a sheet of paper. "Parental consent."

"I'll sign," Rudy said quickly, pulling out a pen from his shirt pocket. It was the gold pen his wife had given him for his last promotion. Now Arlene wanted to jab it into his stomach. I love him, I love him, she told herself, trying to remove the hostile emotions from her system. Why did he always need to get his way?

"Don't you want to know what you're signing?" Jennifer asked with a puzzled expression on her face.

"Miss Teen Canada ... Miss Canada ... Miss World ... Miss Universe," the proud father chanted in happy singsong. It was so easy for him to imagine Jennifer as a beauty queen.

"You don't have to sign for that yet. I have plenty of time to make up my mind about entering. I was thinking, maybe Mom's right."

The father and mother, totally baffled, looked at Jennifer. Suddenly Lori ran into the kitchen crying. During a half-completed somersault in the living room, she had tumbled into a coffee table and bruised her elbow. Keynes started barking, denying any responsibility for the accident. Rudy quieted the dog with a firm gesture. Arlene could never get Keynes to obey her.

Both parents moved towards the crying child and the third-string quarterback deftly scooped up his daughter and kissed the hurt better. The mother dried Lori's tear-stained cheeks as her father tightened his embrace. Arlene wanted to say, she's not a sack of potatoes, but couldn't. In her daydreams she demolished Rudy in debates and arguments and tennis matches.

Amid the confusion Eddie burst into the kitchen, a perpetual jack-in-the-box refusing to stay lidded. He was wearing an "I Love Olivia Newton-John" sweatshirt and carrying a new record album. Last month, both parents recalled, it was "I Love Linda Ronstadt." He immediately demanded centre state. The assertive personality and impregnable confidence of his father were in clear display in the boy. Eddie, at thirteen, was already answering "a millionaire" when people asked him what he wanted to be when he grew up.

"The record was on sale," he said before his parents could accuse him of wasting his allowance.

"Who's breaking the sound barrier this time?" Rudy asked good-naturedly.

Eddie held up an album by Martha and the Muffins.

"Mmmmmmmmm....Makes me hungry. Bran or English?" The father chuckled at his own pun.

The son smiled but wasn't exactly certain what was funny. Arlene refused to change her resolute expression. Jennifer began waving her sheet of paper and Lori surveyed the family gathering from her preferred vantage point, in the air.

The timing buzzer on the stove sounded and ignited the dog's protesting bark until Arlene clicked off the knob. Lori and Eddie resumed arguing over a week-old grievance, calling each other nincompoops and creeps. The father attempted to act as referee as the mother urged him to allow the brother and sister to work things out by themselves. There seemed to be a hundred people in the kitchen, not three kids, two adults, and one huge dog.

"I need your permission to try out for the boys' hockey league next season," Jennifer said into the tumult. "There's going to be a special training program this summer I don't want to miss. I want to be the first girl at our school to make a boys' team. I can do it."

The mother began to laugh, at first nervously, then without restraint; the laughter became pure and joyous. Rudy was stunned. Arlene hugged her oldest child. For an instant she thought she detected the smell of fresh vegetables in Jennifer's long blond hair.

"I'll sign, my dear," Arlene said and grabbed the pen out of her husband's hand. He put Lori down, as if she had become too heavy, and tried to grab the pen back, but Arlene would not let him have it. Now if Rudy insisted they move to Timbuktu, she would simply say no.

ENTRY POINTS

1 (a) What is your first impression of Arlene? Support your response with specific references from the first three paragraphs. Is she a happy woman?

(b) Does your response begin to change after your first impression? When? How? Specify with references.

2 Describe and analyze Arlene's relationship to her husband, Rudy, and her children, Lori, Eddie, and Jennifer. Is she a happy woman? Discuss with your group.

3 Arlene announces: "I don't find beauty contests acceptable anymore." Why doesn't she? What arguments does she present against them? Contrast her opinion with that of Rudy and that of her daughter, Jennifer.

4 Why, according to Arlene, is being a beautiful woman "not enough anymore"? Do you agree more with her or with Rudy? Debate within your group.

5 "He had a conqueror's brazen, gloating smile on his face."

(a) To a great degree, this story is about power, manipulation, and control beyond the surface images of a happy family. How does Rudy attempt to "control" his wife and defeat her, like a "conqueror"?

(b) Analyze Rudy's argumentation techniques. Is he playing fair?

(c) How does Arlene attempt to break free from Rudy's control and "her own ingrained self-control"? To what degree does she succeed?

(d) In your opinion, why had Arlene developed that "ingrained self-control" in the first place? In terms of attitudes towards anger, argument, and debate, does traditional society socialize men and women differently?

6 Why is Rudy "stunned" and Arlene joyful at Jennifer's decision to try out for the boys' hockey team?

7 (a) How has Arlene changed since her high school and beauty contest days? Does she still love her husband as she claims near the end of the story?

(b) Will Arlene be able to say "no" to Rudy next time or will she regress back into old patterns? Speculate and discuss with your group.

8 Define the words "stereotype" and "sexism" as they apply to female and male roles and images. Apply these definitions to the story through a discussion within your group. To what degree does our society promote and perpetuate false images?

9 Have your group collect and bring in images of "beautiful" women and "handsome" men from newspapers and magazines. Analyze and decode their messages and then make a satirical collage. Relate these "print" messages to those in the electronic media, including T.V. commercials and music videos. For further insights into how the media control and mold our perceptions of female beauty, read *The Beauty Myth* by Naomi Wolf (1991), and *Where the Girls Are: Growing Up Female With the Mass Media* by Susan J. Douglas (1994). For an interesting view on stereotyped perceptions of men, read *A Choice of Heroes: The Changing Faces of American Manhood* by Mark Gerzon (1982).

10 Write a short story about manipulation and control. Read Tony Bell's "The Image Maker" (page 7).

11 Write a satirical fairy tale in which the roles of the beautiful princess and the handsome prince are reversed. Create a final moral. Do they live happily ever after?

FROM BEHIND THE VEIL

DHU'L NUN AYYOUB

The street, although wide, was inconveniently full of strollers passing to and fro. The situation was not helped by the sleek swift cars, which sped by from time to time. They carried wealthy occupants, young women and ladies, who protected from the curiosity of the outside world, displayed radiant faces. Their shining gaze roved across the street, smiling or frowning as they took in sights which pleased or displeased them.

Among the surging crowd was an amazing mixture of different clothes and contrasting shapes, which, if nothing else, serve to emphasize the varying tastes of these passers-by.

A European who had never been to the East before might be excused for thinking that its people were in the middle of a great festival. As time goes by, however, he is moved to say in amazement, "What long carnival celebrations you have in this country!" Our Western friend would think that people wear these amazing clothes for a festival, just as they would do in his own country.

You can also see women in the crowd, both veiled and unveiled. A man can be surprised to find himself turning involuntarily towards those figures, wearing long silk gowns, which give them such an enticing and alluring shape, and make the observer yearn to uncover the magic and the secrets which lie beneath them.

His desire is only increased when his gaze falls on the filmy veil. Behind it he can catch a fleeting glimpse of fine features and pencilled eyebrows, which serve to inflame the fires of his heart. It makes him want to devote the rest of his life to the exploration of this world full of shame-faced beauty.

Ihsan was one of those who would stroll along with the crowd displaying his smart and tasteful suit over his slim figure, patting his dark gleaming hair whenever he felt that the evening breezes had ruffled it, or spread a curl over his clear forehead.

This Ihsan was a young man of eighteen, good-looking with fine features which made him attractive to a number of women. Naturally he was aware of his appeal and attraction, and he had the youthful capacity to exploit it. That's why you can see him now, with his eyes wandering in search of a quarry.

Ihsan was not interested in chasing unveiled girls. They exuded poise, which he found unattractive, and they were always looking anxiously to avoid criticism so they never looked the passers-by directly in the face. They would walk by without turning their heads, paying no attention to the expressions of flattery which came their way from the gallants, who, after getting as much out of them as a dog gets out of barking at clouds, would give them no further attention.

This is the reason that makes Ihsan always sidle up to the girls with the long cloaks and the secret little movements which attract him: the burning sighs and the gentle laughter and the concealed glances.

Siham had gone out on the evening of that day as usual to take the air and stroll through the streets. This evening stroll had become a part of her life to such an extent that it was now indispensable. She couldn't remember exactly the date when she first set out to saunter through the street, and did not really know the reason why she kept up her evening appointments. If she did, she did not admit it. Whatever the case, no sooner had Siham seen the bustle in the middle of the street than she headed for the pavement. She looked cautiously left and right until she saw Ihsan in the distance, and suddenly she felt the blood coursing through her veins.

She found herself unconsciously moving towards him until she was almost parallel with him, saw him staring at her from top to bottom, and felt a tremor throughout her body. When she saw his burning stare almost penetrating the cloak which covered her slender body her heart beat violently. She was used to seeing him every day at this time, and she used to stare at him freely each time until she had memorized his face. Of late, she had begun to feel her heart pounding whenever she saw him, and her face flushed with confusion. There was nothing to stop her from feasting her eyes on him, however, because she knew that the veil covered her face and concealed the overwhelming attraction she felt for him.

We cannot be certain what it was that made this youth know that the girl was interested in him, and whether his first overture to her came in the course of one of his habitual overtures, which he made to any girl. Whatever it was, he went up to the girl boldly on that first day, and sidled up to her, greeted her, and saw her turning round to look at him cautiously before hurrying on her way.

He knew immediately that she was not angry with him, and emboldened, he carried on behind her and saw her going into one of the public parks. She knew that he was following her, and hastened on her way, trembling with conflicting emotions of joy, fear, and caution.

He followed her into the park for a short distance, until he saw her sitting on her own, behind a big tree. He went up to her and spoke to her smilingly.

"Good evening."

"Good evening," she replied shyly.

Then she raised her veil from her brown face and her dark eyes, and Ihsan was captivated by the long dark eyelashes which cast a shadow over her features.

The features of her face were fine, and inspired the beholder with the strongest feelings of awe and worship. She was fearful and breathless, turning from side to side like a timid gazelle. She knew that what she was doing amounted to an unpardonable crime, but drew comfort from one thing—the knowledge that this boy had not seen her before and did not know her. She was having an adventure, nothing more, and she was drawn into it by her youth and by the warm blood which coursed in her veins.

The boy's mind worked on some expressions of flattery and endearment. For his opening shot, he ventured: "I've seen you often, as you've passed by this street and then gone to walk among the trees. I wasn't able to talk to you because I respect you, and your whole appearance tells me that you are from a good family."

She replied, a little resentfully: "But I suppose you always try to talk with ordinary girls as well? Why don't you just chase the common girls, and satisfy your passions on them?"

"I'm sorry, really, I don't mean you any harm. But I'm alone, as you see, and I can't find a companion to share my walks with me. I saw that you were the only girl who found pleasure in these strolls, and so I felt that there was a link between us. Anyway, if you find my presence unpleasant in any way, I'll move off right now."

He made a move to get up, but she checked him and asked: "Do you know who I am?"

"I haven't the least idea, but this doesn't stop me from believing that I share your spirit," he replied softly.

"If you want to accompany me on these innocent walks, I don't see any objection," she mused. "There's no harm in strolling around with you for an hour or so, at intervals which we can agree on, on condition that you promise me that you won't try to follow me and try to find out who I am. I don't want you trying to contact me at any other times."

"I respect your wish and I shall honour it," he replied formally.

The two of them sat side by side on one of the stone benches, and a deep silence reigned over them, in which each felt the beating of their own hearts. This silence continued for a long time. Both of them had been overcome by the novelty of their strange and singular situation.

Ihsan, however, was a youth accustomed to flirtations, although he realized that this time he was faced with a girl who was pure and virtuous. There was something about her, a certain strength of purpose and character, which confused him, and stopped him from going too far. His mind worked to collect his thoughts and to rescue him from the situation into which he had unwittingly walked.

At length, he spoke, somewhat confused.

"What is your name, please?"

"Have you forgotten my condition that you should not try to identify me?"

"Of course. I'm sorry. But surely…in view of our future friendship…?"

"Have you forgotten? We live in a society in which this situation is unforgivable. If my people knew anything of this they'd kill me. While society is like this, we must learn to deceive. We must use the follies of our society in order to break its shackles!"

"What a penetrating mind you have!" said Ihsan admiringly.

"Thank you. Time's getting on and I must be getting back to the house. I will see you again in two days."

As she said goodbye he tried to put his arm around her waist, but she rebuffed him sharply. Then she relented slightly, saying: "I don't know who you are. You might be one of those mean boys who take delight in trapping girls for their own pleasure and sport."

She went back to the house invigorated, but somewhat disturbed, for she had broken with the most binding and serious of traditions in one fell swoop. She didn't understand how it had begun and how it had ended, until it seemed to her that everything that had happened that day was a disturbing dream.

She threw her cloak on one side, and went to help her mother with the housework. She flattered her mother, made herself agreeable, and took delight in carrying out her orders and her arrangements. When her father returned home from work she welcomed him with smiling face, then she went to her room to get on with her studies.

She set about her work mechanically, with nervous high spirits, and had disturbing dreams at night.

The meetings went on longer, and the subjects of their conversations diversified. The relationship between them developed, and things became deeply involved. She no longer felt that there was anything strange or unusual about the meetings, but she kept her head, using her lively mind to conceal her relationship with this boy, and to prevent him from trying to find out who she was and getting in touch with her.

One day Siham was sitting with her father, talking to him after supper, while he was scanning the evening paper. His eye fell on a long article about women who had abandoned the veil, and, deciding to have his daughter's view, he read the article out loud. No sooner had he finished than Siham roundly abused the author for trying to break with convention and introduce modern heresies. Her father felt a greatly increased regard for his intelligent, well-brought-up daughter, who obviously knew the value of traditions and respected them. Such a difference between her and the rest of her irresponsible, scandalous friends, who, no sooner had they learned to read and write, went around throwing overboard society's conventions without shame or respect!

Impulsively, he moved towards his daughter and kissed her forehead.

"God preserve you as a treasure for your father."

When she reached her room Siham could barely stop herself from laughing out loud. She picked up her veil and danced with glee, then stopped in the middle of the room and began to whisper to the veil: "You black shroud, you know how I despise you and make use of you to keep him apart from me! I don't care about you, and I feel nothing for you. I defy you. But I love you too. These poor girls take refuge behind you in order to preserve their virginity, and their honour, and good morals. If they were more truthful they would say that they love you because you hide faults and scandals. I love you because you help me to enjoy my life in a way that only those who wear the veil can appreciate. I pity those wretched unveiled women. I scorn them."

Translated by S. Al-Bazzazz

1   "Our Western friend would think that people wear these amazing clothes for a festival...."
   (a) Why does the author feel that he should include such comments on Western/European perception? What is his purpose in terms of this story?
   (b) Why do you think many Westerners have distorted perceptions

of the Middle East and Asian countries? How can this problem be corrected? Make recommendations for your school system.

2 "You can also see women in the crowd, both veiled and unveiled."
   (a) In an encyclopedia, research the cultural significance of the veil within the religion of Islam or record and share your own personal knowledge.
   (b) Why can a man "be surprised to find himself turning involuntarily towards those figures" (the women who are veiled)? Do you agree with this statement? Would men in the West be any different? Discuss the possible cultural differences with your group.

3 "Ihsan was not interested in chasing unveiled girls." Why not? What seems to excite Ihsan in the opposite sex? How would you characterize Ihsan's personality? Refer to specific details in the story.

4 Characterize Siham. Why does she always go out for an evening stroll? How does she react on seeing Ihsan? How would you characterize their conversation on the park bench?

5 Why won't Siham identify herself to Ihsan? How does she suggest that they deliberately contravene their society's traditions?

6 Why do you think Siham begins to have "disturbing dreams"?

7 (a) Comment on and assess Siham's final words to her "black shroud," her veil. Is she being hypocritical or is she being realistic?
   (b) Write a short monologue in which *you* speak to something inanimate, but significant, in your own life.

8 Compare and contrast the concepts of love and beauty as presented in the story, "A Beautiful Woman" (page 140), set in Canada, and in this story set in Iraq. Note the role of power and control in both stories.

9 Discuss this statement with your group: "We all hide behind masks, revealing only what we want to reveal." Read Anwer Khan's "The Pose" (page 205) for further ideas on this statement.

ARRANGED MARRIAGE

when i was almost twelve
the Romanian boy i met at the roundup
wrote me to say, he guessed we'd be
married soon

as a token of his intent
he sent me a gauze hankie
hemmed in gold & smelling
of stale perfume
he said he'd send a ring soon

i hid in my room
i swear, mother, i did nothing
never even kissed him
i don't remember kissing him
i remember kicking his shins
when he grabbed my wrists
he laughed then & i do remember
his strong white teeth & tanned face
like my uncles at the ranch
his hands were strong too
i didn't like that

i admit i kicked him
i admit i'd had my first period
had small beginnings of breasts
inside a little brassiere
i wore so i wouldn't jiggle playing ball
(spider size cup, my brother said,
the mean bastard)

i hid for a month
nothing happened, so i came out
he must have changed his mind
no one ever needed to know

BARBARA SAPERGIA

i burned the letter in the jacket heater
& hid the hankie so well
i still haven't found it
i could just hear my mother saying:
you must have done something
to encourage him

then one fine day
grandpa came to town
& spilled the beans
the father had come to grandpa
to talk cows & sheep
how many i was worth
& so forth
& what my family would give with me
she's only eleven! *my mother shrieked*
wait till i get ahold of her!

but they were laughing
i couldn't believe it
it seems his folks knew us
back in the old country

my mother gave firm instructions
i was not for sale
grandpa looked a little sad—
it had sounded like a good deal
& he didn't like to offend old friends

there were no more letters
no hankies, no rings, no offers
i was not blamed
i was only a little girl, after all

soon i couldn't remember
the letter or the words on the hankie
only the weight of his brown arms
& hot dry dust on his skin

1 Comment on the twelve-year-old girl's reaction to the Romanian boy's announcement of his impending marriage plans. What would *your* reactions be to such a proposal?

2 What is her mother's reaction to the proposal? What has changed since her family moved from Romania, "the old country," to Canada? Explain. Rethink assimilation and multiculturalism.

3 What final impressions are you left with in the girl's reminiscences in the final stanza?

4 Why were "arranged marriages" quite common in most countries before the twentieth century, and are still the norm in some countries today? Speculate and then research an encyclopedia's article on marriage customs through history to verify your response.

5 Given the divorce rate today, is romantic love before marriage superior to arranged marriages? Discuss or debate fully with your group.

6 As the young girl, write a diary item expressing your feelings about the boy's sudden proposal.

7 For other views on love and arranged marriages, read Amy Tan's *The Joy Luck Club*, Katherine Alexander's *The Children of Byzantium* (also published under the name Katherine Vlassie), Barbara Sapergia's *Foreigners*, Thorton Wilder's *The Matchmaker*, or view the musical, *Fiddler on the Roof*.

OUTSIDE THE MARRIAGE BUREAU

HE XIAOHU

People all say that I've made a good match and should be grateful to the marriage bureau. In reality, our marriage was not arranged inside, but outside the bureau. You don't believe me? Then listen to this.

Marriage between men and women is necessary. But although I had met half a dozen possible partners and was approaching the age of twenty-nine, I was still single. Unmarried youths are especially sensitive about their ages. The greater the number, the heavier the pressure on their hearts.

Was it because I was ugly? No, last year, when I was named as an advanced teacher, a newspaper reporter described my appearance thus: "Although he cannot be considered handsome, his pair of black, shining eyes, under long eyelashes, radiate the vitality of youth, and his strong athletic physique makes him an attractive young man."

The principal reason for my failure in love was my profession. I am a primary-school sports teacher. My reversals in the affairs of the heart provided me with a mirror, in which I could clearly see my position in the eyes of some people.

My first love was an old schoolmate, a worker in a textile factory. I often walked with her hand-in-hand by the banks of the river, looking at the orange-yellow setting sun, the magnificent evening clouds, feeling that our two hearts were beating in time together. Songs of joy reverberated round us. Ah, those were really golden days, the days of youthful dreams. Once, she put her head on my shoulder and said in a tender, soft voice, "Weiyang…can't you get another job? My friends at work are all making fun of me."

My heart felt as if it had been pierced.

She urged, "Please change your job. My father can help you…" and she pressed more closely against me.

A wave of coolness rose in my heart. I looked at her eyes; I saw her pleading. But I saw more distinctly her pity for me, and it was just this which I could not bear. It was really a contempt for my work, destroying my self-respect. Many scornful words rose in my throat, but I managed to choke them back. We parted without an angry word.

My last discussion like this occurred last year. A neighbour had introduced me to a fashionable young girl. When we met, her two large, alluring eyes blinked and looked at me as if I was some rare animal. When she learned of my profession, her eyes suddenly became dim, like fading electric light bulbs. She moved away without any explanation. I followed her. Outside my neighbour's window, I heard her giving vent to her anger, "Auntie, you treat me like dirt! You said you were introducing me to an athlete. Some athlete! He's a primary-school sports teacher. What sort of a job is that? Primary-school teachers are looked down on as second-class citizens. Useless!"

The setting up of a marriage bureau was announced in a match-box-sized advertisement on the lower right-hand corner of the fourth page of the local newspaper. The reaction this aroused far surpassed any front-page news! The office was located in Huasheng Lane, a quiet, small back street known to very few people. It suddenly became full of beautiful colours as many young girls in flowery dresses and many young men appeared. The lane was filled with the tinkling of bicycle bells, laughter, smiles, soft guitar music, taped electronic music and songs of famous singers. Some poets romantically called this ordinary small lane the "road of love and beauty."

Urged repeatedly by my mother, I found my residence card, work permit and a photograph of myself. Dressed in a brand-new woollen suit, I proceeded to the "road of love and beauty."

My thoughts were cut short by a burst of electronic music. Three or four long-haired, fashionable young men, with tape recorders in their hands, rushed in ostentatiously. One of them I knew was a well-known young hooligan in the northern city district. My high spirits were at once dampened. Should I try to find love in the company of such bad characters? The love I required was evidently of a different kind from theirs.

As I was hesitating, I heard a melodious, charming voice asking, "Teacher Wang, where are you going?" A tall, slim, graceful girl was standing before me.

She was the elder sister of a pupil of mine. I only knew that her surname was Bai. "Ah, Xiao Bai, I'm going to…." Damn! How could I tell a strange girl that I was going to the marriage bureau to look for a mate? "I...I'm going to visit the parents of one of my pupils. And you...where are you going?"

Xiao Bai smiled, "I'm going to a hardware shop in the east city."

"I see," I nodded, and hurriedly took my leave.

I walked a little distance, and, supposing that Xiao Bai had gone, turned back. I espied that she had also turned back. She shook her pigtails, turned and stepped briskly through the vermilion door of the bureau. I was overjoyed. "With girls like Xiao Bai there, I'll find true love," I thought to myself. The unpleasant impression made by the young men a moment earlier was at once dispelled. I stepped quickly through the door and entered the reception room for men.

I stood at the window and looked into the reception room opposite for women. Among the crowd of girls in pretty clothes was one who looked like Xiao Bai. She was filling in a form, her head down. I watched until she had completed it and left.

I smiled.

One of the staff of the bureau, a man of about forty years of age, came over and patted my shoulder, "Don't looked so dazed. Fill in the forms first. You can depend on me. My name's Chen. I'll find you happiness." I nodded my head gratefully and took the two forms he handed me. Newly printed, they still smelled of ink. The first form was easy to fill in, like filling in a curriculum vitae. The second one, however, gave me quite a headache. It was headed "Requirements for a Partner." Underneath were ten columns, including the girl's possible occupation, age, character, appearance, financial situation, height, native place, nationality, hobbies and general family circumstances. Through these abstract entries I saw a concrete, lively human being, a warm-hearted girl, from whose rosy, oval face shone a pair of bright, black eyes, expressing the purity of her mind. Moreover, she had an easy manner, a graceful figure and a bewitching black mole under her left ear.

How could I forget her, although I hardly knew her name and had only met her three times?

The first time I had met her had been in the winter of last year. I had taken my pupils skating in the park. One boy went outside the boundary and suddenly fell through a hole in the ice. Alarmed, I jumped into the water and got him out. Fortunately, I saved him in time; after his clothes were changed, he quickly recovered. Another teacher warned me, "Wait till his parents come to complain! Last time when I was giving a P.T. lesson, a pupil sprained his ankle vaulting over a horse. His parents raised hell. You've done worse, nearly drowning a boy!"

Accompanying the boy back home, I was nervous, anticipating a confrontation with an irate parent. On entering the boy's home, the only person who received me was his elder sister, Xiao Bai. Instead of blaming me when she heard my story, she looked at me with grateful eyes, thanked me again and again and brought tea and cigarettes for me. I had become a hero. Feeling very uneasy, I criticized myself. When I left and reached the entrance to their lane, I turned back and could still see, under the dim street light, her graceful figure as she repeatedly waved her hand to me.

The second time I saw her was in the early spring of this year. I took some students to see a gymnastics display in the stadium. After the show, it began to rain so hard that it was impossible for us to go back. This was a difficult problem for a teacher to solve. It would soon be lunch time. As I was wondering what to do, the door of the ticket-office opened. Xiao Bai beckoned to me with her hand. "Teacher Wang, since you can't go back to school yet, come in here and get warm." I refused. "I don't want to interrupt your work." I had only met her once before. How could I give her so much trouble? She had invited me out of politeness. I could not accept.

Xiao Bai, however, came over and insisted, "You're a teacher, but what about your pupils? It's very cold outside and the rain won't stop soon. Come inside and have some hot water to drink. It's almost noon. You can buy some bread for the children. I've money and food coupons here. You can use them."

How carefully she had thought of everything! Seeing that she was sincere, I no longer refused. I let the children cram into her room, while she brought two large kettles and searched for and found some bowls and lunch-boxes for us. Then she suggested, "Teacher Wang, have some water first. I'll go to buy the bread."

Psychologists, when describing the mental state of unmarried youths, have written: "With approaching maturity, the image of an 'ideal person' is gradually formed in the mind, a mixture of one's own character, preferences, behaviour and habits. In chance contacts or conversations with a person of the opposite sex, one is always gauging and guessing about the opposite party in terms of the imagined 'ideal person'." I was then just in such a state. To the sound of the rain, I chatted and ate with Xiao Bai. Our warm glances expressed a tender, fluctuating affection. In our conversation, we were assessing each other, trying to find some common ground.

The rain stopped and the sun came out again. I cursed. Why should the sun be so unaccommodating as to end our interesting conversation?

For several days my mind was in a turmoil. Certain vague longings and anxieties possessed me. My equilibrium was disturbed. I knew what was required to restore it. At last, the holidays came. I went by bike to return the money and food coupons to Xiao Bai, hoping we could continue our conversation.

She was playing volley-ball with two young men on the sports ground in front of the stadium. I knew that one of the men was a well-known centre in the provincial basket-ball team; the other was a top-notch volley-ball player. On seeing me Xiao Bai exclaimed joyfully, "Here's another athlete." She introduced me to the two players. When they heard I was only a primary-school sports teacher, the basketball centre did not conceal his contempt and reluctantly shook hands with me.

I realized the distance between such sportsmen and myself, hearing again the words, "Second-class citizens. Useless!" How could a pretty young girl surrounded by such heroes fall in love with a "second-class citizen" like me? She had acted purely out of kindness, but I, love-sick, had imbued it with a deeper significance. I must control myself. Six girls before her had rejected me. Need there be a seventh?

I therefore returned the money and food coupons to Xiao Bai, gave her a faint smile and immediately went away.

Now, I had spotted her in the marriage bureau. This meant she had not yet found a sweetheart. Wonderful news! Through the marriage bureau, I could continue my conversations with Xiao Bai and discuss things with her more openly and sincerely. Even if it didn't work out, I would not feel humiliated or embarrassed.

"The marriage bureau is really good!" I exclaimed from my heart.

According to what I knew of Xiao Bai, I filled in the second form as follows:

Age: About twenty-five.

Occupation: Connected with sports.

Character: Warm-hearted, kind and tolerant.

Specialty: Eager to help other people.

Appearance: Regular features, graceful and pretty, with a black mole under the left ear.

As for financial conditions and general family circumstances, I just wrote "Doesn't matter," or "No particular demands."

I handed the forms to Old Chen. He asked some questions while looking them over.

"*Ai*? Connected with sports? What does that mean?"

I replied, "I'm a sports teacher. I hope my future wife will appreciate such work."

"Of course," said Old Chen, tapping his head. "You mean occupations like being a salesgirl in a sports shop or a sports advertiser?"

I nodded and added, "Or a ticket-seller in a stadium."

"What's this?" Old Chen queried again. "You put down 'having regular features, graceful and pretty, with a black mole under the left ear.' What does that mean?"

"That is...." I quickly made up a wild answer. "My mother said our native place had such a custom. A black mole under the left ear symbolizes good luck. A girl with such a mark is thought to be dutiful."

"Good, you're a filial son. Not many young men like you around these days." With these words he put the two forms I handed to him into the files. Then he said, "Please leave your telephone number and wait for a happy meeting." He accompanied me out of the door and tightly pressed my hand, adding, "Now don't worry. I was thirty-five years old when I got married. I understand your fears. Although your requirements are rather unusual, we'll do our utmost to find a suitable partner for you."

The days that followed were full of hope and longing. The telephone, to which I normally paid no attention, suddenly dominated my thoughts. Whenever it rang, I was always the first to snatch up the receiver. When I wasn't teaching, I used to sit beside it, stroking the receiver with my hand. It was the first time that I realized the beauty of the telephone: It was of a rosy colour with a chromium-plated dial, which glittered brightly, and a green cord, like a streamer decorating the streets on festive days. This was the coloured thread that would bring me a happy marriage.

Ten days later, the beautiful telephone brought me a message from the marriage bureau: "We've found a possible partner for you. Your first meeting will take place in the pavilion near the eastern gate of the municipal park at three o'clock tomorrow afternoon. The girl will hold a newspaper in her right hand. In order to avoid a mistake, you should carry a magazine."

I lost no time in shaving myself and going to the barber's. Then, in my best suit, I set out for the park as if I were a diplomat going abroad on an important mission.

The result was most disappointing. The girl was not Xiao Bai. She also looked quite graceful and had a black mole under her left ear, but to me, her eyes lacked lustre. Her voice also lacked charm. She spoke in a monotone, swallowing the ends of her words. In short, it was just like listening to funeral music. I simply couldn't stand it.

According to the rules of the bureau, a report had to be made after the first meeting. I went directly there.

"She won't do!" I told Old Chen. "Please find another one for me."

"Why not?" Old Chen took out my forms, looked over them slowly and asked, "She doesn't meet your requirements?"

"Her eyes don't sparkle!" I answered.

"Don't sparkle?" Old Chen smiled generously. Pointing at one of the forms, he went on, "You didn't write that down here! You youngsters are really choosy. You want a girl not only with a black mole under her ear, but also with eyes that sparkle! How odd! Ha! Ha!..."

"Anyway, we're not suited to each other."

"All right, all right! You left one column blank, so I'll help you fill it in right now: 'Her eyes must sparkle.'" Standing up, Old Chen kindly patted my shoulder and saw me off as usual to the door. Shaking hands with me, he added, "Now don't worry. I was thirty-five years old when I got married. I understand your fears. Although your requirements are rather unusual, we'll do our utmost to find a suitable partner for you."

My second date was a champion markswoman. She was good-looking, perhaps even prettier than Xiao Bai. Though she also had a black mole under her left ear, I hadn't the same joyful, comfortable feeling as when I met Xiao Bai. Her eyes were very big, like the muzzles of rifles, and they gleamed with a black light as if she were taking aim at me. I got goose-pimples all over.

Once again I rushed back to the bureau to report to Old Chen. As usual, he smiled at me warmly, saying, "How about it this time? You can't say that her eyes weren't sparkling...."

"Sparkling? They were like laser beams. I couldn't bear them."

As usual, Old Chen saw me off to the door. Shaking hands with me he added, "Now don't worry! I was thirty-five years old...."

The third time I ran away before Old Chen could begin, "Now don't worry!..."

At the entrance to the lane, I sat down miserably on a stone step with my head in my hands. I'd been disappointed three times. It was clear that the "ideal person" in Xiao Bai's mind was not a man like me.

Raising my head, I suddenly saw Xiao Bai. She was smiling at me. Refreshed, I stood up.

"Teacher Wang, where are you going?" Xiao Bai asked in her musical voice.

"I... I'm going to visit the parents of one of my pupils," I answered hastily.

"So why are you sitting here?"

"Oh, I got tired walking...I was just taking a rest." I felt very uneasy: It was obvious I was telling a lie. I tried to conceal my embarrassment, saying lamely, "See you again. I've something to do. Goodbye...." With that, I beat a retreat.

After a few steps, I stood still and cursed myself. "Why should I, a grown-up man, be so timid?" When I had gone to the bureau, I had hoped they would introduce me to Xiao Bai, but now she had been standing before me and I had been too scared to speak to her. Would she eat me?

I turned my head and saw she was still standing there motionless, like a statue of a Greek goddess, staring at me.

I plucked up my courage and walked back to her. After heaving a deep sigh, I fixed my eyes on the ground, saying in a very low voice, "I went to the marriage bureau, but the dates they arranged for me were all useless. This was the third one. I'm feeling very depressed."

"So am I," confessed Xiao Bai. "I also went there and they made three dates for me too. None of them worked out."

"So, you...." An unexpected hope rose in my breast, and my heart beat fast.

Xiao Bai said nothing. We began to walk side by side along the road. I couldn't stop myself from asking, "In your job, you have many opportunities to meet the stars of the sports world. It should be easy for you to find your ideal man. Why do you need to resort to a marriage bureau?"

"A man's position and character are two different things," she argued.

I relaxed like a soldier hearing the command, "At ease!" I felt bold enough to joke, "The marriage bureau gave both of us disappointments. So we're fellow-sufferers!"

"Not necessarily so," she replied. "Arithmetically speaking, one disappointment plus another equals two disappointments. But, in life, the result is sometimes just the opposite. One disappointment plus another may equal a hope."

What she said was amusing, yet it had some philosophical truth. My heart beat rapidly, but I didn't know the right thing to say. I began to taste the exquisite, deep sensation of love, more interesting and magnificent than those dull, matter-of-fact appointments made by the bureau. The words slipped out of my mouth, "The work of the bureau is rather like that of my elder brother. He's studying biogenetics. Every day he writes down on his cards lots of data such as the species, weight, hair colour and so on...."

Xiao Bai giggled, "What a sharp tongue you have!"

"Of course the staff of the bureau work hard. Take Old Chen for instance. Every time I went there, he was always friendly. But I wasn't introduced to a girl I liked. They were all a great disappointment."

"Since you've already got your ideal girl in mind, why didn't you contact her directly. Why give so much trouble to the marriage bureau?"

"Easier said than done. I'd been snubbed too many times. Though I'm keen on a certain girl, how can I be sure she's interested in me? I'm only a primary-school sports teacher." I darted her a meaningful glance.

Her face suddenly turned red.

We were both silent, walking slowly together, staring at the ground. More conjectures....

After a short while, Xiao Bai asked in a low voice, "What do you want then?"

I looked at her. Her head was still down, and she was holding a red handkerchief in her hand. I summoned up my courage and answered, "She must have a black mole under her left ear."

"And?"

"Her job must be connected with sports."

"Anything more?"

"She must be kind-hearted, eager to help others, and her eyes must sparkle...." I poured out all my requirements.

"Anything else?"

"Nothing more. That's all!" I gesticulated vigorously.

"But," Xiao Bai raised her head and cast a sidelong glance at me, "how did you know the girl you fancied had also gone to the marriage bureau?"

I had no answer to that.

Frowning, she went on, "Put yourself in the girl's place. How can she fall in love with a man, who follows her stealthily like a secret agent?"

Greatly alarmed, I hastened to protest loudly, "I didn't follow her. I only spotted her in the reception room for women when I was in the one for men."

Xiao Bai smiled and pointed at me with her red handkerchief, "You beast! I never imagined you could play such a trick...."

One month later, I went to the marriage bureau together with Xiao Bai.

Old Chen received me as warmly as ever. He began as soon as he saw me, "I'm very much concerned about your problem. I've found out that there are eleven girls who fit your requirements. Do you want me to arrange a meeting with one of them?"

Pointing at Xiao Bai, who was standing behind me, I replied, "No, thank you. No need now. I came here specially to tell you I've already found a girlfriend. I won't bother you any more."

"A girlfriend?" In surprise, Old Chen gazed at me and then looked at Xiao Bai, asking, "You didn't register with us, did you?"

"Yes," she answered with a smile. "I did register here, but nothing worked out."

Old Chen was silent. Turning round, he took out a bundle of forms and began to flick rapidly through them.

"Don't look at them any more. It's not easy to classify people according to the ten entries on your forms. Rather create a better life for single people. Let them have more opportunities to meet each other. You should organize tours, dances, get-togethers, many activities. In my opinion, that's the best way."

So my story had a happy ending.

Translated by Hu Zhihui

ENTRY POINTS

1. Why, according to Weiyang, is he a "failure in love"? What do his reasons reveal about Weiyang and his state of mind? What do they reveal about his society? To what degree are these revelations different from Canadian society? Discuss thoroughly with your group.

2. What is Weiyang's first impression of the marriage bureau? Why do he and Xiao Bai lie to each other about their destinations outside the marriage bureau?

3 With your group, assess Chen's procedures for finding a love partner—including his ten "Requirements for a Partner." Do you think such a process could work? Why doesn't it work for Weiyang and Xiao Bai? As Canadians, do we have anything that might be an equivalent to Chen's procedures?

4 What exactly is it that attracts Weiyang to Xiao Bai? Why does she become his "ideal person"? Do you have an "ideal person"? Describe him or her. Reread the psychologists' statement on the mental state of unmarried youths. Do you agree with their theories?

5 Write out your own ten "Requirements for a Partner." Are there any other categories you might add in seeking your "ideal person"?

6 With your group, bring in and discuss popular songs and music videos that deal with love in today's society. Are there any common themes?

7 Write a story or a poem about the frustrations of love that, like this story, has a happy ending.

8 Write a diary item in which you role-play Xiao Bai expressing your interest in Weiyang from a distance.

9 Compare the concepts of love and marriage in this story with those revealed in the Iraqi "From Behind the Veil" (page 151) and the Romanian-Canadian "Arranged Marriage" (page 157). For other interesting views, read Joseph Kuertes's comic novel *Winter Tulips* (about a Greek-Canadian girl from Toronto and a Jewish-Canadian boy from Montreal), and Alice Munro's famous novel, *Lives of Girls and Women*.

CALL ME

JUDY McCROSKY

(A penthouse high above the Big City. The living room is spacious, and contains a white modular sofa with matching chairs and three glass-and-chrome tables. The room is dark and shadowed. On one table stands a telephone and an answering machine. A red light on the answering machine is on. The only other light in the room washes in from the City, through the glass double doors along the back wall. The phone rings.)

Hello. This is telephone answering machine XB 1700. I am currently on my coffee break. If you wish to speak with me, you must make an appointment. Leave a message after the tone, and I'll have my human contact you to set one up.

    —Shawna, it's George. Sorry I missed your call. Listen, I have a free evening next week. Let's get together. Call me.

(A young woman enters. She wears a square-shouldered black jacket and a calf-length skirt and carries a briefcase. She places the briefcase on the floor beside the glass doors. She lifts her arms above her head and stretches, her body a dark silhouette against the shimmering lights of the City below.)

Hi. You have reached George Lipincott's line. This evening I'm at the office for a couple of hours finishing up an account, and then it's off to the ballet. Please leave a message after the beep and I'll get back to you as soon as I can.

—George. Shawna here. Sorry, next week is fully booked. I do have Thursday the 26th free. How about a movie?

Sorry, I can't come to the phone right now. I'm watching all seventy-nine episodes of Star Trek, non-stop. Leave a message after the tone and I'll call you when I beam back to earth.

—Ha ha, great greeting, Shawna. Love it. You Trekkie, you. It's George. The 26th sounds fine. I've marked it in my calendar, and I'll see you then. 8:30?

(The young woman is sitting on a chair. Her briefcase is open on a low table in front of her. It is early evening, and the orange and pink of a magnificent sunset can be seen through the glass doors. The young woman appears to be satisfied with the contents of the briefcase. She nods once and snaps it shut. Standing, she takes a navy blue blazer from where it lies across the sofa, puts it on, and leaves. The phone rings.)

Hello. (There are sounds of children laughing.) As you can hear, I'm a little busy right now. (The sounds intensify.) Leave a message after the tone and I'll get back to you as soon as the kids untie me.

—Hi, it's George. Just wanted to tell you how much I enjoyed the other evening. The movie was good, and sharing it with you made it special. You sitting there in the dark beside me, well, I'll only tell you I had a hard time concentrating on the movie. Your silk-clad leg, so close to mine. Our arms, brushing as they shared the arm-rest. I'd better stop right here. If I say more it might shock those kids I heard. Say, where'd those kids come from, anyway?

You have reached George Lipincott's line. I'm out all day today, no time even to come home to change before dinner tonight. John Crosbie is the speaker. Leave a message after the beep and I'll call you first thing tomorrow.

—I borrowed the kids from my sister. I enjoyed the other evening too. Sorry I had to rush off right after the movie, but the presentation the next day was a success, so I'm glad I put in those extra hours that night. Let's get together again. No movies, though. Let's go somewhere we can talk. I'd like to get to know you, George.

I can't come to the phone right now. Please leave a message after the tone and I'll get back to you as soon as I can. Thank you. This has been a generic, no-name brand message.

—Shawna, Shawna, how do you think of them? And do you think of what your last message did to me? That husky undertone in your voice when you said you want to get to know me. Well. I'll tell you, my heart rate shot up even higher than it does during my aerobics class. By all means, let's go somewhere we can talk. How about we meet for a drink on the 6th? 9:30?

(The apartment is dark. A shaft of light slides across the floor. There is the sound of a door closing. The light disappears abruptly. The young woman enters. She drops her briefcase and walks slowly across the floor. She falls into a seat and takes off her shoes. She rubs one foot. After a while she stands up and exits. The apartment is quiet. Then there is the sound of a shower running. The phone rings.)

I can't come to the phone right now. Please leave a message after the tone and I'll get back to you as soon as I can. Thank you. This has been a generic, no-name brand message.
   —Shawna darling, you must be working too hard. The same greeting again on your machine? Still, I mustn't chide you. Your dedication is one of the things I admire most about you. Thank you for the other night. I've never had a watermelon daiquiri before. Deee-lish. And the band was good too. I liked watching you move to the music. In the dark your red dress shimmered enticingly and your hair was like a pale silver cloud. I liked it even better when the music turned slow and you stepped into my arms. The scent of your hair had my senses reeling. What kind of shampoo do you use? And when can I see you again?

Hi. You have reached George Lipincott's line. I've gone sailing today. George is a lucky devil, you must be thinking. Don't worry, it's business. A new client to entertain. And, lest we forget, it's deductible! Leave a message after the beep and I'll call you the moment I come in, my hair smelling of salt spray, and my eyes filled with sea and sky.
   —Hi George. It's me. (Sounds of heavy breathing.) That's from the thought of you with your hair ruffled by the wind, smelling of the sea. I enjoyed the other night too. Dancing was fun. Still, it's a shame the music was so loud. We weren't really able to talk. And it was dark in there, wasn't it. What colour are your eyes? If they are filled with sea and sky, does that mean they're blue?

No brilliant witty scintillating greeting today. It's your turn. Leave your message after you hear the tone.
   —Sorry about the mixup last night. It's George, by the way. The boss came in just as I was leaving and asked me to go through an account with him. He depends on me, I couldn't let him down. By the time I got to the restaurant, you'd left. Can you ever forgive me?
   I want to tell you something funny that just happened. I was in my car driving home. I was alone. No more car pools for me. I value that time to unwind on my own from my day. Anyway, I got stopped at the 52nd and 8th traffic light, and I happened to glance at the car next

to me. The driver was you! I picked up my car phone to call you. But then I didn't. I was struck by a sudden doubt. What if it wasn't really you? It's always been so dark when we've been together. Is your car a black BMW?

Sorry if this message isn't witty or scintillating enough.

(The apartment is dark. A full moon hangs in the night sky outside the glass double doors. Silver light bathes the modular sofa but the rest of the room is in heavy shadow. Off to one side, the red light of the telephone answering machine glows, a beacon in the dark.)

ENTRY POINTS

1 This story departs from normal short story conventions in presenting its action; in fact, it uses the prose style of stage directions. Comment on its effectiveness in conveying both plot and mood. For another example of experimental form in fiction, read "Vocational Counselling" (page 134).

2 What mood is being conveyed through the description of the penthouse, the characters, and their "dialogues"? Do you find this mood appealing or distancing?

3 Given their dialogue through the answering machines and their consequent actions, how would you describe George and Shawna? How would you describe their relationship?

4 "I was struck by a sudden doubt. What if it wasn't really you?"
   (a) Given George's doubts, what does this reveal about the relationship he has with Shawna?
   (b) What comment about today's society is Judy McCrosky making? Do you agree with her in view of the relationship of George and Shawna? Discuss with your group.

5 "…the red light of the telephone answering machine glows, a beacon in the dark."
   (a) Analyze and discuss this final metaphor and relate it to the romantic "relationship" in the story.
   (b) To what extent is the answering machine a more important character in this story than the human beings are?

6 Compare and contrast the romantic relationship in this story with that presented in Xiaohu's "Outside the Marriage Bureau" (page

160). Can direct romantic love continue to take place in our bureaucratic, technological society?

7 Debate: "Technology is becoming too dominant and is robbing us of real human contact." For further insights into this issue, read Dr. Ursula Franklin's *The Real World of Technology* (1990) in which she examines the foundations of technology and its pervasive interventions in our daily lives. Note her ideas on "pseudorealities" and "pseudocommunities": "And what seems extraordinary...is that these media images have so permeated every facet of life that they are no longer perceived as external intrusions or as pseudorealities except by media professionals....".

8 Write an experimental short story like "Call Me" using the same stage directions structure. Think about using as a central object or character one of the newer forms of communication: an answering machine, a FAX machine, a computer network, a VCR, a virtual reality game.

MY MOTHER, A CLOSET FULL OF DRESSES

In Poland, needing a dress
for the potato masher to become a doll,
she cut out a patch from somebody's
Sunday skirt—black silk, good enough
to be buried in; waterfalling folds—
no one would notice. Before the whole church,
Baba bent to kiss the icons; her skirts
fanned, the missing patch a window
to her starched white drawers.
My mother whipped until she could not sit;
the baba never setting foot
in church again.

In Canada, her sewing teacher
called it shameful—a girl of such gifts
entering a factory! Sent her
to design school instead, dressed
in her castoffs. My mother, slashing
stitches from priggish Liberty prints—
everyone else flaunting
palm leaves, cabbage roses.

JANICE KULYK KEEFER

The Story of a Dress *at the Exhibition.*
She sat in a small display-cage, designing,
cutting out, sewing a dress.
The man who grilled her on each
click of the scissors, till she bit
blistered lips, blood
drooling down her chin.
Watched for a week,
then hired her like that—
though it was still Depression,
designers a dime a dozen.

The wedding dress she sketched
and sewed herself: 'The bride in peau de soie
with a delicate rose tint and beading
in the shape of scattered leaves.'
Satin peignoirs from the honeymoon—
tea-coloured stains; folds creased
as with a knife.

A closet full of dresses for weddings,
anniversaries,
funerals—

And occasions for which she didn't dress:
children with high fevers, and husband
off playing golf or bridge as husbands did;
the miscarriage when she bled
faster than the ambulance; migraines
in dark rooms at noon;
and all the nights
when she rummaged, naked,
through steel hangers in an empty closet.

1. Contrast the attitude of "the baba" (her grandmother) to the attitude of the Canadian sewing teacher in respect of the poet's mother's "gifts."

2. What is the poet's attitude towards her mother and her "gifts"? Is she stereotyping her mother as a one-dimensional person? Discuss fully.

3. "And occasions for which she didn't dress." Why does the poet conclude her poem with such vivid, negative images?

4. Write your own poem in which you complete your own metaphor: "My Mother, A Closet Full of _____." Use stark or vivid images and your own personal anecdotes about your own mother or closest female relative.

5. Write a personal essay on *your* relationship to your mother or your closest female guardian. Use a title such as "My Mother, My Friend" or My Mother, Myself."

6. Compare the mother-daughter relationship in this poem with those found in the following stories: "A Beautiful Woman" (page 140); "Two Kinds" (page 178); "A Proper Goodbye" (page 194); "The Answer Is No" (page 214).
   (a) What similarities do you detect? Explain.
   (b) What differences do you find? Explain.

TWO KINDS

AMY TAN

My mother believed you could be anything you wanted to be in America. You could open a restaurant. You could work for the government and get good retirement. You could buy a house with almost no money down. You could become rich. You could become instantly famous.

"Of course you can be prodigy, too," my mother told me when I was nine. "You can be best anything. What does Auntie Lindo know? Her daughter, she is only best tricky."

America was where all my mother's hopes lay. She had come here in 1949 after losing everything in China: her mother and father, her family home, her first husband, and two daughters, twin baby girls. But she never looked back with regret. There were so many ways for things to get better.

We didn't immediately pick the right kind of prodigy. At first my mother thought I would be a Chinese Shirley Temple. We'd watch Shirley's old movies on TV as though they were training films. My mother would poke my arm and say, "*Ni kan*"—You watch. And I would see Shirley tapping her feet, or singing a sailor song, or pursing her lips into a very round O while saying, "Oh my goodness."

"*Ni kan*" said my mother as Shirley's eyes flooded with tears. "You already know how. Don't need talent for crying!"

Soon after my mother got this idea about Shirley Temple, she took me to a beauty training school in the Mission district and put me in the hands of a student who could barely hold the scissors without shaking. Instead of getting big fat curls, I emerged with an uneven mass of crinkly black fuzz. My mother dragged me off to the bathroom and tried to wet down my hair.

"You look like Negro Chinese," she lamented, as if I had done this on purpose.

The instructor of the beauty training school had to lop off those soggy clumps to make my hair even again. "Peter Pan is very popular these days," the instructor assured my mother. I now had hair the length of a boy's, with straight-across bangs that hung at a slant two inches above my eyebrows. I liked the haircut and it made me actually look forward to my future fame.

In fact, in the beginning, I was just as excited as my mother, maybe even more so. I pictured this prodigy part of me as many different images, trying each one on for size. I was a dainty ballerina girl standing by the curtains, waiting to hear the right music that would send me floating on my tiptoes. I was like the Christ Child lifted out of the straw manger, crying with holy indignity. I was Cinderella stepping from her pumpkin carriage with sparkly cartoon music filling the air.

In all of my imaginings, I was filled with a sense that I would soon become *perfect*. My mother and father would adore me. I would be beyond reproach. I would never feel the need to sulk for anything.

But sometimes the prodigy in me became impatient. "If you don't hurry up and get me out of here, I'm disappearing for good," it warned. "And then you'll always be nothing."

Every night after dinner, my mother and I would sit at the Formica kitchen table. She would present new tests, taking her examples from stories of amazing children she had read in *Ripley's Believe It or Not*, or *Good Housekeeping, Reader's Digest*, and a dozen other magazines she kept in a pile in our bathroom. My mother got these magazines from people whose houses she cleaned. And since she cleaned many houses each week, we had a great assortment. She would look through them all, searching for stories about remarkable children.

The first night she brought out a story about a three-year-old boy who knew the capitals of all the states and even most of the European countries. A teacher was quoted as saying the little boy could also pronounce the names of the foreign cities correctly.

"What's the capital of Finland?" my mother asked me, looking at the magazine story.

All I knew was the capital of California, because Sacramento was the name of the street we lived on in Chinatown. "Nairobi!" I guessed, saying the most foreign word I could think of. She checked to see if that was possibly one way to pronounce "Helsinki" before showing me the answer.

The tests got harder—multiplying numbers in my head, finding the queen of hearts in a deck of cards, trying to stand on my head without using my hands, predicting the daily temperatures in Los Angeles, New York, and London.

One night I had to look at a page from the Bible for three minutes and then report everything I could remember. "Now Jehoshaphat had riches and honor in abundance and...that's all I remember, Ma," I said.

And after seeing my mother's disappointed face once again, something inside of me began to die. I hated the tests, the raised hopes and failed expectations. Before going to bed that night, I looked in the mirror above the bathroom sink and when I saw only my face staring back—and that it would always be this ordinary face—I began to cry. Such a sad, ugly girl! I made high-pitched noises like a crazed animal, trying scratch out the face in the mirror.

And then I saw what seemed to be the prodigy side of me—because I had never seen that face before. I looked at my reflection, blinking so I could see more clearly. The girl staring back at me was angry, powerful. This girl and I were the same. I had new thoughts, willful thoughts, or rather thoughts filled with lots of won'ts. I won't let her change me, I promised myself. I won't be what I'm not.

So now on nights when my mother presented her tests, I performed listlessly, my head propped on one arm. I pretended to be bored. And I was. I got so bored I started counting the bellows of the foghorns out on the bay while my mother drilled me in other areas. The sound was comforting and reminded me of the cow jumping over the moon. And the next day, I played a game with myself, seeing if my mother would give up on me before eight bellows. After a while I usually counted only one, maybe two bellows at most. At last she was beginning to give up hope.

Two or three months had gone by without any mention of my being a prodigy again. And then one day my mother was watching "The Ed Sullivan Show" on TV. The TV was old and the sound kept shorting out. Every time my mother got halfway up from the sofa to adjust the set, the sound would go back on and Ed would be talking. As soon as she sat down, Ed would go silent again. She got up, the TV broke into loud piano music. She sat down. Silence. Up and down, back and forth, quiet and loud. It was like a stiff embraceless dance between her and the TV set. Finally she stood by the set with her hand on the sound dial.

She seemed entranced by the music, a little frenzied piano piece with this mesmerizing quality, sort of quick passages and then teasing lilting ones before it returned to the quick playful parts.

"*Ni kan*," my mother said, calling me over with hurried hand gestures. "Look here."

I could see why my mother was fascinated by the music. It was being pounded out by a little Chinese girl, about nine years old, with a

Peter Pan haircut. The girl had the sauciness of a Shirley Temple. She was proudly modest like a proper Chinese child. And she also did this fancy sweep of a curtsy, so that the fluffy skirt of her white dress cascaded slowly to the floor like the petals of a large carnation.

In spite of these warning signs, I wasn't worried. Our family had no piano and we couldn't afford to buy one, let alone reams of sheet music and piano lessons. So I could be generous in my comments when my mother bad-mouthed the little girl on TV.

"Play note right, but doesn't sound good! No singing sound," complained my mother.

"What are you picking on her for?" I said carelessly. "She's pretty good. Maybe she's not the best, but she's trying hard." I knew almost immediately I would be sorry I said that.

"Just like you," she said. "Not the best. Because you not trying." She gave a little huff as she let go of the sound dial and sat down on the sofa.

The little Chinese girl sat down also to play an encore of "Anitra's Dance" by Grieg. I remember the song, because later on I had to learn how to play it.

Three days after watching "The Ed Sullivan Show," my mother told me what my schedule would be for piano lessons and piano practice. She had talked to Mr. Chong, who lived on the first floor of our apartment building. Mr. Chong was a retired piano teacher and my mother had traded housecleaning services for weekly lessons and a piano for me to practice on every day, two hours a day, from four until six.

When my mother told me this, I felt as though I had been sent to hell. I whined and then kicked my foot a little when I couldn't stand it anymore.

"Why don't you like me the way I am? I'm *not* a genius! I can't play the piano. And even if I could, I wouldn't go on TV if you paid me a million dollars!" I cried.

My mother slapped me. "Who ask you be genius?" she shouted. "Only ask you be your best. For you sake. You think I want you be genius? Hnnh? What for! Who ask you!"

"So ungrateful," I heard her mutter in Chinese. "If she had as much talent as she has temper, she would be famous now."

Mr. Chong, whom I secretly nicknamed Old Chong, was very strange, always tapping fingers to the silent music of an invisible orchestra. He looked ancient in my eyes. He had lost most of the hair on top of his head and he wore thick glasses and had eyes that always looked tired and sleepy. But he must have been younger than I thought, since he lived with his mother and was not yet married.

I met Old Lady Chong once and that was enough. She had this peculiar smell like a baby that had done something in its pants. And her fingers felt like a dead person's, like an old peach I once found in the back of the refrigerator; the skin just slid off the meat when I picked it up.

I soon found out why Old Chong had retired from teaching piano. He was deaf. "Like Beethoven!" he shouted at me. "We're both listening only in our head!" And he would start to conduct his frantic silent sonatas.

Our lessons went like this. He would open the book and point to different things, explaining their purpose: "Key! Treble! Bass! No sharps or flats! So this is C major! Listen now and play after me!"

And then he would play the C scale a few times, a simple chord, and then, as if inspired by an old, unreachable itch, he gradually added more notes and running trills and a pounding bass until the music was really something quite grand.

I would play after him, the simple scale, the simple chord, and then I just played some nonsense that sounded like a cat running up and down on top of garbage cans. Old Chong smiled and applauded and then said, "Very good! But now you must learn to keep time!"

So that's how I discovered that Old Chong's eyes were too slow to keep up with the wrong notes I was playing. He went through the motions in half-time. To help me keep rhythm, he stood behind me, pushing down on my right shoulder for every beat. He balanced pennies on top of my wrists so I would keep them still as I slowly played scales and arpeggios. He had me curve my hand around an apple and keep that shape when playing chords. He marched stiffly to show me how to make each finger dance up and down, staccato like an obedient little soldier.

He taught me all these things, and that was how I also learned I could be lazy and get away with mistakes, lots of mistakes. If I hit the wrong notes because I hadn't practiced enough, I never corrected myself. I just kept playing in rhythm. And Old Chong kept conducting his own private reverie.

So maybe I never really gave myself a fair chance. I did pick up the basics pretty quickly, and I might have become a good pianist at that young age. But I was so determined not to try, not to be anybody different that I learned to play only the most earsplitting preludes, the most discordant hymns.

Over the next year, I practiced like this, dutifully in my own way. And then one day I heard my mother and her friend Lindo Jong both talking in a loud bragging tone of voice so others could hear. It was after church, and I was leaning against the brick wall wearing a dress with stiff white petticoats. Auntie Lindo's daughter, Waverly, who was about my age, was standing farther down the wall above five feet away. We had grown up together and shared all the closeness of two sisters squabbling over crayons and dolls. In other words, for the most part, we hated each other. I thought she was snotty. Waverly Jong had gained a certain amount of fame as "Chinatown's Littlest Chinese Chess Champion."

"She bring home too many trophy," lamented Auntie Lindo that Sunday. "All day she play chess. All day I have no time do nothing but dust off her winnings." She threw a scolding look at Waverly, who pretended not to see her.

"You lucky you don't have this problem," said Auntie Lindo with a sigh to my mother.

And my mother squared her shoulders and bragged: "Our problem worser than yours. If we ask Jing-mei wash dish, she hear nothing but music. It's like you can't stop this natural talent."

And right then, I was determined to put a stop to her foolish pride.

A few weeks later, Old Chong and my mother conspired to have me play in a talent show which would be held in the church hall. By then, my parents had saved up enough to buy me a second-hand piano, a black Wurlitzer spinet with a scarred bench. It was the showpiece of our living room.

For the talent show, I was to play a piece called "Pleading Child" from Schumann's *Scenes from Childhood*. It was a simple, moody piece that sounded more difficult than it was. I was supposed to memorize the whole thing, playing the repeat parts twice to make the piece sound longer. But I dawdled over it, playing a few bars and then cheating, looking up to see what notes followed. I never really listened to what I was playing. I daydreamed about being somewhere else, about being someone else.

The part I liked to practice best was the fancy curtsy: right foot out, touch the rose on the carpet with a pointed foot, sweep to the side, left leg bends, look up and smile.

My parents invited all the couples from the Joy Luck Club to witness my debut. Auntie Lindo and Uncle Tin were there. Waverly and her two older brothers had also come. The first two rows were filled with children both younger and older than I was. The little ones got to go first. They recited simple nursery rhymes, squawked out tunes on miniature violins, twirled Hula Hoops, pranced in pink ballet tutus, and when they bowed or curtsied, the audience would sigh in unison, "Awww," and then clap enthusiastically.

When my turn came, I was very confident. I remember my childish excitement. It was as if I knew, without a doubt, that the prodigy side of me really did exist. I had no fear whatsoever, no nervousness. I remember thinking to myself, This is it! This is it! I looked out over the audience, at my mother's blank face, my father's yawn, Auntie Lindo's stiff-lipped smile, Waverly's sulky expression. I had on a white dress layered with sheets of lace, and a pink bow in my Peter Pan haircut. As I sat down I envisioned people jumping to their feet and Ed Sullivan rushing up to introduce me to everyone on TV.

And I started to play. It was so beautiful. I was so caught up in how lovely I looked that at first I didn't worry how I would sound.

So it was a surprise to me when I hit the first wrong note and I realized something didn't sound quite right. And then I hit another and another followed that. A chill started at the top of my head and began to trickle down. Yet I couldn't stop playing, as though my hands were bewitched. I kept thinking my fingers would adjust themselves back, like a train switching to the right track. I played this strange jumble through two repeats, the sour notes staying with me all the way to the end.

When I stood up, I discovered my legs were shaking. Maybe I had just been nervous and the audience, like Old Chong, had seen me go through the right motions and had not heard anything wrong at all. I swept my right foot out, went down on my knee, looked up and smiled. The room was quiet, except for Old Chong, who was beaming and shouting, "Bravo! Bravo! Well done!" But then I saw my mother's face, her stricken face. The audience clapped weakly, and as I walked back to my chair, with my whole face quivering as I tried not to cry, I heard a little boy whisper loudly to his mother, "That was awful," and the mother whispered back, "Well, she certainly tried."

And now I realized how many people were in the audience, the whole world it seemed. I was aware of eyes burning into my back. I felt the shame of my mother and father as they sat stiffly throughout the rest of the show.

We could have escaped during intermission. Pride and some strange sense of honor must have anchored my parents to their chairs. And so we watched it all: the eighteen-year-old boy with a fake mustache who did a magic show and juggled flaming hoops while riding a unicycle. The breasted girl with white makeup who sang from *Madama Butterfly* and got honorable mention. And the eleven-year-old boy who won first prize playing a tricky violin song that sounded like a busy bee.

After the show, the Hsus, the Jongs, and the St. Clairs from the Joy Luck Club came up to my mother and father.

"Lots of talented kids," Auntie Lindo said vaguely, smiling broadly.

"That was somethin' else," said my father, and I wondered if he was referring to me in a humorous way, or whether he even remembered what I had done.

Waverly looked at me and shrugged her shoulders. "You aren't a genius like me," she said matter-of-factly. And if I hadn't felt so bad, I would have pulled her braids and punched her stomach.

But my mother's expression was what devastated me: a quiet, blank look that said she had lost everything. I felt the same way, and it seemed as if everybody were now coming up, like gawkers at the scene of an accident, to see what parts were actually missing. When we got on the bus to go home, my father was humming the busy-bee tune and my mother was silent. I kept thinking she wanted to wait until we got home before shouting at me. But when my father unlocked the door to our apartment, my mother walked in and then went to the back, into the bedroom. No accusations. No blame. And in a way, I felt disappointed. I had been waiting for her to start shouting, so I could shout back and cry and blame her for all my misery.

I assumed my talent-show fiasco meant I never had to play the piano again. But two days later, after school, my mother came out of the kitchen and saw me watching TV.

"Four clock," she reminded me as if it were any other day. I was stunned, as though she were asking me to go through the talent-show torture again. I wedged myself more tightly in front of the TV.

"Turn off TV," she called from the kitchen five minutes later.

I didn't budge. And then I decided. I didn't have to do what my mother said anymore. I wasn't her slave. This wasn't China. I had listened to her before and look what happened. She was the stupid one.

She came out of the kitchen and stood in the arched entryway of the living room. "Four clock," she said once again, louder.

"I'm not going to play anymore," I said nonchalantly. "Why should I? I'm not a genius."

She walked over and stood in front of the TV. I saw her chest was heaving up and down in an angry way.

"No!" I said, and I now felt stronger, as if my true self had finally emerged. So this was what had been inside me all along.

"No! I won't!" I screamed.

She yanked me by the arm, pulled me off the floor, snapped off the TV. She was frighteningly strong, half pulling, half carrying me toward the piano as I kicked the throw rugs under my feet. She lifted me up and onto the hard bench. I was sobbing by now, looking at her bitterly. Her chest was heaving even more and her mouth was open, smiling crazily as if she were pleased I was crying.

"You want me to be someone that I'm not!" I sobbed. "I'll never be the kind of daughter you want me to be!"

"Only two kinds of daughters," she shouted in Chinese. "Those who are obedient and those who follow their own mind! Only one kind of daughter can live in this house. Obedient daughter!"

"Then I wish I wasn't your daughter. I wish you weren't my mother," I shouted. As I said these things I got scared. I felt like worms and toads and slimy things were crawling out of my chest, but it also felt good, as if this awful side of me had surfaced, at last.

"Too late change this," said my mother shrilly.

And I could sense her anger rising to its breaking point. I wanted to see it spill over. And that's when I remembered the babies she had lost in China, the ones we never talked about. "Then I wish I'd never been born!" I shouted. "I wish I were dead! Like them."

It was as if I had said the magic words. Alakazam!—and her face went blank, her mouth closed, her arms went slack, and she backed out of the room, stunned, as if she were blowing away like a small brown leaf, thin, brittle, lifeless.

It was not the only disappointment my mother felt in me. In the years that followed, I failed her so many times, each time asserting my own will, my right to fall short of expectations. I didn't get straight A's. I didn't become class president. I didn't get into Stanford. I dropped out of college.

For unlike my mother, I did not believe I could be anything I wanted to be. I could only be me.

And for all those years, we never talked about the disaster at the recital or my terrible accusations afterward at the piano bench. All that remained unchecked, like a betrayal that was now unspeakable. So I never found a way to ask her why she had hoped for something so large that failure was inevitable.

And even worse, I never asked her what frightened me the most: Why had she given up hope?

For after our struggle at the piano, she never mentioned my playing again. The lessons stopped. The lid to the piano was closed, shutting out the dust, my misery, and her dreams.

So she surprised me. A few years ago, she offered to give me the piano, for my thirtieth birthday. I had not played in all those years. I saw the offer as a sign of forgiveness, a tremendous burden removed.

"Are you sure?" I asked shyly. "I mean, won't you and Dad miss it?"

"No, this your piano," she said firmly. "Always your piano. You only one can play."

"Well, I probably can't play anymore," I said. "It's been years."

"You pick up fast," said my mother, as if she knew this was certain. "You have natural talent. You could been genius if you want to."

"No, I couldn't."

"You just not trying," said my mother. And she was neither angry nor sad. She said it as if to announce a fact that could never be disproved. "Take it," she said.

But I didn't at first. It was enough that she had offered it to me. And after that, every time I saw it in my parents' living room, standing in front of the bay windows, it made me feel proud, as if it were a shiny trophy I had won back.

Last week I sent a tuner over to my parents' apartment and had the piano reconditioned, for purely sentimental reasons. My mother had died a few months before and I had been getting things in order for my father, a little bit at a time. I put the jewelry in special silk pouches. The sweaters she had knitted in yellow, pink, bright orange—all the colors I hated—I put those in moth-proof boxes. I found some old Chinese silk dresses, the kind with little slits up the sides. I rubbed the old silk against my skin, then wrapped them in tissue and decided to take them home with me.

After I had the piano tuned, I opened the lid and touched the keys. It sounded even richer than I remembered. Really, it was a very good piano. Inside the bench were the same exercise notes with handwritten scales, the same secondhand music books with their covers held together with yellow tape.

I opened up the Schumann book to the dark little piece I had played at the recital. It was on the left-hand side of the page, "Pleading Child." It looked more difficult than I remembered. I played a few bars, surprised at how easily the notes came back to me.

And for the first time, or so it seemed, I noticed the piece on the right-hand side. It was called "Perfectly Contented." I tried to play this one as well. It had a lighter melody but the same flowing rhythm and turned out to be quite easy. "Pleading Child" was shorter but slower; "Perfectly Contented" was longer but faster. And after I played them both a few times, I realized they were two halves of the same song.

ENTRY POINTS

1 "America was where all my mother's hopes lay."
(a) How did Jing-mei's mother envision the United States?
(b) What were her greatest hopes after leaving China?
(c) How realistic were her hopes and dreams? Elaborate and assess.

2 How does Jing-mei feel about her mother's view of her as a "prodigy"? Is she being fair to her mother and her dreams? Is her mother being too rigid and pushy? Discuss fully with your group.

3 "I won't let her change me, I promised myself. I won't be what I'm not." Why does Jing-mei react this way to her mother's encouragement? To what extent do you agree with her reaction?

4 "Who ask you be genius?...Only ask you be your best."
(a) Is this true? Is Jing-mei's mother only asking her daughter to be the best she can be?
(b) Why does Jing-mei react the way she does? Is she "ungrateful"? Elaborate.
(c) Why does she behave the way she does with Old Chong and the piano lessons?

5 Why does her mother's expression after the piano recital devastate Jing-mei? How does Jing-mei try to get back at her mother? Assess their behaviour towards each other.

6 "Only two kinds of daughters...." Discuss the mother's philosophy. Are there only two kinds—or is there a "middle ground"?

7 Comment on the final two segments of the story. Why did the mother, apparently, give up hope for her daughter? Was an understanding or a reconciliation between mother and daughter ever reached?

8 Compare the mother-daughter relationship in this story with "A Beautiful Woman" (page 140), and "My Mother, a Closet Full of Dresses" (page 175).

9 Write a story of a reconciliation between a mother and a daughter.

10 You are Jing-mei. Write three diary items expressing your feelings about your mother from your perspective as (a) a little girl, (b) a thirty-year-old, and (c) an adult after your mother's death.

11 Read Amy Tan's *The Joy Luck Club* and *The Kitchen God's Wife* for her further insights into mother-daughter relationships.

THE LETTER

LAURA BULGER

Dear mother and father
I hope you are well. We are just fine.

Domingos writes "we" but deep down he does not include her. It is as if she did not exist in his life although they have been living together under the same roof for eighteen years. Eighteen long years. Just a few months before that he had arrived, wearing his dark suit, a **boina** down over his ears and an empty wallet. He met Joaquim Patricio who gave him help, shelter and finally his daughter, Adelaide. They never whispered words of love or things like that, but a year later their first child was born.

Carlos found some work this summer. It's good for him. He won't hang around bad company. He has become a man; he is now taller than I am. He is still making a little money here and there. It's all for him; I don't need it, thank God. The business is doing well. Tininha is still too young to start working. She helps her mother at home.

Her, again.
For the last few days they had spoken only when they couldn't avoid it, because of the children. Adelaide had become more aloof after the birth of the young one, Eduardo. Ed, in English. She had started standing up to him, provoking him and giving herself airs. Now, she

arrives late from work and then spends hours on the telephone chatting with her friends; she drinks teas that really stink just to lose weight. She stopped ironing his shirts and instead sends them to the cleaners. She answers him in English and complains about the children, her job, her migraines. What the hell does she want? She's got everything: a house in the suburbs, a car, a real fur rotting in the closet. Once in a while a slap keeps her quiet for a few days. She even becomes tender, but her hugs and kisses no longer interest him. Then, she lashes out again for no reason at all. "What a brute you are!" "I'm no slave" "I'm fed up." "One of these days I'm leaving." But she won't. While Joaquim Patricio was alive she didn't dare out of fear. With her father's death things had changed. Now, she even steals his money and wastes it on rags; she has a fancy for them. To top it all, his mother-in-law came to live with them; in her sly way she took her side. Daughter, mother and grandmother, they all conspire against him. They don't get anywhere with the boys though. Ed always has a quick answer on the tip of his tongue.

Eduardo has had good marks in school. He reads and writes very well, in English, of course. He's sharp. People say he takes after his grandfather.

He laughs. Yeah, after his maternal grandfather, the swine. He even lent him money for the business. In exchange he married his daughter. Now, Adelaide goes to church on Sundays wearing a hat, just like the **inglesas**; a bowl on her head. Ridiculous!

At times he feels like shouting at her that her father had put one over on him, a trusting newcomer, and that he had never loved her, that everything had been a mistake, **um erro**. But he always ends up slamming the door behind him, choking back his anger.

Last night I was playing cards with Chico das Malhadas. He came back a few months ago and looks good. He told me that he had given you the parcel. Mother, did you like the present the children sent you? While he was there Chico met big Casimiro. He said he had married Aurora. Why didn't you tell me?

Aurora, blonde as ripe sheaves, provocative among the golden ears of wheat. Aurora, gasping, her sensual lips parted. Aurora, her blue-eyed gaze fixed on the infinite sky above them, teasing his thirsty mouth with a blade of wheat. It all seemed liked yesterday. Sweaty shirt sticking to his back. **Terra firme**. Long green dreams on hot summer afternoons.

"I'm going away for good," he said one sombre day. "And me?" she asked, sobbing. "You, you will come later. I'll send for you." Aurora, misty-eyed, waving, already lost in the distance. Aurora—a memory. **A vida é assim**. There were no recriminations. They never saw each other again. He had become engaged to Joaquim Patricio's daughter.

That summer, when he went back—Carlos was still tiny and Tininha was already in her mother's womb—he asked about Aurora. She was working as a maid in the city. No, they never met again.

This year, I cannot go over. I must fix up the house. I'm going to build a bar downstairs. One day, when you come, you'll see what it's like.

He would write the same thing every summer. He didn't want them to see what it was really like between him and Adelaide. He wanted to spare them the disappointment; for the old folks, what was done on earth was done also in heaven. Now he could no longer hide from the children, especially from the eldest. Carlos was already a man.

One of these days Carlos will go over, so as not to forget his grandparents. He doesn't speak Portuguese well, but he will manage once he gets there. He's going to be a **doutor**.

He was smart all right, but didn't work hard enough, according to the teachers. In the beginning, whenever they started to quarrel, Carlos took his mother's side. Then, as he grew older, he got used to the idea that things would never change. He lost interest. Now, he hardly says anything, just the essentials, and always in English. He comes and goes and no one notices. Always locked in his room listening to music. Sometimes he plays it so loud they have to rap on his door.

None of his friends comes to the house. They must meet somewhere else.

After school he works in a restaurant and comes home late. His mother is worried by his indifference. She screams at him outside his door, but Carlos doesn't answer. He keeps people at a distance and gets away with it. Yeah, Carlos is already a man. He had become aware of it during that occasion in which his son caught both of them, he and the **inglesa**, a cute chick he had fallen for. He was, of course, careful in avoiding a scandal. They would never show up in public, although she nagged at him. When they were alone it was a different story. She was all hugs and kisses.

But he never thought his son might suddenly appear in the cubicle behind the workshop. There he found them kissing each other, all messed up. He was really embarrassed in front of the boy. He coughed. He felt like grabbing him right there and explaining...what? Dumbfounded, he started fumbling with his buttons. Carlos behaved like a man. He stepped out and waited until his father could get himself together. The boy respected him. They never spoke of it.

With Ed it would have been different.

Ed often speaks of his grandparents and Tininha wants to go there too. We have to take the car when we go. Chico did that; he had a great time. They went from north to south by car.

Shortly after coming back, Chico was fired. He had been working in the factory for seven years, but was turned out on the street without so much as a word. That's not fair. With three mouths to feed Chico is in a bind, even with the welfare money. It isn't worth a damn! Many people are in serious trouble around here; now, life is really a pain in the neck. Not like the old days when you arrived and someone gave you a hand.

He was lucky. At least he's his own boss. But he cannot help Chico; what with his own mortgage and other payments. Besides, at the moment he doesn't need extra staff; it's every man for himself as far as he's concerned. With his parents it's different; it's a question of duty.

I'm going to send you money to buy Uncle Zé's land. Tell the lawyer to get the papers ready. Then we can build the house, one bright and modern, as it should be, and you can move in. If you need more money let me know. I don't know when we can get there because of the improvements in this house. Maybe next year.

Talvez para o ano...

And really he has no idea if he'll ever go back. One of these days he has to talk to the kids. The grandparents are getting older. The old country seems farther and farther away. We, here, are even becoming indifferent. Who knows how it happens? It isn't worth thinking about what could have been.

Nothing can be done.

He brought the letter to a close. It was getting too long.

I send you many **saudades**. Love from your son

Domingos

ENTRY POINTS

1 "The Letter" is an example of experimental fiction, which advances its plot line through a formulaic structure. Show how this structure is effective in conveying a double reality.

2 What reality is Domingos trying to convey about his life in Canada to his parents in Portugal? Why doesn't he convey the truth? Look up the word "prevarication."

3 "What the hell does she want?"
   (a) Why is Domingos critical of his wife? What does Domingos's attitude reveal about him?
   (b) What do you think Adelaide wants? Why is she changing from the way she used to be?
   (c) With whom do you sympathize more, Domingos or Adelaide— or are they both at fault for the tension in their marriage? Discuss thoroughly with your group.

4 Comment on the children's relationship to their parents and to their "anglo" Canadian society. How could this relationship be improved? Make specific suggestions.

5 Near the closing of "The Letter," Domingos says "Nothing can be done" about his problems and frustrations. Is that really true? With your group, think of strategies that might help repair the damage done to members of this family. Report your recommendations to the class.

6 Research your library's vertical files on marriage and spousal abuse— and relate your findings to this story, as well as the stories, "Skipper" (page 28), "A Beautiful Woman" (page 140), and the poem, "Thinking With the Heart" (page 210).

7 Using the same letter structure as Bulger does to present a double reality, write your own short story. For example, you might write a letter from a university student to his/her parent(s) about how well things are going when, in truth, there are real problems.

8 You are Carlos. Write an interior monologue in which you express your feelings about your father and your mother. Why do you decide never to speak of the time you caught your father with the "inglesa"?

9 Imagine you are Adelaide. Write a letter to your mother expressing your real feelings about Domingos and your children.

A PROPER GOODBYE

KATHERINE ALEXANDER

Eleni was on her knees in the garden when the phone started ringing. She was kneading the earth around the freshly planted eggplant seeds and trying to decide whether to cook chicken for the dinner on Sunday or a nice leg of lamb. The grandchildren always asked for chicken, but Costa liked lamb on a festive occasion. Her sons would want to cook outdoors on that contraption they'd bought her the summer before. They'd thought she was being difficult when she'd refused to go near the thing. Would they have understood if she'd told them that in Greece they'd have no choice but to cook in an outdoor oven that had to be watched every minute because in the summer it heated so quickly the food burned, while in winter it needed to be fed a continual supply of twigs so the heat wouldn't give out, and that having her own lovely indoor stove which could be regulated by the switch of a knob meant a sort of freedom to her?

Costa understood. As well as the stove, he'd bought her a huge re-frigerator that made its own ice and needed to be defrosted only once a week, and a washing machine that rumbled quietly in the corner as it filled and emptied itself and even wrung the clothes out so all she had to do was hang them up to dry. He was a good man, her Costa. She'd make the lamb. After all, the family dinner was for his birthday. They'd already had his annual Name Day party for family and friends, but the children liked the Canadian custom of celebrating birthdays.

Her Stephano would've been thirty-four now. And the baby, the one she barely remembered—there hadn't even been time to photograph her before God took her away—would've been thirty-five. It was hard to mourn an infant she'd known for only a few months so long ago, but with Stephano it was different. She'd asked Costa over and over to find out where their son was so they could visit, take flowers, but all he'd say was it was better left alone.

The feeling that she'd let her children down wouldn't leave Eleni, not with two of them gone and Angela over thirty and still unmarried. It was something she could never put into words. All she could do was pray to the Virgin, asking forgiveness for she knew not what. Yet even with all her prayers, the deaths of two children continued to hang like a cloud over the happiness her others gave her, and the goodness of her husband.

The phone was still ringing. Didn't Angela realize it might be her Papa? He liked to go to the store every day—to keep an eye on things, he'd say—but he'd often tire quickly and call Angela to pick him up.

Eleni sighed, rocked back on her knees. She'd better go in and see what was going on. Anyway, there was nothing more to be done in the garden for now. The eggplant was being stubborn as usual. Unlike the zucchini that blossomed beautifully year after year, nothing seemed to work with the eggplant. She'd tried different mixes of soils, different patches of garden for a little more sunlight or a little less, but the result was always the same: leathery lumps the size of walnuts. The worst thing was they seemed to lie there, contentedly nestling among the dark green leaves, mocking her.

The phone finally stopped ringing as she got up off her knees. She rubbed the loose dirt from her hands, went to the side of the house, turned on the hose and washed her hands. When she came around the corner, shaking her dripping hands, Angela was standing on the porch steps.

"Who was on the phone?"

Angela reached out to her mother.

"Did you answer?"

Angela took her mother's hands.

"You'll get all wet." Eleni was getting impatient.

Angela put her arms around her mother, drew her close.

Eleni stiffened, then quickly pulled away, saw her daughter's eyes brimming with tears. "Your Papa?" she whispered.

Angela nodded. "I'll take you, Mama."

Eleni rushed into the house, grabbed a light coat to cover her old housedress and ran out the front door. Angela was waiting for her in the car.

They drove in silence. Eleni pulled her coat tight around her. She shouldn't have let Costa go this morning. Some days, when he seemed more tired than others, she would get after him to stay home. Not that he would. But she'd try. This morning though, he had seemed almost his old self, joking with her as she'd helped him pick out a tie. He'd probably done too much at the store, tried to help out when he should've just sat quietly and let his sons do the work.

"Why didn't you answer the phone right away?"

"I was taking the *koulourákia* out of the oven—I was afraid they'd burn if I left them to answer the phone."

"Burnt cookies are more important than your Papa!"

"I'm sorry, Mama."

"I didn't…oh, never mind." She couldn't sit still, couldn't move, it was taking forever. Costa had never been sick, apart from the recent tiredness, and that had only started after the trip to Greece.

Visiting their homeland after so many years had been difficult for both of them. Their parents had been dead for years, and the relatives and friends they'd met after so long had been unrecognizable. The stern middle-aged women who'd said they were her sisters had nothing in common with the laughing children she'd left behind. For Costa it had been worse; he'd found one of his brothers dying, another a sickly old man, and three of his aging sisters swathed in widow's black.

After a few days, Eleni had grown accustomed to her adult sisters and to being back in Greece, but Costa had been on edge no matter what they did or who they saw. When he'd suggested she take her sisters on a holiday to Rhodes, she hadn't wanted to leave him, but he'd insisted, saying it would give him a chance to visit some of the people and places from his youth that would have no meaning for her. Whatever past he'd relived while she was gone had done nothing but bring him sorrow, and she'd always regretted leaving him alone that time.

"Can't you go faster?" Eleni said. Angela was always so careful.

"We'll be there in a minute, Mama."

Eleni smoothed down her hair. She had to look nice for Costa. "Why are you going this way?"

"He's not at the store, Mama." When Eleni saw they were turning into the entrance of the Miseracordia, her breath caught in her throat. She'd only been to the hospital to visit others, never for anyone in her family, except the grandchildren, but childbirth was different. Her sons were walking quickly toward the car. Why weren't they with their papa?

Paul held the car open and Tim helped her out. They huddled around her on the sidewalk in front of the entrance, but neither one spoke. Then she looked at their faces. She clutched at the lapels of her coat, pulling it even tighter around her throat. She knew what they couldn't tell her. "I want to see him."

""Mama, he's…"

"I know. I want to see him."

They led her to a room and she saw her husband lying on a cot, his head turned to one side, his mouth slightly open as if he was asleep. His tie had been pulled away, and his shirt collar unbuttoned. In their bedroom that morning, he'd held out two ties to Eleni, and she'd picked the grey striped one, teasing him about how distinguished he looked in his new light-grey summer suit. They never talked about how tired he seemed so much of the time, how haggard. He didn't look haggard any longer, lying as though asleep, the care finally gone from his face.

Eleni had never seen death before. She'd known it, but she'd never seen it. Her Stephano had died far away in a strange place. As for the baby, one day she was there, sick and crying, and the next she was gone. She used to think sometimes that if only she'd known some English she might have been able to find out where they'd taken her dead baby and where her son had been buried. But Costa had always said it wasn't necessary for her to know more than a few words of English to do the shopping. He looked after everything else, didn't he? He did. He had. He'd looked after her from the time she'd come to him as a bride of sixteen.

She reached a hand to him. Her sons tried to hold her back, but she pushed them away. His cheek was warm, soft; he'd shaved in the morning before Angela had driven him downtown. She'd had his usual cornflakes with sliced peaches ready for him in the kitchen when he'd come downstairs and a second cup of coffee for Eleni. He hadn't seemed tired at all. They'd talked about the dinner on Sunday and how he was looking forward to seeing the grandchildren. Eleni stroked his face, re-arranged his tie so that it was resting nicely on his shirt, leaned over and kissed his brow. Then she sat down beside him. She began to whisper. Soon strong hands lifted her and led her away.

After, at home, a glass of brandy in her hand, at her lips, the worried looks and hushed voices of family, friends, Priest, drew in closer and closer until she gasped out in suffocation. Even Matina, who'd been her first friend when she'd come to Canada, and was still the person she felt closest to, could say nothing to appease her. She ran out of the room, upstairs, threw off her clothes. Her old chenille bathrobe felt good. She started for the bathroom. Angela was waiting in the hall. "Let me help, Mama, please."

"I'm going to have a bath."

"Don't lock the door, Mama." Angela was clenching her hands, a habit she'd acquired lately.

"I'm going to have a bath!"

"In case you need anything." Angela never raised her voice from the whining tone. It was enough to drive a person crazy.

"Fine. I'll leave the door wide open so you can all come and watch!"

She slammed the door shut, locked it, and turned the faucets on full force. She poured a handful of bath salts into the water and tossed in some bubble bath capsules—gifts from tiny grandchildren at

Christmas—lowered herself into the water, let the tub fill, turned off the faucets, lay back and closed her eyes.

People came and went, walking up to the casket, crossing themselves, whispering words to Eleni sitting stiffly between her two sons in the dark-panelled room.

Costa was laid out in ivory satin inside a dark mahogany box, baskets of white lilies on either side. His hair was neatly combed. He had on his good black suit and black tie. She'd wanted to dress him herself, but her sons had said it wasn't allowed. And so strangers had tended to his final needs, the way they had for her son. She closed her eyes to the image of Stephano and tried to focus on Costa as she'd seen him earlier on that last day, helping him on with his tie, or at breakfast. She shouldn't have let him go out, he was tired, but she'd been thinking about her gardening, and so had paid him little attention. She liked her garden, liked the feel of the house when the men were gone, only she and Angela quietly going about their work, sometimes not talking for hours.

"We should go now, Mama." Paul, sombre, like his father, squeezed her hand. Tim, on the other side, had his arm linked through hers. Their wives sat across from them.

"Where's your sister?"

"Right here, Mama." Angela leaned across Tim.

"Go now, all of you. I want to talk to your Papa."

Ignoring the whispers, nudges, looks of concern, Eleni insisted on her time alone with her husband. Matina paused on her way out. "I'll be fine," Eleni assured her.

The Priest grasped her hands. "Think of your children now, *Kyría Eléni*," he said. "*Zoí se más*, life to the living."

The living, always the living. But the dead lingered on. She would have liked to have explained to the Priest that she'd never properly said her goodbyes to the dead—her parents in Greece, her infant child buried in an unknown cemetery right here in this city, her son somewhere in Europe—but he'd only murmur men's words of faith that meant nothing to her. It was to the Virgin she prayed nightly, the Virgin who offered her comfort.

"I'd like to stay here with Costa a little longer, *Páter*."

He left her finally to join the others. They would all wait for her so they could go to the house together. Once there, Paul and Tim would preside over bottles of liquor and their wives would be in the kitchen with Angela preparing coffee and filling plates with *paximádia*, the crisp biscuits always served at times like these. Eleni knew she was holding everyone up, but she couldn't leave, not yet. She needed to say a proper goodbye to Costa and this was their last chance to be alone.

She tried looking down at him, at the stiff, white figure in the casket, surrounded by floral tributes from family and friends, the prayers of the Priest still fresh in the air, but all Eleni could see was her son, her Stephano, dead, alone in a foreign land with no one to mourn him, no one to take flowers to his grave, no one to brush away the leaves in autumn, the snow in winter. "Not even a headstone," she whispered, "nothing to mark the place."

She started to cry. "It's not right. Those people who sent him to war should've been able to find him for us." She wiped her eyes with the back of her hand. "It's not right, Costa, not right." She fumbled in her pocket for a handkerchief, blew her nose. "Remember how tall he was, Costa, how handsome? He had your eyes, always smiling. Remember his letters, the way he described the places he visited? Such beautiful words, Costa. Like poems."

The room was getting very warm. Eleni took off her coat, pushed the veiled hat off her head. She searched in her purse for a clean handkerchief. "Forgive me, Costa. I shouldn't be telling you these things, upsetting you." She wiped her eyes, paused to collect her thoughts. "You were a good husband, Costa. That's what I started to say. My prayers go with you." She crossed herself. "Keep his soul safe, *Panagía*. Amen."

Eleni sat quietly, letting the silent tears flow, not knowing any more whether she was crying for a lost son or a dead husband. For a moment, she wished someone was with her, someone who would help her understand. But who? Even Matina could do nothing now. For all her kindness, she hadn't been able to help when Stephano had been taken from her, or the first tiny baby. Like everyone else, she'd hover, shush her when she'd try to speak, murmur condolences, talk about God's will. It was better this way, at least for a little while.

She sat for a long time; then, when she couldn't bear either the silence or her own thoughts any longer and was getting ready to face the others, a voice intruded. "Oh, Eleni, Eleni." Both the voice and the ample body that almost covered hers in an embrace were instantly recognizable.

Tasia was one of the oldest of what the children called the old-timers. Since her own husband had been dead for years and she'd had no children of her own, everyone else's life was Tasia's concern. Out of respect, no one excluded her from any occasion, be it wedding, christening, name-day celebration, even funeral.

"*Paidí mou*, my child," old Tasia cried. "My dear, my child," she crooned. "Such a loss. Such a fine man."

As wearisome as Tasia was even at the best of times, Eleni was relieved to see her now, for the old woman's lament would force Eleni to concentrate on mourning Costa instead of indulging her own confused thoughts.

"Ah," Tasia wailed. "Such a loss, such a terrible loss…a fine man…a good man." Eleni let herself drift away from the words, searching her cluttered mind for memories, happy memories, while Tasia droned on—"good man...well-loved...pillar of the community"—but all her memories were shrouded in pain. She tried to think about Costa and the way he'd been before he'd taken her to Greece and had begun looking ill, but that always took her to Stephano and the awful day the first telegram arrived.

She didn't want to think about Stephano any more today. It wasn't fair to Costa. She needed to grieve for Costa, pray for his soul. "So brave...at his age...honour his son." Tasia's words were slowly coming into focus. "Poor boy...taken so young...honour his son...brave man...travel so far...honour his son."

Eleni grabbed the old woman, stared her full in the face.

"My dear, you mustn't blame yourself," Tasia said. "It was right of him to go. Take comfort, my child, take comfort. Costa did the right thing."

"Right?" Eleni echoed.

"At his age, and ill, to travel so far to honour his son." Tasia was patting her hand, smiling through tears. "Stephano will rest now."

Eleni jerked away. "Leave me. Go now. Please. Go."

She heard the soft intake of breath, the abrupt closing of a door, and she was alone with the cruel words the old woman had thrown in her face. Unbelievable words. They horrified her. Costa had known where Stephano was; worse, he'd gone there without her. No. He wouldn't have done that. It was a mistake, Tasia was wrong, she'd misunderstood, was repeating malicious gossip.

Eleni shivered. She huddled back into her coat. Costa had never been a cruel man. He would not have denied her a final goodbye to her son. But the seed the old woman had planted wouldn't be rooted out, and Eleni's thoughts flew to the early years when their first baby had died and Costa had taken her away in the night. Perhaps Costa had been right to try and protect her then; she had been a very young bride and the baby a mere infant. But Stephano? She'd raised him to manhood. Surely Costa would've seen the difference!

Suddenly her children were surrounding her. "Tell me the truth," she cried. Pavlo bowed his head. "You can't look me in the face," she accused.

"Papa didn't want you to know," he mumbled.

Eleni grasped her son's lapels. "It's true? You mean it's true? Everyone knew? Even that old crone?" She clutched at him, gasping in anger. "Your Papa went to the grave? Did you go too? Did you? And me? What about me?

"Mama, don't." Tim was holding her arms. "It's not Paul's fault. Papa made us promise."

She pushed them both away. "Why?" she screamed at them. "Why?" She turned on her husband. "Why?" She tore her hands through her hair. "Why?"

"He didn't want to upset you," Paul said.

"Like you are now," Tim added.

"He wanted to spare you, Mama, to protect you," Paul added.

"Protect? Upset? How could you, Costa! How could you!" She screamed and cried and Matina came, tried to hold her, shush her, but she wouldn't be stopped. Propriety meant nothing to her now. Neither the words nor the feelings of others mattered any longer. Nothing mattered except this betrayal. She clutched Matina's arm. "Did you know?" she demanded.

Matina shook her head.

"I want to talk to your Papa," she cried to her sons.

"But, Mama..."

"Now."

"Mama, please..."

"Alone."

"Eleni..."

"I have to."

Whispers, nudges, looks of concern; all of them smugly thinking they knew what was best for her. Like Costa. But she'd have it out with him when the others were gone. She took the glass of water someone handed her, but refused the tiny pills probably meant to calm her down. She wouldn't be calm. She waved everyone away, shaking her head, refusing to speak or to listen to any of them, children, friends, relatives, even the Priest.

When they finally left, she crossed herself, begged forgiveness of the Virgin for what she was about to say, and turned on her husband.

"What I said before, about you being a good husband, I always thought you were, even when I didn't agree with everything you said but now I'm not so sure." Eleni's voice was low. "You gave me many things, Costa, a nice house, there were no other women—at least I don't think so—and you never gambled or came home drunk, so I should be grateful. But you did other things I didn't like and I never spoke out. Well, I'm going to speak now."

She paused, swallowed, took off her coat and laid it on the bench. Her hat was there too; when did it come off? She would have liked to have got rid of the black dress as well. She yearned to be back home, in her floral housedress, a scarf around her head, digging in the earth in her backyard, tending to her flowers, struggling with the eggplant. But she wasn't. She was here, and there were things that had to be said. She crossed herself once more. "Forgive me, *Panagía*," she said again.

She stood up, leaned her hands on the arms of the bench next to her. "You kept me in darkness, Costa. Yes, in darkness. I came to you a young girl and it was your duty to teach me about this new country. When I'd tell you I wanted to learn English, you'd say we were Greek, what did I need to know English for? So I could speak properly to people at stores when I went shopping, or to the neighbours, or read about what was happening in the world, that was why, Costa!"

"I don't know what's going on so much of the time, Costa, because you kept me in darkness. When the children were young, I didn't notice so much because we all spoke Greek, but once the boys grew up and went into business with you, it was different. After supper you'd send me into the kitchen with Angela so you could talk with your sons, and it was always English, English, English! Why, Costa? So I wouldn't know what you were talking about? And you wanted Angela like me. I was so proud, Costa, when you praised me to our daughter and told her you wanted her to grow up to be as wonderful a woman as her mother. Proud! That's how stupid I was. And what did Angela learn? All the things I knew, things any fool can do, cook, and clean and sew. And now our daughter's growing old, with no husband, heaven knows why, and no life outside the house because you wouldn't allow it. When she started growing up you said she mustn't go out with Canadian boys because they weren't like us and wouldn't respect her. Maybe you were right, I don't know; I would've felt strange with a *xéno* son-in-law, it's true. But, Costa, there weren't many Greek boys to choose from, and she's getting old now, what's to become of her?"

"Something else, Costa. Do you know how I feel when my little grandchildren come up to me, hold out an English book and say *"giagía* read" and I have to pretend I can't find my glasses, or they're broken or my head hurts."

"Even the little babies can read the language of this country, but not their ignorant *giagía*. Remember when those papers and medals and letters came about Stephano? You said they were expressions of condolence. They were more though, Costa. They told you where our son was, but you wouldn't tell me. Paul and Tim say this was to protect me. Was I so delicate, Costa? I gave birth to five children and never mind how many I lost that you never knew about. Did you know how hard that was, Costa, one baby after another, and no machines then for the piles of washing day after day? How could I have done all that if I was so weak? And what about crossing the ocean all by myself to come to you when I was only sixteen?"

"Did you never wonder how a delicate flower could carry loads of washing up and down stairs and go for days without sleep because of sick children? I was strong, Costa, couldn't you see how strong? But I was stupid, wasn't I? Yet you said you respected me. How could you respect a stupid woman who can't read and write like everyone else? And how can I respect you now, Costa, and keep your memory pure, when you've left me with this bitterness?"

Eleni turned and stood silently until she was composed again. "All those years I told myself I was lucky to have such a good husband," she said quietly, her back still to him. She took a deep breath. "I can forgive you for keeping me stupid and in darkness, Costa. I can even forgive you for taking my baby away from me, but may the Virgin excuse me, I will never, ever, forgive you for keeping the truth from me about my son."

She turned to him, her fists clenched by her sides. "You paid your final respects to him, Costa, but you would not allow me to do that. You did not have that right, Costa, do you hear? Do you hear me? *You did not have that right!*"

She slumped onto the bench, closed her eyes for a moment. "Forgive me, *Panagía*, she whispered, crossing herself, "but I had to tell him."

She picked up her coat, hat, gloves and purse, got up, and without looking toward the coffin, walked steadily out of the room.

Later that evening, after the others had done with their whispering and staring and hovering and had gone home, Eleni called Angela to sit on the couch with her.

"Did you know about Stephano?"

"No, Mama. Truly. No one said anything."

"Your Papa wanted to protect you as well, it seems," Eleni said, her mouth dry.

"It's all right, Mama. I understand."

"I raised you well, didn't I, daughter?"

Eleni pushed off her black shoes, loosened her belt. She removed the rings from her fingers, the diamond Costa had given her on their twenty-fifth wedding anniversary—it was wartime; Stephano had just left for overseas and Paul was in training school—and the cocktail ring for her fiftieth birthday two years ago, but she left the plain gold wedding band in its place. She lay her head on the back of the couch, soft blue brocade to pick up the blue in the Persian carpet Tim's wife had suggested when she'd asked for help in picking out fabric.

She had much to be thankful for. She ought, like a good woman, to dwell on that. For it seemed, from all she'd heard from her sons in the past few hours, anything their papa had done, or not done, had always been with her best interests at heart. And so he'd flown to visit Stephano's grave that week he'd sent her to Rhodes with her sisters. They'd all known, of course. And for a long time before that there had been a stone to mark her son's grave, and a foreign woman paid to keep it clean and covered in flowers. Her sons seemed to think she'd take comfort in the knowledge that another woman had been looking after her child's grave these many years. What strange creatures these men she'd been living with, how distorted their ideas.

Eleni looked over at her daughter. Something had to be done, at least for her. It wasn't clear to Eleni how, or what, but she knew she had to try. But first she needed one final gesture from her daughter.

"Would you go with me to visit your brother's grave?"

"Go to France?" Angela seemed surprised. "On our own?"

"Yes," Eleni said. "On our own."

1 What are your first impressions of Eleni as you listen to her thoughts while she tends the backyard garden? What appears to be her relationship to her husband, Costa, and the rest of her family?

2 "Visiting their homeland after so many years had been difficult for both of them."
(a) Why had it been so difficult visiting their homeland, Greece?
(b) Define "nostalgia" and apply it to this story and the whole concept of an adult who "can't go home again."

3 "For a moment, she wished someone was with her, someone who could help her understand."
(a) At her husband's funeral, what is it that Eleni wants to understand?
(b) What confusions and resentments have built up in her after all these years in Winnipeg?

4 What was Eleni's reaction to Tasia's revelation that Costa had known all along where Stephano had been buried? Why had Costa kept this information from his wife? Analyze thoroughly Costa's self-defined role as husband and father.

5 "I want to talk to your Papa...." In her final words to her dead husband, Eleni lays out her long-standing complaints. Outline those grievances and assess them. Are they applicable to other husband-wife relationships? Refer to the stories, "A Beautiful Woman" (page 140), and "The Letter" (page 189).

6 During the final segment of the story, how is Eleni beginning to break free from her "darkness"?

7 Write a sequel in which we hear Eleni's and Angela's thoughts as they visit Stephano's grave in France.

8 "...what did I need to know English for?" Write an argumentative paper on the value and power of being able to communicate effectively in English in Canada.

9 For further insights into Greek-North American families, read Katherine Alexander's *The Children of Byzantium* (also published under the name Katherine Vlassie), Nicholas Gage's *Eleni*, and Dennis Koromilas's *East Rockaway Station*.

THE POSE

ANWER KHAN

God knows what got into her head. She abruptly broke her stride and slipped into Shandar Cloth Store. Then she opened the door of the show window and, deftly, removing the lovely mannequin, stood herself in the plastic dummy's place and assumed its pose.

It was evening. The street was packed with people, but they were so preoccupied as they went their way that none of them noticed what she had just done.

Why did she do it? She probably didn't know that herself. True, she was something of a daredevil in her childhood. But now she was a grown young woman, a college student, smart, sophisticated, urbane. Even the most daring boys at the college got cold feet walking with her. What she'd just done, well, it just happened. It was entirely unpremeditated.

Standing in the show window she felt a strange sense of comfort wash upon her. She was now, after all, a part of this bustling marketplace. She could also look closely at the place, the whole of it, standing in just one spot, without having to move. Walking as one of the crowd or while shopping, she never felt herself a part of the life around her—the buoyant, strident life, full of vigour and excitement.

Her tense body gradually became unstrung, and an unprovoked smile came to her lips. She quite liked it—standing with one foot slightly forward, the hem of her sari going over her head and then dropping down to wrap itself around the joint of her right elbow. She looked positively ravishing. She could stand in her new posture forever, she thought, overcome by a sudden impulse, although her knees had already begun to ache from the pressure.

She was just considering easing up on her heels a little when her eyes caught sight of a peasant who suddenly cut through the crowd on the sidewalk and came over to the show window and began gawking at her with eyes at once full of lust and wonder. His eyes seemed to say: Incredible! These craftsmen can be so skilful! How they make statues that look like real people!

It was good the glass panel stood between them, otherwise the country bumpkin would certainly have ventured to touch her.

The peasant perhaps wanted to linger on for a while, but the scouring glances of the passersby forced him to move on. As soon as he had moved away, she relaxed her feet a little. Even shook them a bit. But now her lips began to feel dry. "Just a little while longer," she told her lips under her breath, "and then I'll take you to a restaurant and treat you to a glass of ice water, followed by a steaming cup of some finely brewed tea." Her thirst let up a bit and she slipped back into her former pose.

She certainly had no wish to exhibit herself like this to the pedestrians. Perhaps the thought had never even entered her mind. Rather, it pleased her to think that she was now a full participant in the teeming life around her. It was a strange feeling. She had never experienced it before.

"Oh God!"—the expression came from the lips of two college girls—"how lifelike!"

Their voices, travelling along the glass panels and filtering through the holes in the steel strips holding the frame, came upon her softly, as if from a great distance.

The two girls gawked at her with admiration as they exchanged a few words among themselves, while she looked at them with tenderness. She was happy. Incredibly happy. No one had looked at her so appreciatively before. At least not in her presence. Like a kind and caring queen receiving the adulation of her subjects, she sustained her regal pose until the girls had once again melted into the crowd and disappeared from view.

"Let's see who comes next?" she thought to herself.

Her feet had again started to protest. This time around, though, she sent them a warning, a rather stern one: Scoundrels, stay put! Can't you wait even a little? She wouldn't care a hoot about their protest, she decided.

She was still congratulating herself on her firmness when she caught sight of a cop who had just separated from the crowd and after taking a pinch of chewing tobacco from a box he held was rubbing it with his thumb. The moment he saw her, his hand stopped dead, his mouth fell open, and his eyes widened. She stared at the cop sweetly. The cop's eyelashes began to flap frantically; he rubbed the tobacco hastily and stuffing it between his lower lip and tooth practically stuck his eyes against the glass of the show window.

She was overcome by a powerful urge to laugh, but managed to stop herself with the greatest difficulty. Suddenly her feet began to itch uncontrollably. There was even a slight, involuntary tremble. But the cop thought it was a mere illusion, or the effect of the tobacco.

The cop stared at her for a long time. He would withdraw a little, then come back and inspect her closely. This went on for so long that she began to tire. Is the idiot going to leave the place at all?—she wondered. She was feeling uncomfortable. She knew she couldn't go on standing in that pose. All the same, she also knew that she was safe inside the show window. Where would she find such protection outside?

Thank God the cop finally decided to leave, and she drew a breath of relief, loosened her hands and feet, straightened up her tense back, indeed even massaged it a bit. Night was approaching and the crowd had thinned down to a few swift-footed pedestrians.

Soon it will grow dark, she thought. She'd better get out of here while there was still some light. The cloth store must be emptying out. Somebody might see her getting out of the show window. She'd have to be very careful…and fast. And yet there was such comfort inside the show window! How she wallowed in that pleasure! Another ten minutes? Why not…

She was still mulling over this when she spotted her girlfriend Sheyama on the sidewalk. Right away she sprang into her former pose and held her breath. Sheyama threw an inattentive look in her direction and because her thoughts were elsewhere, the danger, luckily, was averted. The thought that some of her acquaintances might spot her here had not occurred to her until Sheyama came along. This was precisely the time when her older brother returned from work, she recalled with horror. He's already suffering from a heart ailment. What if he saw the family's honour exposed so shamelessly out on the street? Wouldn't he drop dead?

Two boys appeared in her field of vision. They were returning from school, their satchels glued to their backs. They looked with zesty curiosity and pasted their faces—eyes and all—flat against the glass.

"Hey, she's real," the voice of one of the boys entered her ear faintly. Once again she wanted to laugh.

"Punk—it's plastic," the other boy said. "Whoever uses a live model?"

"But she looks so real. Seems she'd open her mouth and start speaking any moment."

"That's because of the evening. In proper light, you'd see."

"Hi!" the boy said as he winked at her mischievously.

The other one broke into a gale of laughter. Then he too waved at her and said "Bye!" and the two walked out of her field of vision.

As soon as they were gone, she suddenly began to laugh, but just as suddenly, became very nervous.

A young man was looking at her with perplexed eyes from across the glass. When their eyes met, he smiled. She smiled back, if only to hide her trepidation. She quickly grabbed the plastic dummy, and tried to install it, pretending to be one of the store attendants.

The youth's eyes were still riveted on her.

Arranging the sari around the mannequin she looked at the youth from the corner of her eye to see who he was looking at. His eyes lingered briefly at the plastic figure, then bounced off it and became glued to her.

She backed up, supremely confident, opened the door to the show window and walked out.

None of the store attendants saw her go out, or if they did, she was so agile and so fast that they couldn't figure out what had happened. The doorman didn't notice as he was busy talking to one of the sales clerks.

Confidently she strode away, briskly but lightly, happy and satisfied. As though she'd just unloaded the entire pestering weight of her body and soul. After she had walked away some distance, she turned around and looked back. The youth was still staring at her, perhaps with wonder.

She quickly turned down another street.

Translated by Muhammad Umar Memon

ENTRY POINTS

1. "God knows what got into her head."
   (a) What do *you* think got into the young woman's head? Do you approve of her actions? Explain.
   (b) Have you ever thought of doing something "entirely un-premeditated"? Why?

2. Why does she begin to feel "a strange sense of comfort" in her pose? Analyze her character and her background for clues.

3. What is the young woman's reaction to the following people who look or gawk at her in the window of the Shandar Cloth Store: the peasant, the two college girls, the policeman, Sheyama, the two school boys, the youth?

4 Why was the young woman so "happy and satisfied" at the end? Discuss with your group.

5 Read "The Image Maker" (page 7), and compare O'Brien, the political consultant, with the young woman in this story. How do their purposes compare? How do their "deceptions" compare? What do their actions serve to reveal about the people they deceive?

6 Stephen Leacock, one of Canada's earliest social satirists, once called humour "a recognition of disharmony" wherein the "accepted norm" of behaviour is juxtaposed with "abnormal," bizarre actions. How does this story illustrate Leacock's definition of humour? Be specific in your analysis. Apply this definition to the following stories: "There Was Once" (page 3), "The Ex-Magician from the Minhota Tavern" (page 17), "Borders" (page 77) and "Balthazar's Marvellous Afternoon" (page 254).

7 Imagine you are the young woman. Write in your diary your feelings about turning yourself into a mannequin that people stare at. Read "A Beautiful Woman" (page 140), and "From Behind the Veil" (page 151), to think through the paradox of appearance and reality, of surface and depth.

8 Write a fairy tale in which a princess transforms herself into something else. Does she live happily ever after?

9 For an interesting reversal of this story, look up the Greek myth of "Pygmalion" in which an artist's statue of a beautiful woman comes to life.

THINKING WITH THE HEART

FOR MARY DI MICHELE

*"I work from awkwardness. By that I mean I don't like to arrange
things. If I stand in front of something, instead of arranging it, I arrange
myself."*

Diane Arbus.

"The problem with you women is, you think with your hearts."

Policeman.

BRONWEN WALLACE

How else to say it
except that the body is a limit
I must learn to love,
that thought is no different from flesh
or the blue pulse that rivers my hands.
How else, except to permit myself
this heart and its seasons,
like the cycles of the moon
which never seem to get me anywhere
but back again, not out.

Thought should be linear.
That's what the policeman means
when I bring the woman to him,
what he has to offer for her bruises, the cut
over her eye: charge him or we can't help you.
He's seen it all before anyway. He knows
how the law changes, depending on what you think.
It used to be a man could beat his wife
if he had to; now, sometimes he can't
but she has to charge him
and nine times out of ten
these women who come in here

ready to get the bastard
will be back in a week or so
wanting to drop the whole thing
because they're back together,
which just means a lot of paperwork
and running around for nothing.
It drives him crazy, how a woman
can't make up her mind and stick to it,
get the guy out once and for all.
'Charge him,' he says, 'or we won't help.'

Out of her bed then, her house, her life,
but not her head, no, nor her children,
out from under her skin.
Not out of her heart, which goes on
in its slow, dark way, wanting
whatever it is hearts want
when they think like this;
a change in his, probably,
a way to hold what the heart can't
without breaking: how the man who beats her
is also the man she loves.

I wish I could show you
what a man's anger makes
of a woman's face,
or measure the days it takes
for her to emerge from a map of bruises
the colour of death. I wish there were words
that went deeper than pain *or* terror
for the place that woman's eyes can take you
when all you can hear
is the sound her heart makes
with what it knows of itself
and its web of blood.

But right now, the policeman's waiting
for the woman to decide.
That's how he thinks of it; choice
or how you can always get what you want
if you want it badly enough.
Everything else he ignores,
like the grip of his own heart's red
persistent warning that he too is fragile.
He thinks he thinks with his brain
as if it were safe up there
in its helmet of bone
away from all that messy business
of his stomach or his lungs.
And when he thinks like that
he loses himself forever.

But perhaps you think I'm being hard on him,
he's only doing his job after all,
only trying to help.
Or perhaps I'm making too much of the heart,
pear-shaped and muscular, a pump really,
when what you want is an explanation or a reason.
But how else can I say it?
Whatever it is you need
is what you must let go of now
to enter your own body
just as you'd enter the room where the woman sat
after it was all over,
hugging her knees to her chest,
holding herself as she'd hold her husband
or their children, for dear life,
feeling the arm's limit, bone and muscle,
like the heart's.
Whatever you hear then
crying through your own four rooms,
what you must name for yourself
before you can love anything at all.

1 The poet used to work in a centre for abused women and children in Kingston, Ontario. Through specific references, show how this poem reflects her experiences. What major techniques does she use to convey her frustration and anger?

2 "Thought should be linear."
(a) How does this line reflect the attitude of the policeman and by extension, the legal system in dealing with spousal abuse?
(b) How does the poet's attitude to the same situation differ? Refer to and analyze both the epigraphs and the first stanza.

3 Explain the title by, in part, referring to stanza three. Can everything be reduced to a simple "*choice*"? How does the policeman "lose(s) himself forever"? Is the poet being too "hard on him"—or are her points valid in terms of how many men might think? Discuss thoroughly with your group.

4 What must you "name for yourself/before you can love anything at all"? Is this a poem about love, or about power, rage, and control? Discuss.

5 (a) Explore your library's vertical files on spousal abuse and its causes. How have the laws changed to deal with this crime in a more effective manner? What more would you recommend to help decrease the incidence of violent abuse against women in our society? Make recommendations in your group and present them to the class.
(b) Write an editorial using your research and recommendations on ending violence against women.

6 Write a poem which deals with the conflict between the emotions (the heart) and thought (the brain). Use the same narrative techniques as Bronwen Wallace.

7 Love has been defined as "caring for someone else's well-being more than your own." Do you agree with this definition? Why or why not? What would your definition of "love" be? If possible, use relationships from the stories and poems in this collection to illustrate your answer. The examples you choose may be either positive or negative models.

THE ANSWER IS NO

NAGUIB MAHFOUZ

The important piece of news that the new headmaster had arrived spread through the school. She heard of it in the women teachers' common room as she was casting a final glance at the day's lessons. There was no getting away from joining the other teachers in congratulating him, and from shaking him by the hand too. A shudder passed through her body, but it was unavoidable.

"They speak highly of his ability," said a colleague of hers. "And they talk too of his strictness."

It had always been a possibility that might occur, and now it had. Her pretty face paled, and a staring look came to her wide black eyes.

When the time came, the teachers went in single file, decorously attired, to his open room. He stood behind his desk as he received the men and women. He was of medium height, with a tendency to portliness, and had a spherical face, hooked nose, and bulging eyes; the first thing that could be seen of him was a thick, puffed-up mustache, arched like a foam-laden wave. She advanced with her eyes fixed on his chest. Avoiding his gaze, she stretched out her hand. What was she to say? Just what the others had said? However, she kept silent, uttered not a word. What, she wondered, did his eyes express? His rough hand shook hers, and he said in a gruff voice, "Thanks." She turned elegantly and moved off.

She forgot her worries through her daily tasks, though she did not look in good shape. Several of the girls remarked, "Miss is in a bad mood." When she returned to her home at the beginning of the Pyramids Road, she changed her clothes and sat down to eat with her mother. "Everything all right?" inquired her mother, looking her in the face.

"Badran, Badran Badawi," she said briefly. "Do you remember him? He's been appointed our headmaster."

"Really!"

Then, after a moment of silence, she said, "It's of no importance at all—it's an old and long-forgotten story."

After eating, she took herself off to her study to rest for a while before correcting some exercise books. She had forgotten him completely. No, not completely. How could he be forgotten completely? When he had first come to give her a private lesson in mathematics, she was fourteen years of age. In fact not quite fourteen. He had been twenty-five years older, the same age as her father. She had said to her mother, "His appearance is a mess, but he explains things well." And her mother had said, "We're not concerned with what he looks like; what's important is how he explains things."

He was an amusing person, and she got on well with him and benefited from his knowledge. How, then, had it happened? In her innocence she had not noticed any change in his behavior to put her on her guard. Then one day he had been left on his own with her, her father having gone to her aunt's clinic. She had not the slightest doubts about a man she regarded as a second father. How, then, had it happened? Without love or desire on her part the thing had happened. She had asked in terror about what had occurred, and he had told her, "Don't be frightened or sad. Keep it to yourself and I'll come and propose to you the day you come of age."

And he had kept his promise and had come to ask for her hand. By then she had attained a degree of maturity that gave her an understanding of the dimensions of her tragic position. She had found that she had no love or respect for him and that he was as far as he could be from her dreams and from the ideas she had formed of what constituted an ideal and moral person. But what was to be done? Her father had passed away two years ago, and her mother had been taken aback by the forwardness of the man. However, she had said to her, "I know your attachment to your personal independence, so I leave the decision to you."

She had been conscious of the critical position she was in. She had either to accept or to close the door forever. It was the sort of situation that could force her into something she detested. She was the rich, beautiful girl, a byword in Abbasiyya for her nobility of character, and now here she was struggling helplessly in a well-sprung trap, while he looked down at her with rapacious eyes. Just as she had hated his strength, so too did she hate her own weakness. To have abused her innocence was one thing, but for him to have the upper hand now that she was fully in possession of her faculties was something else. He had said, "So here I am, making good my promise because I love you." He had also said, "I know of your love of teaching, and you will complete your studies at the College of Science."

She had felt such anger as she had never felt before. She had rejected coercion in the same way as she rejected ugliness. It had meant little to her to sacrifice marriage. She had welcomed being on her own, for solitude accompanied by self-respect was not loneliness. She had also guessed he was after her money. She had told her mother quite straightforwardly, "No," to which her mother had replied, "I am astonished you did not make this decision from the first moment."

The man had blocked her way outside and said, "How can you refuse? Don't you realize the outcome?" And she had replied with an asperity he had not expected, "For me any outcome is preferable to being married to you."

After finishing her studies, she had wanted something to do to fill her spare time, so she had worked as a teacher. Chances to marry had come time after time, but she had turned her back on them all.

"Does no one please you?" her mother asked her.

"I know what I'm doing," she had said gently.

"But time is going by."

"Let it go as it pleases, I am content."

Day by day she becomes older. She avoids love, fears it. With all her strength she hopes that life will pass calmly, peacefully, rather than happily. She goes on persuading herself that happiness is not confined to love and motherhood. Never has she regretted her firm decision. Who knows what the morrow holds? But she was certainly unhappy that he should again make his appearance in her life, that she would be dealing with him day after day, and that he would be making of the past a living and painful present.

Then, the first time he was alone with her in his room, he asked her, "How are you?"

She answered coldly, "I'm fine."

He hesitated slightly before inquiring, "Have you not ... I mean, did you get married?"

In the tone of someone intent on cutting short a conversation, she said, "I told you, I'm fine."

Translated by Denys Johnson-Davies

1 How does Mahfouz reveal to his readers that there is something unsettling the mind of the young female teacher? How does she try to cope with her anxiety?

2 "How could he be forgotten completely?"
   (a) How did she remember Badran Badawi, the new headmaster? Comment on his behaviour when she was fourteen years old.
   (b) How was the young girl victimized? Can such an incident ever be forgotten? Discuss thoroughly with your group with references to the story.

3 "Just as she had hated his strength, so too did she hate her own weakness."
   (a) Explain this sentence in your own words.
   (b) How does the young woman overcome her perceived weakness? To what extent is she successful?

4 Why do you think the woman feels she must "sacrifice marriage"?

5 "I told you, I'm fine."
   (a) Is she? To what extent is she happy?
   (b) Who has control and power at the end, the headmaster or the woman he once abused?

6 Although brief, this story deals in an extraordinary way with complex issues of child abuse and its long-term effects, of power, and of control of one's own life. Show, with specific examples from the text, how Mahfouz has handled these issues with subtlety and force.

7 Imagine you have survived Badawi's irresponsible and criminal behaviour. Write a diary item as (a) the young girl, and (b) the same girl as an older woman. What changes do you detect in yourself?

8 Compare the thoughts of the poem, "Thinking With the Heart" (page 210), with this story. How does the title, "The Answer Is No," speak to both pieces?

A MATTER OF BALANCE

W. D. VALGARDSON

He was sitting on a cedar log, resting, absentmindedly plucking pieces from its thick layer of moss, when he first saw them. They were standing on the narrow bridge above the waterfall. When they realized he had noticed them, they laughed, looked at each other, then turned their backs. In a moment, the short, dark-haired one turned around to stare at him again. His companion flicked a cigarette into the creek.

Bikers, he thought with a mixture of contempt and fear. He had seen others like them, often a dozen at a time, muscling their way along the road. These two had their hair chopped off just above the shoulders and, from where he sat, it looked greasy for it hung in tangled strands. They both had strips of red cloth tied around their heads. The dark-haired boy, he thought, then corrected himself, man, not boy, for he had to be in his middle twenties, was so short and stocky that he might have been formed from an old-fashioned beer keg. They both wore black leather vests, jeans, and heavy boots.

He was sorry that they were there but he considered their presence only a momentary annoyance. They had probably parked their bikes at the pull-off below the waterfall, walked up for god knows what reason—he could not imagine them being interested in the scenery—and would shortly leave again. He would be happy to see them go. He was still only able to work part time and had carefully arranged his schedule so that his Wednesdays were free. He didn't want anything to interfere with the one day he had completely to himself.

The tall blond man turned, leaned against the railing and stared up at Harold. He jabbed his companion with his elbow and laughed. Then he raised his right hand, pointed two fingers like he would a pistol, and pretended to shoot.

The action, childish as it was, unsettled Harold and he felt his stomach knot with anxiety. He wished that he had been on the other side of the bridge and could simply have picked up his pack and walked to his station wagon. The only way across the river, however, was the bridge and he had no desire to try to force his way past them. They reminded him of kids from his public school days who used to block the sidewalk, daring anyone to try to get by. He had been in grade two at the time and had not yet learned about fear. When he had attempted to ignore them and go around, they had shifted with him to the boulevard, then to the road and, finally, to the back lane. As his mother was washing off his scrapes and bruises and trying to get blood off his shirt, he had kept asking her why, why did they do it? Beyond saying that they were bad boys and that she would speak to the principal, she had no answers. Only later, when he was much older, had he understood that their anger was not personal and, so, could not be reasoned with.

Every Wednesday for the last six months, he had hiked to the end of this trail and then used his rope to lower himself to the river bank. Before the winter rains began and flooded the gorge, he wanted to do as much sniping as possible. The previous week, he had discovered a crack in the bedrock that looked promising but, before he had a chance to get out all the gravel, the day had started to fade and he had been forced to leave. The gorge was no place to spend the night. Even at noon, the light was filtered to a pale grey. He dressed warmly, wearing a cotton shirt, then a wool shirt and, finally, a wool jack-shirt; yet, within a few hours he was always shaking with cold. As strenuous as the panning was, it could not keep out the chill. The air was so damp that when he took a handful of rotting cedar and squeezed it, red water ran like blood between his fingers. On the tree trunks, hundreds of mushrooms grew. At first, because of their small size and dark grey colour, he thought they were slugs, but then he pried one loose with his fingernail and discovered its bright yellow gills.

Although he had been nowhere near the bottom of the crack, he had found a few flakes of gold which he meticulously picked out of his pan with tweezers. Panning in the provincial parks was illegal so he always went right to the end of the path, then worked his way along the river for another hundred yards. Recently, he had started taking as much as half-an-ounce of dust and small nuggets out of the river in a day and he wondered if someone had found out, but he immediately dismissed the idea. Only Conklin knew. When they met each Thursday he always showed Conklin his latest find. As far as his friends and colleagues were aware, he spent his days off hiking, getting himself back into shape after having been ill for over a year.

As he studied the two men below, he told himself he was letting his imagination run away with him again and to get it under control. There was no good in borrowing trouble. He stood up, swung his pack onto his shoulders and, being careful not to look like he was running away, resumed his hike.

From this point on, the trail was a series of switchbacks. If the two on the bridge were planning on following him and stealing his equipment or wallet, they would probably give up after a short distance and wait for easier prey. Unless they were in good condition, the steep climb would leave them gasping for breath.

Large cedars pressed close to the path, blocking out the light. Old man's beard hung from the branches. The ground was a tangle of sword fern, salal, and Oregon grape. In a bit of open space, an arbutus twisted toward the sun. Its bark, deep earth-red, hung in shreds. Here and there, the new pale green bark was visible. That was the way he felt, like a snake or an arbutus, shedding his old skin for a new, better one. The previous year, when nothing else had seemed to work, he had taken his pack and hiked from sunrise to sunset, exhausting himself so completely that he could not stay awake. The sniping, looking for gold in cracks, under rocks, among the roots of trees, had come when he had started to feel better.

At the next bend he stopped and hid behind a rotting stump. In a couple of minutes his pursuers—he told himself not to be foolish, not to be paranoid—appeared. They were walking surprisingly fast. If the trail had been even slightly less steep, they would have been running.

He wished there were a cutoff that would allow him to circle back. He could, he realized, use his equipment, if necessary, to lower himself to the river but to do so, he would need to gain enough of a lead to have time to untie and uncoil the rope, to set it around a tree, to climb down, and then to pull his rope down after him so that it could not be taken away or cut. He then would be faced with the problem of finding a route up. He had to be back by seven. It was the agreed upon time. Since their mother had been killed, the children became upset if he were even a few minutes late.

He looked at his watch. It was ten o'clock. It was a two-hour hike to the end of the trail, but he could hike out in an hour and a half. That did not leave him much time. First, he wanted to clean out the crack and, if possible, begin undercutting a large rock that sat in the centre of the river. Undercutting was dangerous. It would require that he move rocks and logs to divert the shallow water to either side of where he was going to work. Then he would need more logs to prop up the rock. He didn't want to get the work partly done and have half a ton of stone roll onto him. The nuggets that might be clustered around the base were worth some risk but there was no sense in taking more chances than necessary.

Ahead, through a gap in the trees, he saw the railway trestle. The two behind him would, he told himself, stop there. Hardly anyone went further. The trestle was an inexplicable focal point. Every weekend dozens of people hiked to it, then dared each other to cross over the gorge. Many, terrified of heights, balked after the first few steps and stood, rigid, unable to force themselves to go any further.

That, he reassured himself, was what those two were coming for. They would cross the trestle and scare each other by rough-housing like a couple of adolescents.

He had hoped, unreasonably, that there would be hikers or a railway crew on the tracks. Normally, it was a relief when there was no one there. Hikers were inclined to talk about their experiences and, in the past, he had been afraid that if he were frequently seen on the same trail his weekly visits might come to the attention of a park warden. To avoid that, he had deliberately arranged to come when the park was empty.

He did not stop but crossed over the tracks and entered the forest on the far side. The path dwindled to a narrow line of crushed ferns. The trees were shagged with wind-blown moss and deadfall was everywhere. It was old forest and, in all the times he had come, he had never seen a bird or animal. As a child he had dreamed of living in the forest. In his dreams, his hunting had always been rewarded with game. The discrepancy between what he had hoped for and reality still astounded him.

While he was able to see the railway tracks he stopped and waited. His legs had begun to tire and cramp. He stretched them, then kneaded his right calf with his thumb and forefinger. Always before he had valued the silence and the isolation. Now, however, as he watched the two bikers look up and down the roadbed then cross to the path, Harold felt the forest close around him like a trap.

He hurried away. Even as he fled he reassured himself that they had done nothing. Anyone was free to hike wherever he wanted. If he just stopped, they would catch up and pass him by without paying any attention to him.

He kept his eyes on the path. He had no intention of tripping over a vine or slipping on a log. His fear, he chided himself, was not rational. If a mountie suddenly appeared and asked him what was the matter, what could he say? That he hadn't liked the way they had looked at him earlier? That they had threatened him? And how was that, sir? He could hear the question. And the answer? The blond one pointed his finger at me. Any mountie would think him mad.

The moss was so thick that his feet made no sound. There was only the creak of his pack, the harsh sound of his breathing. He would, he decided, abandon his plans, and when he got to the end of the granite ridge that ran along on his left, he would double back through the narrow pass on its far side. People don't assault other people without good reason, he told himself, but it did no good. His panic fluttered like dry leaves in a rising wind.

He wished that he had brought a hunting knife. It would have made him feel better to have had a weapon. His mind scurried over the contents of the pack as he tried to determine what he could use in a fight. The one possibility was his rack of chock nuts. It wasn't much. A dozen aluminum wedges, even clipped together on a nylon sling, would not be very effective.

As he came to the end of the ridge he turned abruptly to the left. The pass was nearly level and, unlike the area around it, contained only a few, scattered trees. There were, he remembered, circles of stone where people had made campfires. One day he had poled about and discovered used condoms, some plastic sandwich bags, and four or five beer bottles. A broken beer bottle, he thought, would serve as a weapon. He was just beginning to search for one when he saw a movement at the far end of the pass.

He became absolutely still. He felt so weak that he thought he was going to fall down. He craned his neck for a better look. If there were two of them, he could circle back the other way. In a moment, he realized that there was only one. That meant the other was on the path he had just left. He spun on his heel and ran back to the fork. No more than a quarter of a mile away the path ended. At that point, there was nothing to do but return the way he had come or descend to the river. In either case, he was trapped. His mouth, he realized, was so dry he could not swallow.

Behind him, he heard someone ask a question that sounded like "Where did he go?" and a muffled reply but he could not be sure of the words. The ground was nearly level. He was running when he burst out onto an area where the rock fell from the side of the trail like a frozen set of rapids. There were few places here for trees to root. Leaves and pine needles were swept from the pale green lichen by the winter rains. Rather than continue to what he knew was a dead end, he clambered down the slope. He had not explored this area. In the back of his mind was the hope that the rough rock continued all the way to the river. By the time they found out he was no longer on the path, he could have climbed the other cliff. All at once, he stopped. The rough, black rock turned into sixty feet of smooth slab.

There was no time to go back. He glanced over his shoulder, then at the slab. It was, he realized, deceptive. It angled down toward the river then stopped at a ragged edge. No steeper than a roof at the outset, it curved just enough that every few feet the angle increased. Patches of lichen and the smooth texture of the stone guaranteed that anyone who ventured out on it would be engaged in a test of balance.

There was a chance, because of his friction boots, that he could work his way onto the steepest part of the slope. If the two behind him were not pursuing him, they would pass by and he would never see them again. If they were, for whatever reason, meaning him some harm, they would have great difficulty reaching him.

Quickly, he unzipped the right hand pocket of his pack and pulled out a section of three-millimetre rope. He tied a figure eight knot in both ends, wrapped the rope around his left hand, then crept down to a small evergreen. Ten feet to the right, in a completely exposed area, there was a gnarled bush. Here and there, stunted trees, their trunks nearly as hard as the rock itself, protruded from cracks.

There was little room for error. If he began to slide, it would be difficult to stop before he went over the edge. At this part of the river, the fall would not be great, but height would not make any difference. Even a twenty-foot fall onto the scattered boulders of the river bed would certainly be fatal. He leaned out, brushed away some dust that had collected on the rock, then took his first step.

Above him someone whistled sharply. It startled him but he kept his eyes fixed on the surface of the rock. He fitted the toe of his boot onto a small nubbin, then his other toe onto a seam of cracked quartz. The greatest danger was that, for even a split second, he would allow himself to be distracted. For his next move, he chose a pebbled area no bigger than a silver dollar. From there, he moved to a depression that was only noticeable because of its slight shadow. He had crossed more difficult areas than this but always with the security of a harness and rope and a belayer he could trust. A fall in those circumstances meant no more than some scraped skin and injured pride.

When he was within two feet of the bush he felt a nearly overwhelming urge to lunge forward. He forced himself to stay where he was. On the rock there could be no impetuous moves. Patience, above all else, was to be valued. There seemed to be no place for him to put his foot. He scanned the surface. Just below him there was a hairline crack. If he pressed down hard on it, it would hold him long enough for him to step to the side and up and catch hold of the bush.

Slowly, he pirouetted on his left foot, then brought his right foot behind him. He took a deep breath, forced the air out of his lungs, then in one fluid movement, stepped down, up and across. Even as his hand grasped the wooded stem, he felt his feet begin to slide.

While he unwrapped the three-millimetre rope from his arm, he sat with his legs on either side of the stem. He fitted a loop of rope around an exposed root, then slipped the second loop around his wrist. Unless the root gave way, the most he was going to fall was a couple of feet.

Only then did he allow himself to look back. There was still no sign of anyone. The area of tumbled rock ran on for a fair distance and, he realized, would take awhile to search. Realizing this, he cursed himself for not taking a chance and running back the way he had come.

He hooked his pack to the bush, took out the sling with the hardware on it, then eased himself out onto the steepest section of slab he could reach. Here he crouched, with his back to the trail, his hands splayed against the rock.

There was a sharp whistle above him. It was immediately answered from some distance back toward the trestle. With that, he realized that they had split up. One had blocked the trail while the other had done the searching.

He looked back again. Thirty feet behind him was the dark-haired biker. His blond companion was swinging down from the left. Both of them, Harold could see, were tired. He had, he thought with a distant kind of pleasure, given them a good run for their money. If they had been carrying packs, he would have outdistanced them.

They both stopped at the rough edge, some ten feet apart, looked at each other and smirked.

"Did you want something?" he asked. He had meant to make it a casual question, even offhand, as though he had no idea they had followed him, but panic sharpened his voice.

They both laughed as if at a joke.

"What do you want?" He was no longer sure that what he had planned would work. The blond-haired man had a small leather purse attached to his belt. He unsnapped it and took out a bone-handled clasp knife. He pried out a wide blade.

"Are you crazy?" Harold cried. "What's the matter with you? I don't even know you."

They both grinned foolishly and studied their boots. They looked, he thought wildly, like two little boys caught in the middle of a practical joke.

Panic made him feel like he was going to throw up. "Are you nuts?" he shouted. "Are you crazy or something?"

Their answer was to start down the slab, one on each side of him. Their first steps were confident, easy. The surface of the rock was granular and bare at the edge and provided plenty of friction. He could see that neither was experienced. They both came down sideways, leaning into the rock, one hand pressed to the surface. He gripped the nylon sling in his right hand and concentrated on keeping his balance.

The dark-haired one was closest. He was coming down between the tree and the shrub, taking little steps, moving his left foot down, then his right foot, then his left, dangerously pressing all his weight onto the edge of his boot and, even more dangerously, leaning backwards, throwing off his centre of balance. Suddenly, a piece of lichen peeled away and his left foot slid out from under him. Instead of responding by bending out from the rock and pressing down with his toes, he panicked. He was sliding faster and faster. His body was rigid, his face contorted with fear, his eyes, instead of searching for a place he could stop his slide, were desperately fixed on the safe area he had just left behind. He made no sound. When he was finally even with Harold, he reached out his hand as though expecting it to be taken. There was,

Harold saw, on the back of the hand, a tattoo of a heart pierced by a knife. A red and blue snake wound up the arm and disappeared beneath the sleeve. It was only by luck that his one foot struck a piece of root and he stopped. He was no more than a foot from the edge.

The blond man had come at an angle, picking his way along by fitting his knife blade into a crack. Just before his companion had lost control, the blond man had started to work his way across an area where there were no cracks. He seemed frozen into place.

"Why?" Harold shouted at him.

The sound seemed to wake the blond man from a stupor. He turned his head slowly to look at Harold. He squinted and formed his mouth into a small circle, then drew his chin down and ran his tongue along his lower lip. For a moment, Harold thought the biker was going to turn and leave.

"Get me out of here," his companion cried. Fear made his voice seem as young as a child's.

The blond man shook his head, then half-snarled, stood up, and tried to walk across the intervening space. It was as though momentum and will held him upright; then Harold swung the nylon sling over his head, lunged forward, and struck his opponent on the upper arm. The blow was not powerful and, normally, it would have been swept aside. But there, as they both teetered on the steep surface, it was enough to knock them both off balance.

As the blond man skidded down the rock, he jabbed at it with his knife, trying to find an opening. Six feet from the edge, he managed to drive the blade into a crack. The knife held. He jammed the tips of his fingers into the crack.

Harold had slipped, fallen, then been caught by the rope around his wrist. He pulled himself back to the shrub and knelt with his knee against the stem.

"Help us up," the dark-haired man begged. He looked like he was on the verge of weeping.

Harold loosened the rope, then untied it. Carefully, giving his entire attention to the task, he retraced his original route. Once at the evergreen, he knew he was safe. His sides were soaked with sweat and he could smell his own fear, bitter as stale tobacco. The two men never stopped watching him.

When Harold reached the top of the slab, the blond man called, in a plaintive voice, "For God's sake, don't leave us here."

Fear had softened their eyes and mouths but he knew it was only temporary. If he drew them to safety, they would return to what they had been.

"Pull us up," the dark-haired man whined. His red head-band had come off and was tangled in his hair.

Around them, the forest was silent. Not a bird called, not an animal moved. The moss that covered the rock and soil, the moss that clung thickly to the tree trunks, the moss that hung in long strands from the branches, deadened everything, muted it, until there were no sharp lines, no certainties. The silence pressed upon them. Harold had, for a moment, a mad image of all three of them staying exactly as they were, growing slowly covered in moss and small ferns until they were indistinguishable from the logs and rocks except for their glittering eyes.

"Tell somebody about us," the dark-haired man asked.

The words tugged at him like little, black hooks. He looked down. Their faces were bleached white with fear. He could tell someone, a park warden, perhaps, but then what would happen? If he had been certain they would be sent to prison he might have dared tell somebody, but he knew that would not happen. If charges were laid he would have to testify. They would discover his name and address. And, from then on, he would live in fear. Afraid to leave his house. Afraid to go to sleep at night. Afraid for his children. And what if they denied everything, turned it all around? He had the necessary equipment to rescue them and had refused. What if one of them had fallen by the time someone came? He could be charged with manslaughter and the children would be left without mother or father. No matter how he tried to keep Conklin out of it, he would become involved. Harold knew how people thought. His short stay in hospital for depression, his weekly visits to a psychiatrist to siphon off pain and, automatically, he was crazy.

"You bastard," the blond man screamed. "You bastard. Get us out of here." He kept shifting his feet about, trying to find a purchase where there was none. "If you don't, our friends will come. They'll get us out. Then we'll start looking for you. There's thousands of us. We'll find you."

The screaming startled him for a moment but then he thought about how soon the little warmth from the sun would disappear, of how the fog would drift down with the darkness, of how the cold would creep into everything, of how few people came this way.

"No," he said. He wondered if his wife had screamed like that. Six of her fingernails had been broken. *Unto the third generation*, Conklin had said. His children and his grandchildren, should he have any, would feel the effects. Alone on a dark parking lot, desperately fighting for her life, and he had been sitting in his study, reading. "Help never comes when it is needed most."

Then with real regret for the way things were but which couldn't be changed, he hefted his pack so that it settled firmly between his shoulders and returned the way he had come.

1 How does Valgardson build an atmosphere of tension and fear in the opening four paragraphs? Be specific.

2 "...he felt his stomach knot with anxiety."
(a) If nothing has yet happened, why does Harold feel this way? Look closely at the brief flashback to his childhood.
(b) "...why did they do it?" How did Harold's mother respond to his question? How would Harold himself answer this question later in life?
(c) Why do you think people engage in unprovoked violence against strangers? What is the implication about certain people's nature? Discuss with your group.

3 Discuss the following questions with your group:
(a) Is this kind of unprovoked violence against strangers more of a problem in North America than elsewhere? Investigate and study crime statistics and information from other countries to see how Canada compares.
(b) What do you think is the prevailing attitude within Canadian society toward violence? What does this attitude reveal about our culture? In your response, refer to the popular media (movies, television, music videos, computer games) and their uses of violence. How have your school and community taken action against violence?

4 This story forces Harold and, by extension, the reader to make a very difficult decision in which matters of conscience and pragmatic considerations come into conflict with each other. What would you have done in similar circumstances? Is it true, as Harold claims, that some things can't be changed?

5 Did your opinion of Harold, and his decision change after you read his description of his wife's death in the second last paragraph?

6 As Harold, write in your journal your reflections on the day's events in the woods. Do you have any regrets about your actions?

7 For more insights into violence by males against other males, and its ultimate effects, read the following novels: William Golding's *Lord of the Flies*, William Butler's *The Butterfly Revolution*, John Knowle's *A Separate Peace*, and Robert Cormier's *The Chocolate War*. For further comparisons examining the effects of bullies on their victims, read Gregory Clarke's "The Bully" and James Reaney's "The Bully."

THE NONREVOLUTIONARIES

YU-WOL CHONG-NYON

Revolution, counterrevolution, nonrevolution.

The revolutionaries are executed by the counter-revolutionaries and the counterrevolutionaries by the revolutionaries.

The nonrevolutionaries are sometimes taken for revolutionaries and executed by the counterrevolutionaries, sometimes taken for counterrevolutionaries and executed by either the revolutionaries or the counterrevolutionaries for no apparent reason at all.

—Lu Hsun (1881–1936)
Translated from Chinese by Chi-chen Wang

Cursed be the men of the East. Cursed be the men of the West. Cursed be those who have left my beloved homeland bleeding and torn.

They banged on the doors. They hammered at the walls. Out! *Out!* Everybody out! Everybody to the playfield.

With fear and with trembling we all got up, we got up out of our blankets into the chilly dawn. My father and my mother, my sisters and my brother. Out. *Out.* The shouting and the hammering continued. Out to the playfield.

"What about Ok-Sun?" my mother said to my father, pointing to me. "They don't know she's here. Maybe she should hide?"

"No, no," said my father. "They'll surely find her."

"But why? If we keep her hidden in the back, no one will see her."

"They will, they will. They're breaking in without warning. Only the night before they broke into twelve houses in our district. In the middle of the night, at two and three in the morning. They banged at the doors and pushed their way in, stamped into the houses with their muddy boots on, and dragged the men away."

"With their boots on!" My mother was silent for a moment, shocked at this revelation of incredible boorishness. The poorest rag-picker, the most unlearned peasant, would never dream of entering another's home without removing his footwear.

But she returned to the argument. "I'm sure we can hide her safely—"

"No! No!" my father again protested. "Too dangerous. Better she go with all of us."

"But—"

But there was no time to argue. Out! *Out!* The shouting and the banging went on. They were still there, rounding up every man, woman, and child. Out I went, too, with my sisters and brother, my father and mother, out to the playfield.

I had returned home only a month ago. My year's scholarship had ended, and I was coming back to bring the wisdom of the West to my "underdeveloped" homeland. The boat had arrived at Seoul a day earlier than expected, but late at night. When I had reached home after midnight, none of the neighbours had seen me come. My father, glad as he and all the family were to see me, had said, "Enough. We'll go to bed and talk in the morning. She must be tired."

Tired I was, tired of the long, long voyage, still ill-adjusted to the many-houred change in time, so tired that I developed a fever of exhaustion that night. It was as though I had been holding it in until I could get back to my own bed before letting it go. For weeks I lay there sick.

It was at the beginning of my illness that the armies suddenly and without warning swarmed down from the north, blasting their way through my homeland, leaving us overnight under a strange regime, ruled by men of our own nation, but men warped and twisted by their training in a foreign land, by the rule of an oppressive hand, of cruel and unfeeling heart and mind.

In a faraway country on the other side of the globe, the President of the United States, the Prime Minister of the His Majesty's Government, and the chairman of the Supreme Soviet, accompanied by their Chiefs of Staff and other experts on human welfare, had met. The map had glistened brightly before them with greens and reds and yellows and blues.

The fate of the world was decided. Here a cut, there a snip, and here a line. "For purposes of military convenience," the history books say, my beloved homeland was cut in two. Our minds and hearts, our families and lives, were cut into shreds.

My beloved homeland! Will your rice and your wine ever taste the same again? Will your flutes and your harps ever sound the same again?

We were at the playfield once more. The playfield of so many mixed memories, now to be the site of the most sharply etched memory of them all. The playfield where with the girls of my class I had spent so many happy hours of childhood and adolescence. The playfield which had been built during the days of our Japanese lords, the days where here as everywhere in Korea we were taught to speak, write, and think only in a foreign tongue, when a phrase spoken in our mother tongue in a public place brought a slap on the face from the lords or their Korean vassals. The playfield where my father with all the other fathers had had to go so often to prostrate himself before the Shinto shrines. The playfield where our masters revealed a change of heart to us, where they suddenly called us brothers, members of the same race, fruit of the same cultural heritage, and "invited" our young men to join their armies to fight for the glory of our "common primordial ancestors." Then we knew that the war was truly going badly for them, that their men were dying.

The playfield! We waited in the chilly dawn for our new lords to guide us. We were there by the thousand, fathers and mothers, children and elders. I saw many neighbours I hadn't seen for well over a year, but they were too preoccupied to be surprised at my sudden reappearance. We waited in the chilly dawn for our new lords to guide us.

They came. They came with their heavy boots and their heavy rifles. They came dragging twelve men behind them. Twelve men we all knew. Twelve men we had grown up with.

The men with the boots and the rifles distributed themselves among the crowd. A hundred men or more. A man here, a man there. Everyone felt the alien presence close to his skin, everyone felt the gnawing cancer digging into his soul.

Their leader climbed up on the platform and slowly turned his eyes over us, at the sea of faces all around him. A signal, and one the twelve men was set up next to him, one of the twelve men we knew. He was a clerk in our municipal office, a man as inoffensive as he was inefficient, a man who did his insignificant work as well as his limited abilities permitted him, a man whose main interest in his job consisted in receiving his pay regularly and going home to his family at the end of each day.

I had noticed his wife and children in the crowd.

"Comrades!" bellowed the leader. "Behold a traitor to the people. As you all know, the man you see before you has for years held in his hands the lives and well-being of all the people of this community. It is he who handles the rationing records, he who can decide how much rice you are to receive and when you are going to get it. Comrades, an investigation of his records has revealed gross mismanagement of the rationing system of our community. When this treacherous criminal was directed to mend his ways, he offered nothing but resistance and reactionary proposals. For ten days now he has deliberately and malevolently sabotaged every effort on our part to establish the system of food distribution in this community on a rational and an honest basis. Comrades," he cried out again to the crowd, "what shall we do with this traitor?"

"Kill him!" The hundred men who had distributed themselves among the crowd had raised their fists and roared out this response with a single voice: *"Kill him!"*

The leader on the platform nodded in approval. "Thank you, comrades. That is indeed the only proper treatment for traitors."

He took his heavy pistol out of its holster, held it against the man's temple, and pulled the trigger. The clerk slumped to the boards of the platform. The crowd gasped.

"Death to traitors!" roared the hundred men. The man's blood trickled through the cracks between the boards and stained the soil of the playfield.

Another man was hoisted up onto the platform to take his place.

"Comrades," again cried the leader, "behold a traitor to the people...."

An excited murmur went through the crowd as we recognized the man. I heard my brother whisper to my father, "Daddy! Isn't he the leader of the Communists?"

"Yes!"

"Then why?"

"Three kinds—Communists who've been in South Korea all the time; those trained in Russia and China; those trained in North Korea since the partition. They're fighting among themselves already."

The leader had finished his charges. Again he cried to the crowd: "Comrades, what shall we do with this traitor?"

"Kill him!" the hundred shouted as before.

But this time the leader looked displeased. "Comrades, I ask you what to do with a traitor and there is hardly any response! Comrades, think it over well. Take your time and reflect on the matter. I will ask once again a minute from now."

The hundred men glared at us, swung around in their places, and looked us each in the eye in turn. "I wonder if there could be any traitors here among us," they said for all to hear.

Then again the leader turned to the crowd. "Comrades," he bellowed once more, "What shall we do with this traitor to the people?"

"Kill him!" roared the hundred.

"Kill him!" we cried with our lips.

The leader looked pleased. He again unholstered his pistol, pressed it to the man's head, and his blood joined that of the other, dripping down to the soil of the playfield.

Ten more times did the leader harangue us. Ten more times did we shudder as we cried aloud with our lips, *"Kill him!"* Ten more times did the blood of a Korean stain the soil of Korea.

We watched and we trembled as the chilly dawn unfolded into the chilly day.

> My beloved homeland!
> Will your rice and your wine
>   ever taste the same again?
> Will your flutes and your harps
>   ever sound the same again?
> Cursed be the men of the East.
>   Cursed be the men of the West.
> Cursed be those
>   who have left my beloved homeland
>   bleeding and torn.

Translated by the Author and Daniel L. Milton

ENTRY POINTS

1 The Korean War began on June 25, 1950, with a sudden attack by the North, supported by the U.S.S.R. and China, upon the South, supported by the United States and the United Nations.
   (a) How does the opening sequence personalize the larger national conflict?
   (b) Compare the atmosphere of tension and fear in the opening of this story with that created in W. D. Valgardson's "A Matter of Balance" (page 218). Which story's opening has a greater impact upon you? Explain your response.
   (c) Does the epigraph by Lu Hsun detract from or add to the impact of the opening? Explain. Compare the use of the epigraph in this story with Murilo Rubião's use in "The Ex-Magician from the Minhota Tavern" (page 17).

2 (a) What is the young narrator's view of her education in the West?
   (b) What is her view of the armies and men "from the north"? Elaborate fully.
   (c) What is her view of the way her country "was cut in two" by international powers in 1945? Refer to specific lines and note her use of exclamations and rhetorical questions.

3 Compare the narrator's memories of the "playfield" when she was a little girl with her observations of the present realities. Comment on the irony of the setting.

4 (a) Does Ok-Sun believe the municipal clerk is a traitor? Explain with specific references to the story. What might the communists' real reasons be for killing the "inoffensive" clerk?

(b) What is your reaction to the killing of the clerk? Discuss with your group the psychology of political terror that permeates this story. How would *you* react under similar circumstances?

5 (a) Why was the "leader of the Communists" executed? Refer back to the epigraph and explain the irony.

(b) Why does the crowd, including the narrator's family, go along with the leader and cry out for the execution?

(c) What would or could you do in similar circumstances? Discuss with your group.

6 Harold in "A Matter of Balance" (page 218) and Ok-Sun in this story both feel they have "no choice" in what they do. Do they have a choice? In what ways are their choices different?

7 On July 27, 1953, the civil war ended after an armistice was signed dividing Korea at the thirty-eighth parallel. Currently plans exist to unite the North and the South. Research the history of Korea in the library. Explore the vertical files to obtain information on today's plans for unification. Present a report to your class and relate your information to the story.

8 Relate and compare the use of irony and manipulation within a political context in this story with George Orwell's novels, *Animal Farm* and *1984*. In the same manner, refer also to "Lies" (page 1) and "The Image Maker" (page 7) in this anthology. On a more personal level, compare the techniques of intimidation and use of power in this story with those revealed in "Skipper" (page 28).

9 For filmic presentation of civil wars, view *The Killing Fields, Apocalypse Now, Glory,* or *Gone with the Wind*. Write a film review detailing your impressions.

10 You are Ok-Sun. Write a brief sequel to the story in which you articulate, the next day, your feelings of what happened on the "playfield." How do you feel after your "participation" in the executions?

11 Write a political speech in which you condemn injustice and political terrorism. Present your speech in a dramatic manner to the "crowd" in your classroom.

HOCKEY PLAYERS

AL PURDY

What they worry about most is injuries
        broken arms and legs and
fractured skulls opening so doctors
can see such bloody beautiful things almost
not quite happening in the bone rooms
                as they happen outside
And the referee?
                He's right there on the ice
not out of sight among the roaring blue gods
of a game played for passionate stockbrokers
children wearing business suits
and a nation of television agnostics
who never agree with the referee and applaud
when he falls flat on his face

            On a breakaway
the centreman carrying the puck
his wings trailing a little
            on both sides why
I've seen the aching glory of a resurrection
            in their eyes
            if they score
but crucifixion's agony to lose
—the game?

We sit up there in the blues
bored and sleepy and suddenly three men
break down the ice in roaring feverish speed and
we stand up in our seats with such a rapid pouring
of delight exploding out of self to join them why
their and our orgasm is the rocket stipend
for skating thru the smoky end boards out
of sight and climbing up the appalachian highlands
and racing breast to breast across laurentian barrens
over hudson's diamond bay and down the treeless tundra where
auroras are tubercular and awesome and
stopping isn't feasible or possible or lawful
but we have to and we have to
                                        laugh because we must and
stop to look at self and one another but
            our opponent's never geography
                                        or distance why

                it's men
              —just men?

And how do the players feel about it
this combination of ballet and murder?
For years a Canadian specific
to salve the anguish of inferiority
by being good at something the Americans aren't
And what's the essence of a game like this
which takes a ten year fragment of a man's life
replaced with love that lodges in his brain
          and substitutes for reason?
Besides the fear of injuries
is it the difficulty of ever really overtaking
a hard black rubber disc?
—Boys playing a boy's game in a permanent childhood
with a screaming coach who insists on winning
sports-writer-critics and the crowd gone mad?
—And the worrying wives wanting you to quit and
your aching body stretched on the rubbing table
thinking of money in owners' pockets that might be yours
the butt-slapping camaraderie and the self indulgence
of allowing yourself to be a hero and knowing
everything ends in a pot-belly

Out on the ice can all these things be forgotten
in swift and skilled delight of speed?
—roaring out the endboards out the city
streets and high up where laconic winds
whisper litanies for a fevered hockey player
Or racing breast to breast and never stopping
over rooftops of the world and all together
sing the song of winning all together
sing the song of money all together

          (and out in the suburbs
there's the six-year-old kid
whose reflexes were all wrong
who always fell down and hurt himself and cried
and never learned to skate
          with his friends)

1 This poem seems to want to elevate hockey to a myth-like status, revealing both its glories and its pain. Explore the poem with your group and set up a comparison chart indicating words and incidents that reflect this duality of hockey as seen by Al Purdy. Discuss the validity of Purdy's dualities and add to them.

2 To what degree is Purdy critical of the hockey players and of the spectators? To what degree is he critical of the violence that seems to surround the game of hockey? Do you agree that hockey is a "combination of ballet and murder"? Elaborate on your response.

3 Define "satire." Are there elements of satire in this poem? What is the poet's purpose?

4 What is the purpose of the final stanza? What does it add to the poem's vision?

5 Debate: "Hockey is institutionalized violence and, as such, its violent element should be banned."

6 Watch a game of hockey, making notes on the violent incidents in the game and the spectators' reactions to the violence. Share your observations and conclusions with your class.

7 "...a screaming coach who insists on winning...." Is winning everything? What is lost if winning is everything? Discuss with your class.

8 Write a poem about your favourite sport using the same techniques as Al Purdy: graphic descriptions, rhetorical questions, vivid juxtapositions, and personal commentary. Decide whether or not your poem will be serious or satirical in tone.

9 Think back to when you were a child. Who were your heroes? Did you ever fantasize about being a big-league athlete? Write a personal essay relating your childhood dreams.

10 Read Steven Scriver's *All-Star Poet* and Stan Rogers' song, "Flying," for further poets' insights into hockey. For a child's view of hockey, read Roch Carrier's classic short story, "The Hockey Sweater."

GOALIE

RUDY THAUBERGER

Nothing pleases him. Win or lose, he comes home angry, dragging his equipment bag up the driveway, sullen eyes staring down, seeing nothing, refusing to see. He throws the bag against the door. You hear him, fumbling with his keys, his hands sore, swollen and cold. He drops the keys. He kicks the door. You open it and he enters, glaring, not at you, not at the keys, but at everything, the bag, the walls, the house, the air, the sky.

His clothes are heavy with sweat. There are spots of blood on his jersey and on his pads. He moves past you, wordless, pulling his equipment inside, into the laundry room and then into the garage. You listen to him, tearing the equipment from the bag, throwing it. You hear the thump of heavy leather, the clatter of plastic, the heavy whisper of damp cloth. He leaves and you enter. The equipment is everywhere, scattered, draped over chairs, hung on hooks, thrown on the floor.

You imagine him on the ice: compact, alert, impossibly agile and quick. Then you stare at the equipment: helmet and throat protector, hockey pants, jersey, chest and arm protectors, athletic supporter, knee pads and leg pads, blocker, catching glove and skates. In the centre of the floor are three sticks, scattered, their broad blades chipped and worn. The clutter is deliberate, perhaps even necessary. His room is the same, pure chaos, clothes and magazines everywhere, spilling out of dresser drawers, into the closet. He says he knows where everything is. You imagine him on the ice, focused, intense, single-minded. You understand the need for clutter.

When he isn't playing, he hates the equipment. It's heavy and awkward and bulky. It smells. He avoids it, scorns it. It disgusts him. Before a game, he gathers it together on the floor and stares at it. He lays each piece out carefully, obsessively, growling and snarling at anyone who comes too close. His mother calls him a gladiator, a bullfighter. But you know the truth, that gathering the equipment is a ritual of hatred, that every piece represents, to him, a particular variety of pain.

There are black marks scattered on the white plastic on his skates. He treats them like scars, reminders of pain. His glove hand is always swollen. His chest, his knees and his biceps are always bruised. After a hard game, he can barely move. "Do you enjoy it?" you ask. "Do you enjoy the game at least? Do you like playing?" He shrugs. "I love it," he says.

Without the game, he's miserable. He spends his summers restless and morose, skating every morning, lifting weights at night. He juggles absent-mindedly; tennis balls, coins, apples, tossing them behind his back and under his leg, see-sawing two in one hand as he talks on the phone, bouncing them off walls and knees and feet. He plays golf and tennis with great fervor, but you suspect, underneath, he is indifferent to these games.

As fall approaches, you begin to find him in the basement, cleaning his skates, oiling his glove, taping his sticks. His hands move with precision and care. You sit with him and talk. He tells you stories. This save. That goal. Funny stories. He laughs. The funniest stories are about failure: the goal scored from centre ice, the goal scored on him by his own defenceman, the goal scored through a shattered stick. There is always a moral, the same moral every time. "You try your best and you lose."

He starts wearing his leg pads in September. Every evening, he wanders the house in them, wearing them with shorts and a T-shirt. He hops in them, does leg lifts and jumping jacks. He takes them off and sits on them, folding them into a squat pile to limber them up. He starts to shoot a tennis ball against the fence with his stick.

As practices begin, he comes home overwhelmed by despair. His skill is an illusion, a lie, a magic trick. Nothing you say reassures him. You're his father. Your praise is empty, invalid.

The injuries begin. Bruises. Sprains. His body betrays him. Too slow. Too clumsy. His ankles are weak, buckling under him. His muscles cramp. His nose bleeds. A nerve in his chest begins to knot and fray. No one understands. They believe he's invulnerable, the fans, his teammates. They stare at him blankly while he lies on the ice, white-blind, paralyzed, as his knee or his toe or his hand or his chest or his throat burns.

To be a goalie, you realize, is to be an adult too soon, to have too soon an intimate understanding of the inevitability of pain and failure. In the backyard, next to the garage, is an old garbage can filled with broken hockey sticks. The blades have shattered. The shafts are cracked. He keeps them all, adding a new one every two weeks. You imagine him, at the end of the season, burning them, purging his failure with a bonfire. But that doesn't happen. At the end of the season, he forgets them and you throw them away.

You watch him play. You sit in the stands with his mother, freezing, in an arena filled with echoes. He comes out without his helmet and stick, skating slowly around the rink. Others move around him deftly. He stares past them, disconnected, barely awake. They talk to him, call his name, hit his pads lightly with their sticks. He nods, smiles. You know he's had at least four cups of coffee. You've seen him, drinking, prowling the house frantically.

As the warm-up drills begin, he gets into the goal casually. Pucks fly over the ice, crashing into the boards, cluttering the net. He skates into the goal, pulling on his glove and blocker. He raps the posts with his stick. No one seems to notice, even when he starts deflecting shots. They come around to him slowly, firing easy shots at his pads. He scoops the pucks out of the net with his stick. He seems bored.

You shiver as you sit, watching him. You hardly speak. He ignores you. You think of the cost of his equipment. Sticks, forty dollars. Glove, one hundred and twenty. Leg pads, thirteen hundred dollars. The pads have patches. The glove is soft, the leather eaten away by his sweat.

The game begins, casually, without ceremony. The scoreboard lights up. The ice is cleared of pucks. Whistles blow. After the stillness of the face-off, you hardly notice the change, until you see him in goal, crouched over, staring.

You remember him in the backyard, six years old, standing in a ragged net, wearing a parka and a baseball glove, holding an ordinary hockey stick, sawed off at the top. The puck is a tennis ball. The ice is cement. He falls down every time you shoot, ignoring the ball, trying to look like the goalies on TV. You score, even when you don't want to. He's too busy play-acting. He smiles, laughs, and shouts.

You buy him a mask. He paints it. Yellow and black. Blue and white. Red and blue. It changes every month, as his heroes change. You make him a blocker out of cardboard and leg pads out of foam rubber. His mother makes him a chest protector. You play in the backyard, every evening, taking shot after shot, all winter.

It's hard to recall when you realize he's good. You come to a point where he starts to surprise you, snatching the ball out of the air with his glove, kicking it away with his shoe. You watch him one Saturday, playing with his friends. He humiliates them, stopping everything. They shout and curse. He comes in, frozen, tired and spellbound. "Did you see?" he says.

He learns to skate, moving off of the street and onto the ice. The pain begins. A shot to the shoulder paralyzes his arm for ten minutes. You buy him pads, protectors, thinking it will stop the pain. He begins to lose.

Game after game. Fast reflexes are no longer enough. He is suddenly alone, separate from you, miserable. Nothing you say helps. Keep trying. Stop. Concentrate. Hold your stick blade flat on the ice.

He begins to practise. He begins to realize that he is alone. You can't help him. His mother can't help him. That part of his life detaches from you, becoming independent, free. You fool yourself, going to his games, cheering, believing you're being supportive, refusing to understand that here, in the rink, you're irrelevant. When you're happy for him, he's angry. When you're sad for him, he's indifferent. He begins to collect trophies.

You watch the game, fascinated. You try to see it through his eyes. You watch him. His head moves rhythmically. His stick sweeps the ice and chops at it. When the shots come, he stands frozen in a crouch. Position is everything, he tells you. He moves, the movement so swift it seems to strike you physically. How does he do it? How? You don't see the puck, only his movement. Save or goal, it's all the same.

You try to see the game through his eyes, aware of everything, constantly alert. It's not enough to follow the puck. The position of the puck is old news. The game. You try to understand the game. You fail.

He seems unearthly, moving to cut down the angle, chopping the puck with his stick. Nothing is wasted. You can almost feel his mind at work, watching, calculating. Where does it come from, you wonder, this strange mind? You try to move with him, watching his eyes through his cage, and his hands. You remember the way he watches games on television, cross-legged, hands fluttering, eyes seeing everything.

Suddenly you succeed, or you think you do. Suddenly, you see the game, not as a series of events, but as a state, with every moment in time potentially a goal. Potentiality. Probability. These are words you think of afterwards. As you watch, there is only the game, pressing against you, soft now, then sharp, then rough, biting, shocking, burning, dull, cold. No players. Only forces, feelings, the white ice, the cold, the echo, all joined. A shot crashes into his helmet. He falls to his knees. You cry out.

He stands slowly, shaking his head, hacking at the ice furiously with his stick. They scored. You never noticed. Seeing the game is not enough. Feeling it is not enough. He wants more, to understand completely, to control. You look out at the ice. The game is chaos again.

He comes home, angry, limping up the driveway, victorious. You watch him, dragging his bag, sticks in his hand, leg pads over his shoulder. You wonder when it happened, when he became this sullen, driven young man. You hear whispers about scouts, rumours. Everyone adores him, adores his skill. But when you see his stiff, swollen hands, when he walks slowly into the kitchen in the mornings, every movement agony, you want to ask him why. Why does he do it? Why does he go on?

But you don't ask. Because you think you know the answer. You imagine him, looking at you and saying quietly, "What choice do I have? What else have I ever wanted to do?"

1 (a) What are your first impressions of the young goalie? Point to specific images and actions in the first four paragraphs.

(b) Why do you think that "Win or lose, he comes home angry"? Reread Al Purdy's "Hockey Players" (page 234).

(c) Compare his image at home with his image on the ice.

2 "Do you enjoy the game at least?...I love it...."

(a) Does he love hockey? In what way? Explore the goalie's attitude.

(b) Why is his father's praise and encouragement "empty, invalid"? Do you agree with his assessment? Discuss with your group.

(c) What are the realities of the goalie that the spectators don't see?

3 How does the father remember him as a six-year-old child? Compare this reminiscence to the image of the six-year-old in "Hockey Players." When does the sport become serious and less fun? Is winning everything?

4 When did he become "this sullen, driven man"? What does he want? Is he right: he has no choice, the process is inevitable?

5 Rethink the concepts of control and anger, explored elsewhere in this anthology, and apply them to this story. Do sports both control and create anger and tension? Research the incidence of sports and violence in other countries (for example, soccer in Europe). What are the causes of such incidents? Discuss with your group and share your findings with the class. Provide recommendations for controlling or decreasing such violence among both players and spectators.

6 Write a story about your favourite sport, about winning and losing, about control and chaos.

7 (a) Imagine you are the young goalie. Write a diary piece in which you express your "love" of hockey.

(b) Imagine you are the goalie's mother or father. Write a diary piece in which you express your concern for your son.

(c) Imagine you are a hockey scout for a major league team. Rate the goalie's skills and potential for big-league status.

8 Compare the father-son relationship of this story with the mother-daughter relationships revealed in "The Stolen Party" (page 49), "A Beautiful Woman" (page 140), and "Two Kinds" (page 178).

9 For more insights into the culture of hockey, read the following novels: Roy MacGregor's *The Last Season*, and Paul Quarrington's *King Leary* and *Logan in Overtime*. Write a book report commenting on the author's view of our unofficial national sport.

THE KID NOBODY COULD HANDLE

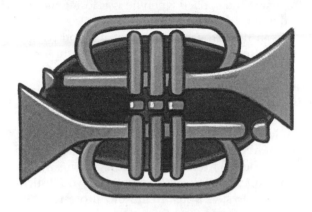

KURT VONNEGUT, JR.

It was seven-thirty in the morning. Waddling, clanking, muddy machines were tearing a hill to pieces behind a restaurant, and trucks were hauling the pieces away. Inside the restaurant, dishes rattled on their shelves. Tables quaked, and a very kind fat man with a headful of music looked down at the jiggling yolks of his breakfast eggs. His wife was visiting relatives out of town. He was on his own.

The kind fat man was George M. Helmholtz, a man of forty, head of the music department of Lincoln High School, and director of the band. Life had treated him well. Each year he dreamed the same big dream. He dreamed of leading as fine a band as there was on the face of the earth. And each year the dream came true.

It came true because Helmholtz was sure that a man couldn't have a better dream than his. Faced by this unnerving sureness, Kiwanians, Rotarians, and Lions paid for band uniforms that cost twice as much as their best suits, school administrators let Helmholtz raid the budget for expensive props, and youngsters played their hearts out for him. When youngsters had no talent, Helmholtz made them play on guts alone.

Everything was good about Helmholtz's life save his finances. He was so dazzled by his big dream that he was a child in the marketplace. Ten years before, he had sold the hill behind the restaurant to Bert Quinn, the restaurant owner, for one thousand dollars. It was now apparent, even to Helmholtz, that Helmholtz had been had.

Quinn sat down in the booth with the bandmaster. He was a bachelor, a small, dark, humorless man. He wasn't a well man. He couldn't sleep, he couldn't stop working, he couldn't smile warmly. He had only two moods: one suspicious and self-pitying, the other arrogant and boastful. The first mood applied when he was losing money. The second mood applied when he was making it.

Quinn was in the arrogant and boastful mood when he sat down with Helmholtz. He sucked whistlingly on a toothpick, and talked of vision—his own.

"I wonder how many eyes saw the hill before I did?" said Quinn. "Thousands and thousands, I'll bet—and not one saw what I saw. How many eyes?"

"Mine, at least," said Helmholtz. All the hill had meant to him was a panting climb, free blackberries, taxes, and a place for band picnics.

"You inherit the hill from your old man, and it's nothing but a pain in the neck to you," said Quinn. "So you figure you'll stick me with it."

"I didn't figure to stick you," Helmholtz protested. "The good Lord knows the price was more than fair."

"You say that now," said Quinn gleefully. "Sure, Helmholtz, you say that now. Now you see the shopping district's got to grow. Now you see what I saw."

"Yes," said Helmholtz. "Too late, too late." He looked around for some diversion, and saw a fifteen-year-old boy coming toward him, mopping the aisle between booths.

The boy was small but with tough, stringy muscles standing out on his neck and forearms. Childhood lingered in his features, but when he paused to rest, his fingers went hopefully to the silky beginnings of sideburns and a mustache. He mopped like a robot, jerkily, brainlessly, but took pains not to splash suds over the toes of his black boots.

"So what do I do when I get the hill?" said Quinn. "I tear it down, and it's like somebody pulled down a dam. All of a sudden everybody wants to build a store where the hill was."

"Um," said Helmholtz. He smiled genially at the boy. The boy looked through him without a twitch of recognition.

"We all got something," said Quinn. "You got music; I got vision." And he smiled, for it was perfectly clear to both where the money lay. "Think big!" said Quinn. "Dream Big! That's what vision is. Keep your eyes wider open than anybody else's."

"That boy," said Helmholtz, "I've seen him around school, but I never knew his name."

Quinn laughed cheerlessly. "Billy the Kid? The storm trooper? Rudolph Valentino? Flash Gordon?" He called the boy.... "Hey, Jim! Come here a minute."

Helmholtz was appalled to see that the boy's eyes were as expressionless as oysters.

"This is my brother-in-law's kid by another marriage—before he married my sister," said Quinn. "His name's Jim Donnini, and he's from the south side of Chicago, and he's very tough."

Jim Donnini's hands tightened on the mop handle.

"How do you do?" said Helmholtz.

"Hi," said Jim emptily.

"He's living with me now," said Quinn. "He's my baby now."

"You want a lift to school, Jim?"

"Yeah, he wants a lift to school," said Quinn. "See what you make of him. He won't talk to me." He turned to Jim. "Go on, kid, wash up and shave."

Robotlike, Jim marched away.

"Where are his parents?"

"His mother's dead. His old man married my sister, walked out on her, and stuck her with him. Then the court didn't like the way she was raising him, and put him in foster homes for a while. Then they decided to get him clear out of Chicago, so they stuck me with him." He shook his head. "Life's a funny thing, Helmholtz."

"Not very funny, sometimes," said Helmholtz. He pushed his eggs away.

"Like some whole new race of people coming up," said Quinn wonderingly. "Nothing like the kids we got around here. Those boots, the black jacket—and he won't talk. He won't run around with the other kids. Won't study. I don't think he can even read and write very good."

"Does he like music at all? Or drawing? Or animals?" said Helmholtz. "Does he collect anything?"

"You know what he likes?" said Quinn. "He likes to polish those boots—get off by himself and polish those boots. And when he's really in heaven is when he can get off by himself, spread comic books all around him on the floor, polish his boots, and watch television." He smiled ruefully. "Yeah, he had a collection too. And I took it away from him and threw it in the river."

"Threw it in the river?" said Helmholtz.

"Yeah," said Quinn. "Eight knives—some with blades as long as your hand."

Helmholtz paled. "Oh." A prickling sensation spread over the back of his neck. "This is a new problem at Lincoln High. I hardly know what to think about it." He swept spilled salt together in a neat little pile, just as he would have liked to sweep together his scattered thoughts. "It's a kind of sickness, isn't it? That's the way to look at it?"

"Sick?" said Quinn. He slapped the table. "You can say that again!" He tapped his chest. "And Doctor Quinn is just the man to give him what's good for what ails him."

"What's that?" said Helmholtz.

"No more talk about the poor little sick boy," said Quinn grimly. "That's all he's heard from the social workers and the juvenile court, and God knows who all. From now on, he's the no-good bum of a man. I'll ride his tail till he straightens up and flies right or winds up in the can for life. One way or the other."

"I see," said Helmholtz.

"Like listening to music?" said Helmholtz to Jim brightly, as they rode to school in Helmholtz's car.

Jim said nothing. He was stroking his mustache and sideburns, which he had not shaved off.

"Ever drum with the fingers or keep time with your feet?" said Helmholtz. He had noticed that Jim's boots were decorated with chains that had no function but to jingle as he walked.

Jim sighed with ennui.

"Or whistle?" said Helmholtz. "If you do any of those things, it's just like picking up the keys to a whole new world—a world as beautiful as any world can be."

Jim gave a soft Bronx cheer.

"There!" said Helmholtz. "You've illustrated the basic principle of the family of brass wind instruments. The glorious voice of every one of them starts with a buzz on the lips."

The seat springs of Helmholtz's old car creaked under Jim, as Jim shifted his weight. Helmholtz took this as a sign of interest, and he turned to smile in comradely fashion. But Jim had shifted his weight in order to get a cigarette from inside his tight leather jacket.

Helmholtz was too upset to comment at once. It was only at the end of the ride, as he turned into the teachers' parking lot, that he thought of something to say.

"Sometimes," said Helmholtz, "I get so lonely and disgusted, I don't see how I can stand it. I feel like doing all kinds of crazy things, just for the heck of it—things that might even be bad for me."

Jim blew a smoke ring expertly.

"And then!" said Helmholtz. He snapped his fingers and honked his horn. "And then, Jim, I remember I've got at least one tiny corner of the universe I can make just the way I want it! I can go to it and gloat over it until I'm brand-new and happy again."

"Aren't you the lucky one?" said Jim. He yawned.

"I am, for a fact," said Helmholtz. "My corner of the universe happens to be the air around my band. I can fill it with music. Mr. Beeler, in zoology, has his butterflies. Mr. Trottman, in physics, has his pendulum and tuning forks. Making sure everybody has a corner like that is about the biggest job we teachers have. I —"

The car door opened and slammed, and Jim was gone. Helmholtz stamped out Jim's cigarette and buried it under the gravel of the parking lot.

Helmholtz's first class of the morning was C Band, where beginners thumped and wheezed and tooted as best they could, and looked down the long, long, long road through B Band to A Band, the Lincoln High School Ten Square Band, the finest band in the world.

Helmholtz stepped onto the podium and raised his baton. "You are better than you think," he said. "A-one, a-two, a-three." Down came the baton.

C Band set out in its quest for beauty—set out like a rusty switch engine, with valves stuck, pipes clogged, unions leaking, bearings dry.

Helmholtz was still smiling at the end of the hour, because he'd heard in his mind the music as it was going to be someday. His throat was raw, for he had been singing with the band for the whole hour. He stepped into the hall for a drink from the fountain.

As he drank, he heard the jingling of chains. He looked up at Jim Donnini. Rivers of students flowed between classrooms, pausing in friendly eddies, flowing on again. Jim was alone. When he paused, it wasn't to greet anyone, but to polish the toes of his boots on his trousers legs. He had the air of a spy in a melodrama, missing nothing, liking nothing, looking forward to the great day when everything would be turned upside down.

"Hello, Jim," said Helmholtz. "Say I was just thinking about you. We've got a lot of clubs and teams that meet after school. And that's a good way to get to know a lot of people."

Jim measured Helmholtz carefully with his eyes. "Maybe I don't want to know a lot of people," he said. "Ever think of that?" He set his feet down hard to make his chains jingle as he walked away.

When Helmholtz returned to the podium for a rehearsal of B Band, there was a note waiting for him, calling him to a special faculty meeting.

The meeting was about vandalism.

Someone had broken into the school and wrecked the office of Mr. Crane, head of the English Department. The poor man's treasures— books, diplomas, snapshots of England, the beginnings of eleven novels—had been ripped and crumpled, mixed, dumped and trampled, and drenched with ink.

Helmholtz was sickened. He couldn't believe it. He couldn't bring himself to think about it. It didn't become real to him until late that night, in a dream. In the dream Helmholtz saw a boy with barracuda teeth, with claws like baling hooks. The monster climbed into a window of the high school and dropped to the floor of the band rehearsal room. The monster clawed to shreds the heads of the biggest drum in the state. Helmholtz woke up howling. There was nothing to do but dress and go to the school.

At two in the morning, Helmholtz caressed the drum heads in the band rehearsal room, with the night watchman looking on. He rolled the drum back and forth on its cart, and he turned the light inside on and off, on and off. The drum was unharmed. The night watchman left to make his rounds.

The band's treasure house was safe. With the contentment of a miser counting his money, Helmholtz fondled the rest of the instruments, one by one. And then he began to polish the sousaphones. As he polished, he could hear the great horns roaring, could see them flashing in the sunlight, with the Stars and Stripes and the banner of Lincoln High going before.

"Yump-yump, tiddle-tiddle, yump-yump, tiddle-tiddle!" sang Helmholtz happily. "Yump-yump-yump, ra-a-a-a-a, yump-yump, yump-yump—boom!"

As he paused to choose the next number for his imaginary band to play, he heard a furtive noise in the chemistry laboratory next door. Helmholtz sneaked into the hall, jerked open the laboratory door, and flashed on the lights. Jim Donnini had a bottle of acid in either hand. He was splashing acid over the periodic table of the elements, over the blackboards covered with formulas, over the bust of Lavoisier. The scene was the most repulsive thing Helmholtz could have looked upon.

Jim smiled with thin bravado.

"Get out," said Helmholtz.

"What're you gonna do?" said Jim.

"Clean up. Save what I can," said Helmholtz dazedly. He picked up a wad of cotton waste and began wiping up the acid.

"You gonna call the cops?" said Jim.

"I—I don't know," said Helmholtz. "No thoughts come. If I'd caught you hurting the bass drum, I think I would have killed you with a single blow. But I wouldn't have had any intelligent thoughts about what you were—what you thought you were doing."

"It's about time this place got set on its ear," said Jim.

"Is it?" said Helmholtz. "That must be so, if one of our students wants to murder it."

"What good is it?" said Jim.

"Not much good, I guess," said Helmholtz. "It's just the best thing human beings ever managed to do." He was helpless, talking to himself. He had a bag of tricks for making boys behave like men—tricks that played on boyish fears and dreams and loves. But here was a boy without fear, without dreams, without love.

"If you smashed up all the schools," said Helmholtz, "we wouldn't have any hope left."

"What hope?" said Jim.

"The hope that everybody will be glad he's alive," said Helmholtz. "Even you."

"That's a laugh," said Jim. "All I ever got out of this dump was a hard time. So what're you gonna do?"

"I have to do something, don't I?" said Helmholtz.

"I don't care what you do," said Jim.

"I know," said Helmholtz. "I know." He marched Jim into his tiny office off the band rehearsal room. He dialed the telephone number of the principal's home. Numbly, he waited for the bell to get the old man from his bed.

Jim dusted his boots with a rag.

Helmholtz suddenly dropped the telephone into its cradle before the principal could answer. "Isn't there anything you care about but ripping, hacking, bending, rending, smashing, bashing?" he cried. "Anything? Anything but those boots?"

"Go on! Call up whoever you're gonna call," said Jim.

Helmholtz opened a locker and took a trumpet from it. He thrust the trumpet into Jim's arms. "There!" he said, puffing with emotion. "There's my treasure. It's the dearest thing I own. I give it to you to smash. I won't move a muscle to stop you. You can have the added pleasure of watching my heart break while you do it."

Jim looked at him oddly. He laid down the trumpet.

"Go on!" said Helmholtz. "If the world has treated you so badly, it deserves to have the trumpet smashed!"

"I—" said Jim. Helmholtz grabbed his belt, put a foot behind him, and dumped him on the floor.

Helmholtz pulled Jim's boots off and threw them into a corner. "There!" said Helmholtz savagely. He jerked the boy to his feet again and thrust the trumpet into his arms once more.

Jim Donnini was barefoot now. He had lost his socks with his boots. The boy looked down. The feet that had once seemed big black clubs were narrow as chicken wings now—bony and blue, and not quite clean.

The boy shivered, then quaked. Each quake seemed to shake something loose inside, until, at last, there was no boy left. No boy at all. Jim's head lolled, as though he waited only for death.

Helmholtz was overwhelmed by remorse. He threw his arms around the boy. "Jim! Jim—listen to me, boy!"

Jim stopped quaking.

"You know what you've got there—the trumpet?" said Helmholtz. "You know what's special about it?"

Jim only sighed.

"It belonged to John Philip Sousa!" said Helmholtz. He rocked and shook Jim gently, trying to bring him back to life. "I'll trade it to you, Jim—for your boots. It's yours, Jim! John Philip Sousa's trumpet is yours! It's worth hundreds of dollars, Jim—thousands!"

Jim laid his head on Helmholtz's breast.

"It's better than boots, Jim," said Helmholtz. "You can learn to play it. You're somebody, Jim. You're the boy with John Philip Sousa's trumpet!"

Helmholtz released Jim slowly, sure the boy would topple. Jim didn't fall. He stood alone. The trumpet was still in his arms.

"I'll take you home, Jim," said Helmholtz. "Be a good boy and I won't say a word about tonight. Polish your trumpet, and learn to be a good boy."

"Can I have my boots?" said Jim dully.

"No," said Helmholtz. "I don't think they're good for you."

He drove Jim home. He opened the car windows and the air seemed to refresh the boy. He let him out at Quinn's restaurant. The soft pats of Jim's bare feet on the sidewalk echoed down the empty street. He climbed through a window, and into his bedroom behind the kitchen. And all was still.

The next morning the waddling clanking, muddy machines were making the vision of Bert Quinn come true. They were smoothing off the place where the hill had been behind the restaurant. They were making it as level as a billiard table.

Helmholtz sat in a booth again. Quinn joined him again. Jim mopped again. Jim kept his eyes down, refusing to notice Helmholtz. And he didn't seem to care when a surf of suds broke over the toes of his small and narrow brown Oxfords.

"Eating out two mornings in a row?" said Quinn. "Something wrong at home?"

"My wife's still out of town," said Helmholtz.

"While the cat's away—" said Quinn. He winked.

"When the cat's away," said Helmholtz, "this mouse gets lonesome."

Quinn leaned forward. "Is that what got you out of bed in the middle of the night, Helmholtz? Loneliness?" He jerked his head at Jim. "Kid! Go get Mr. Helmholtz his horn."

Jim raised his head, and Helmholtz saw that his eyes were oyster-like again. He marched away to get the trumpet.

Quinn now showed that he was excited and angry. "You take away his boots and give him a horn, and I'm not supposed to get curious?" he said. "I'm not supposed to start asking questions? I'm not supposed to find out you caught him taking the school apart? You'd make a lousy crook, Helmholtz. You'd leave your baton, sheet music, and your driver's license at the scene of the crime."

"I don't think about hiding clues," said Helmholtz. "I just do what I do. I was going to tell you."

Quinn's feet danced and his shoes squeaked like mice. "Yes?" he said. "Well, I've got some news for you too."

"What is that?" said Helmholtz uneasily.

"It's all over with Jim and me," said Quinn. "Last night was the payoff. I'm sending him back where he came from."

"To another string of foster homes?" said Helmholtz weakly.

"Whatever the experts figure out to do with a kid like that." Quinn sat back, exhaled noisily, and went limp with relief.

"You can't," said Helmholtz.

"I can," said Quinn.

"That will be the end of him," said Helmholtz. "He can't stand to be thrown away like that one more time."

"He can't feel anything," said Quinn. "I can't help him; I can't hurt him. Nobody can. There isn't a nerve in him."

"A bundle of scar tissue," said Helmholtz.

The bundle of scar tissue returned with the trumpet. Impassively, he laid it on the table in front of Helmholtz.

Helmholtz forced a smile. "It's yours, Jim," he said. "I gave it to you."

"Take it while you got the chance, Helmholtz," said Quinn. "He doesn't want it. All he'll do is swap it for a knife or a pack of cigarettes."

"He doesn't know what it is, yet," said Helmholtz. "It takes a while to find out."

"Is it any good?" said Quinn.

"Any good?" said Helmholtz, not believing his ears. "Any good?" He didn't see how anyone could look at the instrument and not be warmed and dazzled by it. "Any good?" he murmured. "It belonged to John Philip Sousa."

Quinn blinked stupidly. "Who?"

Helmholtz's hands fluttered on the table top like the wings of a dying bird. "Who was John Philip Sousa?" he piped. No more words came. The subject was too big for a tired man to cover. The dying bird expired and lay still.

After a long silence, Helmholtz picked up the trumpet. He kissed the cold mouthpiece and pumped the valves in a dream of a brilliant cadenza. Over the bell of the instrument, Helmholtz saw Jim Donnini's face, seemingly floating in space—all but deaf and blind. Now Helmholtz saw the futility of men and their treasures. He had thought that his greatest treasure, the trumpet, could buy a soul for Jim. The trumpet was worthless.

Deliberately, Helmholtz hammered the trumpet against the table edge. He bent it around a coat tree. He handed the wreck to Quinn.

"Ya busted it," said Quinn, amazed. "Why'dja do that? What's that prove?"

"I—I don't know," said Helmholtz. A terrible blasphemy rumbled deep in him, like the warning of a volcano. And then, irresistibly, out it came. "Life is no damn good," said Helmholtz. His face twisted as he fought back tears and shame.

Helmholtz, the mountain that walked like a man, was falling apart. Jim Donnini's eyes filled with pity and alarm. They came alive. They became human. Helmholtz had got a message through. Quinn looked at Jim, and something like hope flickered for the first time in his bitterly lonely old face.

Two weeks later, a new semester began at Lincoln High.

In the band rehearsal room, the members of C Band were waiting for their leader—were waiting for their destinies as musicians to unfold.

Helmholtz stepped onto the podium, and rattled his baton against his music stand. "The Voices of Spring," he said. "Everybody hear that? The Voices of Spring?"

There were rustling sounds as the musicians put the music on their stands. In the pregnant silence that followed their readiness, Helmholtz glanced at Jim Donnini, who sat on the last seat of the worst trumpet section of the worst band in school.

His trumpet, John Philip Sousa's trumpet, George M. Helmholtz's trumpet, had been repaired.

"Think of it this way," said Helmholtz. "Our aim is to make the world more beautiful than it was when we came into it. It can be done. You can do it."

A small cry of despair came from Jim Donnini. It was meant to be private, but it pierced every ear with its poignancy.

"How?" said Jim.

"Love yourself," said Helmholtz, "and make your instrument sing about it. A-one, a-two, a-three." Down came his baton.

ENTRY POINTS

1 Describe George M. Helmholtz's personality and his "same big dream." Why is he such "a child in the marketplace"? To what degree do you like or admire Helmholtz? Explain.

2 What is your first reaction to Quinn's nephew, Jim Donnini? Does Quinn's background information on Jim change your mind about him? Be specific.

3 Why does Helmholtz take an interest in Jim? How does Jim react? How does Helmholtz's interest in Jim fit in to his "big dream," his belief in the "beautiful" world of music? Do *you* believe in Helmholtz's faith in the power of music?

4 "What good is it?" said Jim.
  (a) Why does Jim want to vandalize the school? Explore the pathology of violence and destruction as depicted in this story.
  (b) Why do you think Jim won't destroy the trumpet? What is the difference to him between that and the destruction of the chemistry laboratory?

(c) How does Helmholtz attempt to cope with the situation and "save" Jim from his own self-destruction? Specify and assess his techniques with your group.

5 Explain the role of the black boots and Sousa's trumpet in this story.

6 "Deliberately, Helmholtz hammered the trumpet against the table edge."
(a) Why did he do this to his "greatest treasure"?
(b) What was the consequence? Is this a credible consequence? Explain.
(c) As a story about the reclamation of a young person's soul, does this story appeal to you? Explain your response.

7 Write a personal essay in which you comment on Helmholtz's philosophy: "Our aim is to make the world more beautiful than it was when we came into it." How can *you* do it? Make specific suggestions.

8 "Love yourself...." Write a story in which your protagonist, after a state of despair and despondency, learns to love himself/herself. Show clearly the possibility of love and harmony even in a potentially violent, chaotic world.

9 Compare the hope and optimism in this story with the bleaker visions of the human heart in other items in this anthology. Is one vision any more realistic than the other? Are they equal? Explain.

10 Imagine you are Jim Donnini. Write in your journal about what your life is like a year after you join Helmholtz's class.

11 For further insights into the positive effects of teachers on their students (and of students on their teachers), view the following films: *The Browning Version*; *To Sir, With Love*; *Why Shoot the Teacher?*; *Stand and Deliver*; *Dead Poet's Society*; *Sister Act II*; *Renaissance Man* and *Mr. Holland's Opus*. Write a film review in which you explore the reasons why students learned effectively from their teachers.

BALTHAZAR'S MARVELLOUS AFTERNOON

GABRIEL GARCÍA MÁRQUEZ

The cage was finished, Balthazar hung it under the eave, from force of habit, and when he finished lunch everyone was already saying that it was the most beautiful cage in the world. So many people came to see it that a crowd formed in front of the house, and Balthazar had to take it down and close the shop.

"You have to shave," Ursula, his wife told him. "You look like a Capuchin."

"It's bad to shave after lunch," said Balthazar.

He had two weeks' growth, short, hard, and bristly hair like the mane of a mule, and the general expression of a frightened boy. But it was a false expression. In February he was thirty; he had been living with Ursula for four years, without marrying her and without having children, and life had given him many reasons to be on guard but none to be frightened. He did not even know that for some people the cage he had just made was the most beautiful one in the world. For him, accustomed to making cages since childhood, it had been hardly any more difficult than the others.

"Then rest for a while," said the woman. "With that beard you can't show yourself anywhere."

While he was resting, he had to get out of his hammock several times to show the cage to the neighbors. Ursula had paid little attention to it until then. She was annoyed because her husband had neglected the work of his carpenter's shop to devote himself entirely to the cage, and for two weeks had slept poorly, turning over and muttering incoherencies, and he hadn't thought of shaving. But her annoyance dissolved in the face of the finished cage. When Balthazar woke up from his nap, she had ironed his pants and a shirt; she had put them on a chair near the hammock and had carried the cage to the dining table. She regarded it in silence.

"How much will you charge?" she asked.

"I don't know," Balthazar answered. "I'm going to ask for thirty pesos to see if they'll give me twenty."

"Ask for fifty," said Ursula. "You've lost a lot of sleep in these two weeks. Furthermore, it's rather large. I think it's the biggest cage I've ever seen in my life."

Balthazar began to shave.

"Do you think they'll give me fifty pesos?"

"That's nothing for Mr. Chepe Montiel, and the cage is worth it," said Ursula. "You should ask for sixty."

The house lay in the stifling shadow. It was the first week of April and the heat seemed less bearable because of the chirping of the cicadas. When he finished dressing, Balthazar opened the door to the patio to cool off the house, and a group of children entered the dining room.

The news had spread. Dr. Octavio Giraldo, an old physician, happy with life but tired of his profession, thought about Balthazar's cage while he was eating lunch with his invalid wife. On the inside terrace, where they put the table on hot days, there were many flowerpots and two cages with canaries. His wife liked birds, and she liked them so much that she hated cats because they could eat them up. Thinking about her, Dr. Giraldo went to see a patient that afternoon, and when he returned he went by Balthazar's house to inspect the cage.

There were a lot of people in the dining room. The cage was on display on the table: with its enormous dome of wire, three stories inside, with passageways and compartments especially for eating and sleeping and swings in the space set aside for the bird's recreation, it seemed like a small-scale model of a gigantic ice factory. The doctor inspected it carefully, without touching it, thinking that in effect the cage was better than its reputation, and much more beautiful than any he had ever dreamed of for his wife.

"This is a flight of the imagination," he said. He sought out Balthazar among the group of people and, fixing his maternal eyes on him, added, "You would have been an extraordinary architect."

Balthazar blushed.

"Thank you," he said.

"It's true," said the doctor. He was smoothly and delicately fat, like a woman who had been beautiful in her youth, and he had delicate hands. His voice seemed like that of a priest speaking Latin. "You wouldn't even need to put birds in it," he said, making the cage turn in front of the audience's eyes as if he were auctioning it off. "It would be enough to hang it in the trees so it could sing by itself." He put it back on the table, thought for a moment, looking at the cage, and said:

"Fine, then I'll take it."

"It's sold," said Ursula.

"It belongs to the son of Mr. Chepe Montiel," said Balthazar. "He ordered it specially."

The doctor adopted a respectful attitude.

"Did he give you the design?"

"No," said Balthazar. "He said he wanted a large cage, like this one, for a pair of troupials."

The doctor looked at the cage.

"But this isn't for troupials."

"Of course it is, Doctor," said Balthazar, approaching the table. The children surrounded him. "The measurements are carefully calculated," he said, pointing to the different compartments with his forefinger. Then he struck the dome with his knuckles, and the cage filled with resonant chords.

"It's the strongest wire you can find, and each joint is soldered outside and in," he said.

"It's even big enough for a parrot," interrupted one of the children.

"That it is," said Balthazar.

The doctor turned his head.

"Fine, but he didn't give you the design," he said. "He gave you no exact specifications, aside from making it a cage big enough for troupials. Isn't that right?"

"That's right," said Balthazar.

"Then there's no problem," said the doctor. "One thing is a cage big enough for troupials, and another is this cage. There's no proof that this is the one you were asked to make."

"It's this very one," said Balthazar, confused. "That's why I made it."

The doctor made an impatient gesture.

"You could make another one," said Ursula, looking at her husband. And then, to the doctor: "You're not in any hurry."

"I promised it to my wife for this afternoon," said the doctor.

"I'm very sorry, Doctor," said Balthazar, "but I can't sell you something that's sold already."

The doctor shrugged his shoulders. Drying the sweat from his neck with a handkerchief, he contemplated the cage silently with the fixed, unfocused gaze of one who looks at a ship which is sailing away.

"How much did they pay you for it?"

Balthazar sought out Ursula's eyes without replying.

"Sixty pesos," she said.

The doctor kept looking at the cage. "It's very pretty." He sighed. "Extremely pretty." Then, moving toward the door, he began to fan himself energetically, smiling, and the trace of that episode disappeared forever from his memory.

"Montiel is very rich," he said.

In truth, José Montiel was not as rich as he seemed, but he would have been capable of doing anything to become so. A few blocks from there, in a house crammed with equipment, where no one had ever smelled a smell that couldn't be sold, he remained indifferent to the news of the cage. His wife, tortured by an obsession with death, closed the doors and windows after lunch and lay for two hours with her eyes opened to the shadow of the room, while José Montiel took his siesta. The clamor of many voices surprised her there. Then she opened the door to the living room and found a crowd in front of the house, and Balthazar with the cage in the middle of the crowd, dressed in white, freshly shaved, with that expression of decorous candor with which the poor approach the houses of the wealthy.

"What a marvelous thing!" José Montiel's wife exclaimed, with a radiant expression, leading Balthazar inside. "I've never seen anything like it in my life," she said, and added, annoyed by the crowd which piled up at the door:

"But bring it inside before they turn the living room into a grandstand."

Balthazar was no stranger to José Montiel's house. On different occasions, because of his skill and forthright way of dealing, he had been called in to do minor carpentry jobs. But he never felt at ease among the rich. He used to think about them, about their ugly and argumentative wives, about their tremendous surgical operations, and he always experienced a feeling of pity. When he entered their houses, he couldn't move without dragging his feet.

"Is Pepe home?" he asked.

He had put the cage on the dining-room table.

"He's at school," said José Montiel's wife. "But he shouldn't be long," and she added, "Montiel is taking a bath."

In reality, José Montiel had not had time to bathe. He was giving himself an urgent alcohol rub, in order to come out and see what was going on. He was such a cautious man that he slept without an electric fan so he could watch over the noises of the house while he slept.

"Adelaide!" he shouted. "What's going on?"

"Come and see what a marvelous thing!" his wife shouted.

José Montiel, obese and hairy, his towel draped around his neck, appeared at the bedroom window.

"What is that?"

"Pepe's cage," said Balthazar.

His wife looked at him perplexedly.

"Whose?"

"Pepe's," replied Balthazar. And then, turning toward José Montiel, "Pepe ordered it."

Nothing happened at that instant, but Balthazar felt as if someone had just opened the bathroom door on him. José Montiel came out of the bedroom in his underwear.

"Pepe!" he shouted.

"He's not back," whispered his wife, motionless.

Pepe appeared in the doorway. He was about twelve, and had the same curved eyelashes and was as quietly pathetic as his mother.

"Come here," José Montiel said to him. "Did you order this?"

The child lowered his head. Grabbing him by the hair, José Montiel forced Pepe to look him in the eye.

"Answer me."

The child bit his lip without replying.

"Montiel," whispered his wife.

José Montiel let the child go and turned toward Balthazar in a fury. "I'm very sorry, Balthazar," he said. "But you should have consulted me before going on. Only to you would it occur to contract with a minor." As he spoke, his face recovered its serenity. He lifted the cage without looking at it and gave it to Balthazar.

"Take it away at once, and try to sell it to whomever you can," he said. "Above all, I beg you not to argue with me." He patted him on the back and explained, "The doctor has forbidden me to get angry."

The child had remained motionless, without blinking, until Balthazar looked at him uncertainly with the cage in his hand. Then he emitted a guttural sound, like a dog's growl, and threw himself on the floor screaming.

José Montiel looked at him, unmoved, while the mother tried to pacify him. "Don't even pick him up," he said. "Let him break his head on the floor, and then put salt and lemon on it so he can rage to his heart's content." The child was shrieking tearlessly while his mother held him by the wrists.

"Leave him alone," José Montiel insisted.

Balthazar observed the child as he would have observed the death throes of a rabid animal. It was almost four o'clock. At that hour, at his house, Ursula was singing a very old song and cutting slices of onion.

"Pepe," said Balthazar.

He approached the child, smiling, and held the cage out to him. The child jumped up, embraced the cage which was almost as big as he was, and stood looking at Balthazar through the wirework without knowing what to say. He hadn't shed one tear.

"Balthazar," said José Montiel softly. "I told you already to take it away."

"Give it back," the woman ordered the child.

"Keep it," said Balthazar. And then, to José Montiel: "After all, that's what I made it for."

José Montiel followed him into the living room.

"Don't be foolish, Balthazar," he was saying, blocking his path. "Take your piece of furniture home and don't be silly. I have no intention of paying you a cent."

"It doesn't matter," said Balthazar. "I made it expressly as a gift for Pepe. I didn't expect to charge anything for it."

As Balthazar made his way through the spectators who were blocking the door, José Montiel was shouting in the middle of the living room. He was very pale and his eyes were beginning to get red.

"Idiot!" he was shouting. "Take your trinket out of here. The last thing we need is for some nobody to give orders in my house. Son of a bitch!"

In the pool hall, Balthazar was received with an ovation. Until that moment, he thought that he had made a better cage than ever before, that he'd had to give it to the son of José Montiel so he wouldn't keep crying, and that none of these things was particularly important. But then he realized that all of this had a certain importance for many people, and he felt a little excited.

"So they gave you fifty pesos for the cage."

"Sixty," said Balthazar.

"Score one for you," someone said. "You're the only one who has managed to get such a pile of money out of Mr. Chepe Montiel. We have to celebrate."

They bought him a beer, and Balthazar responded with a round for everybody. Since it was the first time he had ever been out drinking, by dusk he was completely drunk, and he was talking about a fabulous project of a thousand cages, at sixty pesos each, and then of a million cages, till he had sixty million pesos. "We have to make a lot of things to sell to the rich before they die," he was saying, blind drunk. "All of them are sick, and they're going to die. They're so screwed up they can't even get angry any more." For two hours he was paying for the jukebox, which played without interruption. Everybody toasted Balthazar's health, good luck, and fortune, and the death of the rich, but at mealtime they left him alone in the pool hall.

Ursula had waited for him until eight, with a dish of fried meat covered with slices of onion. Someone told her that her husband was in the pool hall, delirious with happiness, buying beers for everyone, but she didn't believe it, because Balthazar had never got drunk. When she went to bed, almost at midnight, Balthazar was in a lighted room where there were little tables, each with four chairs, and an outdoor dance floor, where the plovers were walking around. His face was smeared with rouge, and since he couldn't take one more step, he thought he wanted to lie down with two women in the same bed. He had spent so much that he had had to leave his watch in pawn, with the promise to pay the next day. A moment later, spread-eagled in the street, he realized that his shoes were being taken off, but he didn't want to abandon the happiest dream of his life. The women who passed on their way to five-o'clock Mass didn't dare look at him, thinking he was dead.

Translated by Gregory Rabassa and J. S. Bernstein

ENTRY POINTS

1 From the very beginning of this story, it is made clear to the reader that Balthazar is, in his own way, gifted. Choose details from the opening two pages that support this statement. Note Balthazar's perception of his own talents and his artistic creation, the cage.

2 Characterize Dr. Octavio Giraldo and his assessment of Balthazar's creation. Why doesn't Balthazar sell him the cage? What is his wife's reaction to Balthazar's actions?

3 Comment on the attitudes of Jose Montiel, his wife, and his son, Pepe, to (a) Balthazar and the other "poor" people in the town, and (b) Balthazar's creation, the cage.

4 Balthazar "never felt at ease among the rich." Why not? Explain fully.

5 Why does Balthazar give the cage to Pepe without accepting payment? What has he "won" as a result of his action?

6 Comment on and evaluate Balthazar's drunkenness at the end of the story. Why does he experience the "happiest dream of his life" in this state even though he is now poorer than he has ever been?

7 Read the notes (page 21) on Latin American literature at the end of the story, "The Ex-Magician from the Minhota Tavern." Although Márquez is a master at magic realism himself, it should be noted that this story follows the other major trend in Latin American literature, realistic fiction. At the same time, much of his writing also reflects a dominant theme in this literature: the plight of the poor dominated by the few rich, and the resultant marked class divisions.
(a) Show how this story reflects both the style of realistic fiction and the themes of poverty and class conflicts.
(b) Compare the theme of this story with the Argentinian "The Stolen Party" (page 49), and the South African "The Bench" (page 57). Emphasize both the similarities and differences.

8 In a sense, both Balthazar, in this story, and Helmholtz, the teacher in "The Kid Nobody Could Handle" (page 243), are "magicians" controlling events and making new meanings. With your group, discuss the following:

   (a) Compare and contrast Balthazar and Helmholtz as "magicians."

   (b) How is Balthazar's gift of the cage similar to and different from Helmholtz's gift of the trumpet? Is the sacrifice the same in both cases? What does each hope to gain?

9 In the same realistic style as "Balthazar's Marvellous Afternoon," write a story where the protagonist scores a victory, breaking free from social constraints and obstacles.

10 As Balthazar, describe the "happiest dream" of your life.

11 Write a personal essay in which you envision and describe your own "Marvellous Afternoon." What did you achieve?

HE SITS DOWN ON THE FLOOR OF A SCHOOL FOR THE RETARDED

I sit down on the floor of a school for the retarded,
a writer of magazine articles accompanying a band
that was met at the door by a child in a man's body
who asked them, "Are you the surprise they promised us?"

It's Ryan's Fancy, Dermot on guitar,
Fergus on banjo, Denis on penny-whistle.
In the eyes of this audience, they're everybody
who has ever appeared on TV. I've been telling lies
to a boy who cried because his favourite detective
hadn't come with us; I said he had sent his love
and, no, I didn't think he'd mind if I signed his name
to a scrap of paper: when the boy took it, he said,
"Nobody will ever get this away from me,"
in the voice, more hopeless than defiant,
of one accustomed to finding that his hiding places
have been discovered, used to having objects snatched
out of his hands. Weeks from now I'll send him
another autograph, this one genuine
in the sense of having been signed by somebody
on the same payroll as the star.
Then I'll feel less ashamed. Now everyone is singing,
"Old MacDonald had a farm," and I don't know what to do

about the young woman (I call her a woman
because she's twenty-five at least, but think of her
as a little girl, she plays that part so well,
having known no other), about the young woman who
sits down beside me and, as if it were the most natural
thing in the world, rests her head on my shoulder.

It's nine o'clock in the morning, not an hour for music.
And, at the best of times, I'm uncomfortable
in situations where I'm ignorant
of the accepted etiquette: it's one thing
to jump a fence, quite another thing to blunder
into one in the dark. I look around me
for a teacher to whom to smile out my distress.
They're all busy elsewhere. "Hold me," she whispers. "Hold me."

I put my arm around her. "Hold me tighter."
I do, and she snuggles closer. I half-expect
someone in authority to grab her
or me; I can imagine this being remembered
for ever as the time the sex-crazed writer
publicly fondled the poor retarded girl.
"Hold me," she says again. What does it matter
what anybody thinks? I put my other arm around her,
rest my chin in her hair, thinking of children
real children, and of how they say it, "Hold me,"
and of a patient in a geriatric ward
I once heard crying out to his mother, dead
for half a century, "I'm frightened! Hold Me!"
and of a boy-soldier screaming it on the beach
at Dieppe, of Nelson in Hardy's arms,
of Frieda gripping Lawrence's ankle
until he sailed off in his Ship of Death.

It's what we all want, in the end,
to be held, merely to be held,
to be kissed (not necessarily with the lips,
for every touching is a kind of kiss).

Yes, it's what we all want, in the end,
not to be worshipped, not to be admired,
not to be famous, not to be feared,
not even to be loved, but simply to be held.

She hugs me now, this retarded woman, and I hug her.
We are brother and sister, father and daughter,
mother and son, husband and wife.
We are lovers. We are two human beings
huddled together for a little while by the fire
in the Ice Age, two hundred thousand years ago.

1 How does the "writer of magazine articles" first approach his assignment at the "School for the Retarded"? Explore his feelings.

2 What is the writer's first reaction to the young woman who sits down beside him on the floor? What would be *your* reaction? Why does he continue to be nervous about this "most natural" situation? How does he resolve his feelings of discomfort?

3 When this poem was written, the word "retarded" had not yet been replaced by the phrase "mentally challenged" or "developmentally disabled" to refer to those people who were slower than the majority of the population in their mental development. Discuss with your group why various words have been replaced by other words today—you may have to research word origins in the library. State and list other examples. What do you think this changing terminology means about us as a culture?

4 *It's what we all want, in the end,*
to be held, merely to be held

Assess the writer's final words and actions in the poem. Express your own feelings about the final moments of this poem.

5 Compare the message of this poem to the messages of "The Middle Ground" (page 68), "The Kid Nobody Could Handle" (page 243), and "Balthazar's Marvellous Afternoon" (page 254). Show how all these pieces represent a victory over negative human tendencies and stereotypes, a breaking free of cynicism.

6 You are the "writer of magazine articles." Write a feature story on your experiences as described in the poem.

7 Write a narrative poem in which you describe an uncomfortable situation. Show the changes that evolve in you.

8 For other views on developmentally disabled people, read Daniel Keyes's *Flowers for Algernon* or view the films, *Bill*, *Rainman*, and *Forrest Gump*. Write a movie or book review commenting on their depiction of developmentally disabled people.

9 Write a short story which depicts the theme of "love conquers all" as your protagonist breaks free of negative social constraints and "lies." Read the first poem at the start of this anthology.

"…we belong to something before we are anything, and we have entered a specific social contract before birth. I was predestined to be, for example, a middle-class mid-twentieth-century male white English-speaking Canadian in the instant of conception. But as the individual develops within his society, all the essential aspects of thought and imagination and experience take place in him. Social freedom, however essential, is general and approximate; real freedom is something that only the individual can experience. The individual grows out of society like a plant out of its soil; but he does not break away from it. The progress of his education includes increasing awareness of his social conditioning and context, and hence a reabsorbing of his society into an individual form, though it may include an absorption of many other influences originating elsewhere."

—Northrop Frye: *The Great Code*

A NOTE ON POST-MODERNISM

Post-modernism is a movement in literature and the arts which holds up to question the basic assumptions that may govern our perceptions of the world and our own culture, and also the origins of those assumptions. It suggests that there is no such thing as totally unbiased, "scientific" knowledge, and questions the very nature of truth—specifically, "universal truths"—and how we perceive these truths. Further, post-modernism asks us to rethink the nature of fiction and our relationship to it as readers.

Within a post-modern reality, we are asked to understand and appreciate that there may be many "truths" and different "truths" from the ones we may have comfortably grown up with because of our own "situation"—our own distinct cultural, community, and national background. In understanding this new perspective, we may begin to respond to Gabriel García Márquez's criticism of conventional European and North American perspectives: that we should measure other peoples in our own land and in far-away lands with a different "yardstick" from that which we use to measure our own individual cultures. In so doing, Marquez feels we may begin to build that Utopia that he envisioned for the world:

> ...tellers of tales who, like me, are capable of believing anything, feel entitled to believe that it is not yet too late to undertake the creation of a minor utopia: a new and limitless utopia for life wherein no one can decide for others how they are to die, where love really can be true and happiness possible, where the lineal generations of one hundred years of solitude will have at last and forever a second chance on earth.

If we take on Marquez's challenge, as readers, we may begin to think more critically and more open-mindedly about the printed page, the assumptions of the author, of the created characters, and our recreations of them in our own minds. We can begin to appreciate in a fuller way the nature of literature as constructed "truths" that we, as thinking readers, have a right to "deconstruct" so that we may understand the authors' ideas within their proper cultural context and highly individualized perspective. In effect, we will have become more thoughtful and more powerful readers, able to comprehend both the page and the world with greater clarity and precision, enabling us not only to survive, but to prevail in our post-modern world.

— John Borovilos

AUTHOR BIOGRAPHIES

JOHN AGARD, born in Guyana in 1949, has been acting and writing since he was a teenager. After touring the Caribbean with the All Ah We acting troupe, he moved to England in 1977 where he now works for the Commonwealth Institute giving talks to schools. As with many other modern Caribbean poets, he uses and promotes the common vernacular and local dialect in his writings. His poetry books include *Limbo Dancer in Dark Glasses* (1983) and *Mangoes and Bullets* (1985) from which "Stereotype" was taken.

KATHERINE ALEXANDER, was born in 1935 in Winnipeg, Manitoba, of Greek parents, and has lived in Athens, Montreal, and Toronto. She received her B.A. and B.Ed. from the University of Manitoba. After being a full-time mother and homemaker, she enrolled in a creative writing programme and received her M.A. from Montreal's Concordia University. "A Proper Goodbye" is taken from her first book, *Children of Byzantium* (1987; then published under the name Katherine Vlassie), a series of linked stories which chronicles the life of a Greek-Canadian family in Winnipeg. She currently resides in Athens, Greece.

JEANNETTE C. ARMSTRONG, a fluent Okanagan speaker, was born on the Penticton Indian Reserve in British Columbia in 1948. Educated at the University of Victoria, her publications include the children's books, *Enwhisteetkwa Walk in Water* (1982), and *Neekna and Chemai* (1984), and the novel *Slash* (1987). She is a Director of En'owkin, a multifaceted Native Education Centre. "History Lesson" appeared in *Breathtracks* (1991), a collection of her poetry.

MARGARET ATWOOD, was born in 1939 in Ottawa of Nova Scotian parents and grew up in northern Quebec and in Toronto (1946–1961). She received her B.A. from Victoria College in 1961 and her A.M. degree from Harvard in 1962. Winner of the Governor General's Award for poetry for the *Circle Game* (1966) and for fiction for *The Handmaid's Tale* (1986), she has written over thirty books, including her most recent novel, *The Robber Bride* (1993). She has also produced two major works of literary criticism dealing with Canadian literature: *Survival: A Thematic Guide to Canadian Literature* (1972) and *Second Words* (1982).

DHU'L NUN AYYOUB, born in 1908, is one of the leading writers of the early generation of realistic short story writing in Iraq. "From Behind the Veil" is from *Modern Arab Stories* and first appeared in *UR*, a literary review published by the Iraqi Cultural Centre in London. The author currently lives in Vienna, Austria.

TONY BELL, born in 1955 in Ontario, grew up in London and Windsor. He received his B.A. from the University of Western Ontario and moved west to do his post-graduate work at the University of Alberta. He currently teaches and lives in Edmonton. A playwright and a novelist, he has twice been runner-up in the Alberta Culture first novel competition. "The Image Maker," his first published story, was included in *Alberta Rebound* (1990).

ELIZABETH BREWSTER, born in Chipman, New Brunswick, in 1922, was educated at the University of New Brunswick, Radcliffe College, King's College, London, the University of Toronto, and Indiana University. She worked as a librarian in a number of provinces before joining the English Department at the University of Saskatchewan in Saskatoon. She is best known for her many collections of poetry including *Passage of Summer* (1969), *In Search of Eros* (1974), and *The Way Home* (1982) from which "Calgary as a Christmas Tree in February" was taken.

LAURA BULGER, born in 1939, in Lisbon, Portugal, received her doctorate from the University of Oporto. After she arrived in Canada in 1966, she taught at the University of Manitoba and the University of Toronto and then became a professor of Portuguese, Spanish, and Comparative Literature at York University. Her first book of short stories, *Paradise on Hold* (1987), was translated by herself from the original Portuguese version of her collection, *Vaivém*. She is currently teaching in the Department of Literature at the University of Tras-Os-Montes E Alto Douro in Portugal.

YU-WOL CHONG-NYON, is the pen name of a little-known Korean female writer. Her name means "Month-of-June-Youth" and refers symbolically to those young Koreans who endured their country's tragic civil war from 1950–1953. "The Nonrevolutionaries" was translated into English and published in *A Treasury of Modern Asian Stories*, edited by Daniel L. Milton and William Clifford.

CYRIL DABYDEEN, born in 1945 in Guyana, South America, moved to Canada in 1970 where he finished his formal education at Queen's University, Kingston, Ontario. A winner of the Okanagan Fiction Prize, his books of poetry and prose include *Goatsong, Islands Lovelier than a Vision*, and *Coastland: New and Selected Poems*. Recipient of many honours, he served as Poet Laureate of Ottawa from 1984 to 1987. He now teaches Creative Writing at the University of Ottawa.

GENNI GUNN, was born in Trieste, Italy, in 1949, and immigrated to Canada in 1959. After gaining an M.F.A. from the University of British Columbia, she began publishing poems, short fiction, and translations in a number of literary magazines, including *Fiddlehead* and *West Coast Review*. She has published two books of fiction: *Thrice Upon a Time* (1990) and *On the Road* (1991). "The Middle Ground" appeared in *Ricordi: Things Remembered* (1989), a seminal anthology of Italian-Canadian fiction, edited by the late C. D. Minni. She currently lives in Vancouver, B.C., and is an instructor in the Department of Creative Writing at U.B.C.

LILIANA HEKER, was born in 1943 in Buenos Aires, Argentina. She quickly established her reputation as an outspoken critic of the military dictatorship in Argentina through her first book of short stories, *Those Who Beheld the Burning Bush* (1966), and as editor-in-chief of a "radical" literary magazine called *The Platypus*. Its motto was Oscar Wilde's ironic line: "One must always be a little improbable."

LAWRENCE HILL, a writer from Oakville, Ontario, has worked for the *Globe and Mail* and the *Winnipeg Free Press*. His short stories have appeared in such publications as *Descant* and *Exile*, and his novel, *Some Great Thing*, appeared in 1992. He has also written the children's history text, *Trials and Triumphs: the Story of African Canadians* (1993) and is currently working on a second novel as well as a history of the Canadian Negro Women's Association.

ANNE JEW, has a degree in English Literature from the University of British Columbia. She is a screenwriter and a columnist for *Disorder* magazine. Her short fiction has been published in *A Room of One's Own* and *Proem Canada*. "Everyone Talked Loudly in Chinatown," which reflects Jew's concern with racism, appeared in *Proem Canada* in the spring of 1989.

JANICE KULYK KEEFER, was born in Toronto in 1952. She grew up in the Ukrainian community and was involved with the Ukrainian Orthodox Church and Youth Associations. Educated at the University of Toronto and the University of Sussex, England, she has taught at various institutions including the Université Sainte-Anne in Nova Scotia and the University of Prince Edward Island. She has been widely published, and in 1987 her critical study of Maritime fiction, *Under Eastern Eyes*, was nominated for a Governor General's Award. She has written a novel, *Constellations* (1988), several collections of short stories, and a collection of poetry, *White of the Lesser Angels* (1986). She now lives in Ontario where she holds the position of Professor of English at the University of Guelph.

GEORGE KENNY, born on the Lac Seul Reserve, grew up in small Northwestern Ontario towns. Many of his stories deal with the ambivalence young people feel trying to respect their ancestors' traditions within a changing cultural milieu. "On the Shooting of a Beaver" first appeared in his book of poetry and short fiction, *Indians Don't Cry* (1977).

ANWER KHAN, born in Bombay, India, holds M.A. degrees in Urdu and Persian and is currently employed at the Bombay Port Trust. Writing since the 1960s, he has published three collections of short stories and a novel. "The Pose" was taken from his collection, *Yad Basere* (1990). It is of interest to note that Urdu, an Indo-European language, is written in the Perso-Arabic script with a sizeable percentage of its vocabulary derived from Persian, Turkish, and Arabic loanwords. Today, it is chiefly spoken in India, Pakistan, and in Western countries such as Great Britain and Canada which have large numbers of South Asian expatriates—and growing literary communities.

THOMAS KING, born in 1943 in Sacramento, California, is of Cherokee, Greek, and German descent. He taught Native Studies and encouraged young Native writers for ten years at the University of Lethbridge in Alberta. In 1989, he became Chair of American Indian Studies at the University of Minnesota. His short stories and poems have been widely anthologized and have appeared in many journals and magazines across Canada and the United States. His novels have also been highly praised: *Medicine River* (1990) and *Green Grass, Running Water* (1993), which was short-listed for the Governor General's Award. He is currently living in Toronto where he is Story Editor for "Four Directions," a CBC-TV dramatic anthology series by and about the First Peoples.

NAGUIB MAHFOUZ was born in Cairo, Egypt, in 1911 and began writing when he was seventeen. He has been one of the most prolific writers in the world having written more than thirty screenplays, several stage plays, and more than forty short story collections and novels—including his masterwork, *The Cairo Trilogy*, a 1500-page epic that spans three generations of Cairo families. He claims to have been influenced by many Western writers such as Dickens, Zola, Camus, Dostoevsky, and Proust. In 1988, he became the first Arabic writer to win the Nobel Prize for Literature. He continues to live in the Cairo suburb of Agouza. "The Answer Is No" comes from his collection, *The Time and the Place* (1991).

GABRIEL GARCÍA MÁRQUEZ was born in 1928 in Aracataca, Columbia, but has spent much of his time in Mexico and Spain. He attended the University of Bogota and immediately began working as an international journalist and editor. His many novels and stories are characterized by "magic realism" which combines realism and fantasy in almost improbable ways. In 1967, he wrote his masterpiece, *One Hundred Years of Solitude*, which depicted a hundred years of a doomed South American family—an idea strongly influenced by the work of the American novelist, William Faulkner. "Balthazar's Marvellous Afternoon," was published originally in 1962, and appeared in his *Collected Stories* in 1984. Márquez was awarded the Nobel Prize for Literature in 1982.

HAROLD MARSHALL was born in 1930 in Barbados and emigrated to Canada in 1956 after journeying to Britain, South America, and Europe. He has been an editor of several journals, newspapers, and other publications in Barbados, British Columbia, and Manitoba. He currently works for the Winnipeg School Division and is also engaged in researching 17th century Barbadian history. His story, "Things in the Silence," appeared in *Other Voices* (1985) and *Breaking Through* (1990).

JUDY MCCROSKY, born in 1956 in Aberdeen, Scotland, won a Major Award for short fiction from the Saskatchewan Writers Guild Literary Competition in 1988 and an Honourable

Mention for Humour in 1989. She has edited *Windscript* magazine and has taught Creative Writing at the University of Saskatchewan. Her stories have been published in numerous magazines and broadcast on CBC Radio. Her first book, *Spin Cycle and Other Stories*, was published in 1990. She currently resides in Saskatoon.

OODGEROO NOONUCCAL (1920–1993) was also known by the non-Aboriginal name of Kath Walker. The first of the modern Australian Aboriginal protest writers, she was of the Noonuccal tribe of Stradbroke Island off the Queensland coast—custodian of the land Minjerribah. Although she was educated only to primary school level, by 1961 she rose to become State Secretary of the Federal Council for the Advancement of Aboriginals and Torres Strait Islanders. She campaigned successfully for the 1967 abolition of Section 52 of the Australian Constitution which discriminated against Aborigines. Her best known books include *We Are Going* (1964), *The Dawn Is at Hand* (1966), *Stradbroke Dreamtime* (1972), and *Father Sky & Mother Earth* (1981). Her poems and stories evoke nostalgia for her Aboriginal past, a sense of loss, and a sense of pride in her native identity.

ALDEN NOWLAN (1933–1983) was born in Windsor, Nova Scotia. He dropped out of school at the age of twelve to work on farms, in lumber camps, and in sawmills. A self-educated man, he later worked as a journalist and editor with several New Brunswick newspapers, and in 1968 became writer-in-residence at the University of New Brunswick. For a time, he was also the manager of a country music band, "George Shaw and the Green Valley Ranch Boys." Among his many collections of poetry, *Bread, Wine, and Salt* won the Governor General's Award in 1967. His published fiction includes *Miracle at Indian River* (1968) and an autobiographical novel, *Various Persons Named Kevin O'Brien* (1973). He died in his beloved Fredericton, New Brunswick, at the age of fifty. "Skipper" appeared in his final collection of short stories, *Will Ye Let the Mummers In?* (1984).

AL PURDY was born in 1918 in Wooler, Ontario. At sixteen, he dropped out of school, working at odd jobs and riding the rails during the Depression, before serving with the RCAF in British Columbia during World War II. He has travelled extensively to the Cariboo, Newfoundland, Baffin Island, Cuba, Greece, and England, and has been writer-in-residence at a number of universities. He has published numerous major collections of his poetry, including *Sex and Death* (1973), *Being Alive* (1978), and *Piling Blood* (1984). Two of his collections have received the Governor General's Award: *The Cariboo Horses* (1965) and *The Collected Poems of Al Purdy* (1986). He currently lives in Ameliasburg, Ontario.

CHRISTA REINIG was born in 1926 in Berlin, Germany. After working as a florist and factory worker during World War II, she studied art history and archaeology at Humboldt University in East Germany. She settled in West Germany after receiving a literary prize there in 1964. Her early works are poems dealing with the horrors and insanity of war. Her later works include *Heavenly and Earthly Geometry* (1975), an autobiographical novel that reveals her animosity against the communist East German state.

RICHARD RIVE (1931–1989) was born in Cape Town, South Africa, and educated at the University of Cape Town, Columbia University, and Oxford University. Educator, academic administrator, editor, and author, Rive was known for his writings about South Africa's racist apartheid system, some of which were banned in his homeland. His works include the short story collection, *African Songs* (1963), and the novels, *Emergency* (1970), and *"Buckingham Palace" District Six* (1986). His autobiography, *Writing Black*, was published in 1982. At the time of his death, he was Head of the English Department at Hewat College of Education in Cape Town.

GABRIELLE ROY (1909–1983) was born in St. Boniface, Manitoba, and studied to be a teacher at the Winnipeg Normal Institute. In 1939, she moved to Montreal, and in 1952 settled in Quebec City where she lived until her death. A prolific and highly-acclaimed writer, her works have been translated into more than fifteen languages, and three of her works won the Governor General's Award: *The Tin Flute* (1947); *Street of Riches* (1957); and, *Children of My Heart* (1977). Although most of Roy's work deals with the lives of French-Canadians, she sometimes wrote about "ex-centric" groups in Canada such as the Chinese, the Doukhobors, and, as in "The Wheelchair," the Inuit.

MURILO RUBIAO was born in 1916 in the state of Minas Gerais in Brazil. He was active in literary circles at the University of Minas and a founder of a number of literary reviews during his education there. After receiving his law degree in 1942, he began writing professionally and attended the First Brazilian Congress of Writers, which called for an immediate halt to censorship and an end to military dictatorships in South America. His off-beat stories combining the natural and the fantastic have become highly admired bestsellers.

BARBARA SAPERGIA, born in 1943 in Moose Jaw, Saskatchewan, received her B.A. from the University of Saskatchewan and her M.A. from the University of Manitoba. She has written for C.B.C. radio and television, for the stage (*Lokkinen* and *Matty and Rose*), and for various periodicals and anthologies, including *The Bridge City Anthology: Stories from Saskatoon* (1991). She also wrote a novel, *Foreigners* (1984), about Romanian immigrants in southern Saskatchewan in the early twentieth century. "Arranged Marriage" first appeared in her poetry collection, *Dirt Hills Mirage* (1980). She now lives in Saskatoon.

EUNICE SCARFE was born in the United States, but now lives in Edmonton, Alberta. She has travelled widely and taught in England and the United States as well as Canada. Her published stories have been included in a number of prestigious magazines and anthologies among which are *The Malahat Review, Room of One's Own*, and *Best Canadian Short Fiction*. Since 1990 she has taught writing classes for the Women's Program and Resource Centre at the University of Alberta. Assisted by the Norwegian Marshall Fund, she currently is interviewing Norwegian women writers whose works have been translated into English. "The Ground Rules," which forces us to see ourselves as outsiders, won *Prism international's* Annual Short Fiction Contest in 1987.

SAMUEL SELVON (1923–1994) was born and educated in Trinidad where he studied at Naparima College. He wrote several acclaimed novels, including *The Lonely Londoners* (1956) and *Moses Ascending* (1975). Many of his novels and stories deal with the experiences of West Indians arriving in Britain—as he did—in the 1950s, and dealing with a society different from that of the Caribbean. "Cane Is Bitter" appeared in his collection of short stories, *Ways of Sunlight* (1957). He last lived in Calgary, Alberta.

WOLE SOYINKA, born in Abeokuta, Western Nigeria, in 1934, studied at Government and University Colleges in Ibadan, Nigeria, and at the University of Leeds in England. Although chiefly known as Africa's leading dramatist, he has achieved prominence as a novelist, critic, poet, and teacher, heading up the Theatre Arts Departments of both Ibadan and Ife universities. Although born to and raised by Christian parents, he was greatly influenced by the cultural forces and beliefs of the Yoruba people, his traditional African group. After returning to Nigeria in 1960 after its independence, in 1967 he was thrown in jail for speaking out against the civil war with Biafra. He recorded his prison experiences in *Poems from Prison* (1969) and in a memoir, *The Man Died* (1972). His plays include *The Lion and the Jewel* (1959) and a *Play of Giants* (1984). In 1986, he became the first African to receive the Nobel Prize in Literature.

J. J. STEINFELD was born in a Displaced Persons camp in Munich, Germany, of Polish Jewish parents, grew up in the United States, and moved to Canada in 1972, living in Ontario during the 1970s. After attaining a B.A. from Case Western Reserve University in Ohio and an M.A. in history from Peterborough's Trent University, he moved to Charlottetown, P.E.I. in 1980. His writing has won him a great number of awards, including first place in Theatre Prince Edward Island's playwriting competition in 1984, 1985, and 1986, and the Okanagan Short Fiction Award in 1984. He has also published a novel,

Our Hero in the Cradle of Confederation (1987), and five short story collections, including *The Apostate's Tattoo* (1983). His latest collection is *Dancing at the Club Holocaust* (1993).

AMY TAN was born in Oakland, California, in 1952, two and a half years after her parents immigrated from China to the United States. She visited China for the first time in 1987. "Two Kinds" first appeared in the *Atlantic Monthly* and then as part of her huge best-seller, *The Joy Luck Club* (1989). She currently resides in San Francisco where she is working on a novel, *The Year of No Flood*.

RUDY THAUBERGER was born in 1961 in Saskatoon, Saskatchewan, and raised in Western Canada. "Goalie" first appeared in *The Rocket, the Hammer, the Flower and Me* (1988), an anthology of hockey stories edited by Doug Beardsley, and was inspired by his brother, a goalie in Victoria, B.C. He attended the Master of Fine Arts programme in Creative Writing at the University of British Columbia and is currently pursuing a writing career in the Vancouver area. He resides in Burnaby, B.C.

W. D. VALGARDSON, born in 1939, grew up in Gimli in the Interlake District of Manitoba near Winnipeg—an area where his Icelandic ancestors settled. Educated at the University of Manitoba and the University of Iowa, he returned to Canada to become a professor of English and Chairman of the Department of Creative Writing at the University of Victoria in British Columbia. He has published three collections of short stories, including *Bloodflowers* (1973) and *Red Dust* (1978). A novel, *Gentle Sinners* won the *Books in Canada* Award for best first novel in 1980. "A Matter of Balance" won first prize for fiction in the CBC literary competition in 1980.

M. G. VASSANJI, born in Kenya and raised in Tanzania, attended M.I.T. in Massachusetts before coming to Canada in 1978. He has won wide acclaim for his novels, *No New Land* (1991) and *The Gunny Sack* (1989), which won a Commonwealth Prize. "Leaving" comes from his collection of linked stories, *Uhuru Street* (1992), which reveals life in Dar es Salaam, a port city on the east coast of Africa. He currently lives in Toronto, Ontario.

KURT VONNEGUT, JR., born in Indianapolis, Indiana, attended Cornell, Carnegie Tech., and the Universities of Tennessee and Chicago. A very popular writer, he is best-known for his off-beat and science fiction stories. His better known books include *Welcome to the Monkey House* (1970), *Slaughterhouse Five* (1974), and *Galapagos* (1985).

BRONWEN WALLACE (1945–1989) was born in Kingston, Ontario, where she taught in the English Department at Queen's University and worked in a centre for abused women and children. Her five books of poetry include *Common Magic* (1985), *The Stubborn Particulars of Grace* (1987), and *Signs of the Former Tenant* (1983), from which "Thinking With the Heart" is taken.

HE XIAOHU, a member of the Chinese Writers' Association, was born in Taiyuan, Shanxi, China, in 1950. After graduating from middle school, he worked in a power plant as a welder. Since 1972, he has published several short stories which try to capture the mood and attitudes of today's Chinese urban youth. "Outside the Marriage Bureau" won high praise and a distinguished award in 1981.

YEVGENY YEVTUSHENKO was born in 1933 of Latvian and Ukrainian origins in Zima Junction, Siberia, Russia. He studied at the Gorky Institute of World Literature in Moscow, where he published his first book, *Prospectors of the Future* (1952). He has continued to write many books of poetry and some prose ever since—and, because of his magnetic performances of his own poems, has been invited over the years to give public readings throughout the world. An outspoken opponent of censorship in the old Soviet Union, he was elected to the then Soviet Congress as a leading proponent of Mikhail Gorbachev's policy of *perestroika*. "Lies" appeared in his *Selected Poems* (1962).

CONTENTS BY THEME

CREDITS

Grateful acknowledgement is given to authors, publishers, and agents for permission to reprint the following copyrighted material. Every effort has been made to determine copyright owners. In the case of any omissions, the Publisher will be pleased to make suitable acknowledgements in future editions.

1 "Lies" from SELECTED POEMS by Yevgeny Yevtushenko, translated by Robin Milner-Gulland and Peter Levi, S J (Penguin Books, 1962) copyright © Robin Milner-Gulland and Peter Levi, 1962. Reprinted with permission; **3** "There Was Once" by Margaret Atwood, © 1992 O. W. Toad Ltd. Reprinted from *Good Bones* by permission of Coach House Press; **7** "The Image Maker" by Tony Bell, used by permission of the author; **17** "The Ex-Magician from the Minhota Tavern" by Murilo Rubião, appeared in *A Hammock Beneath the Mangoes: Stories from Latin America* (ed., trans., Thomas Colchie, Plume Books, Penguin, 1992); **23** "Calgary as a Christmas Tree in February" by Elizabeth Brewster is reprinted from *Selected Poems* by permission of Oberon Press; **28** "Skipper" from WILL YE LET THE MUMMERS IN? by Alden Nowlan. Reprinted with the permission of Stoddart Publishing Co. Limited, Don Mills, Ont; **33** "Cane Is Bitter" by Samuel Selvon, reprinted by permission of the Estate of Samuel Selvon; **45** "On the Shooting of a Beaver" from *Indians Don't Cry*, © 1982 by George Kenny (NC Press, Toronto, 1982); **49** "The Stolen Party" by Liliana Heker, appeared in *Other Fires: Short Fiction by Latin American Women* (ed., trans., A. Manguel, Lester & Orpen Dennys, 1985). Used by permission of the Lucinda Vardey

Agency; **55** "Stereotype" appeared in *Mangoes and Bullets,* © by John Agard (Pluto Press, 1985); **57** "The Bench" by Richard Rive appeared in *African Voices* (ed. Peggy Rutherford, Drum Publications, Johannesburg, 1958); **63** "So What Are You, Anyway?" copyright © 1992 by Lawrence Hill appeared in *Voices: Canadian Writers of African Descent* (ed. Ayanna Black, HarperCollins, 1992). Used by permission of the author; **68** "The Middle Ground" copyright © 1989 by Genni Gunn, first published in *RICORDI: Things Remembered* (Guernica, 1989); **77** "Borders" from *One Good Story, That One* by Thomas King, published by HarperCollins Canada, 1993. Used by permission of The Bukowski Agency; **87** "Multiculturalism" by Cyril Dabydeen, used by permission of the author; **90** "Everyone Talked Loudly in Chinatown" by Anne Jew appeared in *Proem Canada* (Spring, 1989); **96** "Land of No Delight" by Harold Marshall, used by permission of the author; **102** "Telephone Conversation" by Wole Soyinka appeared in *Reflections* (ed. Frances Ademola, African Universities Press); **105** "The Ground Rules" by Eunice Scarfe, © 1990, first appeared as "Jokulhaups" in the April 1988 issue of *Prism International.* Used by permission of the author; **113** "Leaving" from *Uhuru Street* by M. G. Vassanji. Used by permission of the Canadian Publishers, McClelland & Stewart, Toronto; **120** "History Lesson" from *Breathtracks* , copyright Jeannette C. Armstrong (Theytus Books, 1991); **121** Quotation from Antonine Maillet from "My Canada Includes...", *Maclean's Magazine,* Maclean Hunter Ltd., Jan., 3, 1994. ; **122** "Civilisation" by Oodgeroo Noonuccal (Kath Walker), appeared in *Poetry Can* (Heinemann Educational Australia, 1991). Reprinted by permission; **124** "The Wheelchair" by Gabrielle Roy, copyright: FONDS GABRIELLE ROY. Used by permission; **134** "Vocational Counselling" by Christa Reinig appeared in *German Women Writers of the Twentieth Century* (ed. E. R. Herrmann and E. H. Spitz, Pergamon Press, 1978); **140** "A Beautiful Woman" from *The Apostate's Tattoo* (Ragweed Press) by J. J. Steinfeld, copyright © 1983 by J. J. Steinfeld. Used by permission of the author; **151** "From Behind the Veil" by Dhu'l Nun Ayyoub appeared in *Modern Arab Stories* (ed., trans., S. Al-Bazzazz, Iraqi Cultural Centre, London); **157** "Arranged Marriage" by Barbara Sapergia, from *Dirt Hills Mirage,* Thistledown Press, 1980. Reprinted by permission; **160** "Outside the Marriage Bureau" by He Xiaohu, translated by Hu Zhihui, appeared in *Contemporary Chinese Short Stories* (Panda Books, 1983); **170** "Call Me" by Judy McCrosky appeared in *The Budge City Anthology: Stories from Saskatoon* (Fifth House, 1991). Used by permission of the author; **175** "My Mother, a Closet Full of Dresses" by Janice Kulyk Keefer, used by permission of the author; **178** "Two Kinds" from THE JOY LUCK CLUB by Amy Tan. Copyright © 1989 by Amy Tan. Published by the Putnam Publishing Group. Reprinted with permission; **189** "The Letter" by Laura Bulger, used by permission of the author; **194** "A Proper Goodbye" by Katherine Alexander from *Children of Byzantium* (1993) by K. Alexander, published by Cormorant Books Inc; **205** "The Pose" by Anwer Khan, from *Domains of Fear and Desire: Urdu Stories* (ed., trans., Muhammad Umar Memon, TSAR Publications, 1992); **210** "Thinking With the Heart" by Bronwen Wallace is reprinted from *Signs of the Former Tenant,* copyright by permission of Oberon Press; **214** "The Answer Is No" from THE TIME AND THE PLACE AND OTHER STORIES by Naguib Mahfouz. Copyright © 1991 by the American University in Cairo Press. Used by permission of Doubleday, a division of Bantam Doubleday Dell Publishing Group, Inc; **218** "A Matter of Balance," from *What Can't Be Changed Shouldn't Be Mourned* (Vancouver: Douglas & McIntyre, 1990), copyright 1990 by W. D. Valgardson. Used with permission of the author; **228** "The Nonrevolutionaries" by Yu-Wol Chong-Nyon, from *A Treasury of Modern Asia Stories,* edited by D. L. Milton and W. Clifford (Plume Books/New American Library). Used by permission of W. Clifford; **234** "Hockey Players" from *The Collected Poems of Al Purdy* by Al Purdy. Used by permission of the Canadian Publishers, McClelland & Stewart, Toronto; **238** "Goalie" by Rudy Thauberger, from *The Rocket, the Flower, the Hammer and Me* (Polestar Press, 1988), © Rudy Thauberger and used by permission of the author; **243** "The Kid Nobody Could Handle" from WELCOME TO THE MONKEY HOUSE by Kurt Vonnegut, Jr. Copyright © 1961 by Kurt Vonnegut, Jr. Used by permission of Delacorte Press/Seymour Lawrence, a division of Bantam Doubleday Dell Publishing Group, Inc; **254** "Balthazar's Marvellous Afternoon" from NO ONE WRITES TO THE COLONEL... by Gabriel García Márquez. Copyright © 1968 in the English translation by HarperCollins Publishers, Inc. Reprinted by permission of HarperCollins Publishers, Inc; **262** "He Sits Down on the Floor of a School for the Retarded" by Alden Nowlan. Reprinted with the permission of Stoddart Publishing Co. Limited, Don Mills, Ont.